# Western Canadian Native Destiny
## Complex Questions
## on the Cultural Maze

## John W. Friesen, Ph.D., D.Min., D.R.S.
## Virginia Lyons Friesen, Ph.D.

DETSELIG
ENTERPRISES LTD

**Western Canadian Native Destiny**
 **Complex Questions on the Cultural Maze**
 © 2008 John W. Friesen and Virginia L. Friesen

Library and Archives Canada Cataloguing in Publication

Friesen, John W.
  Western Canadian native destiny : complex questions on the
cultural maze / John W. Friesen, Virginia Lyons Friesen.

Includes bibliographical references
ISBN 978-1-55059-355-6
  1. Native peoples – Canada. Friesen, Virginia Agnes Lyons,
1952- II. Title.
E78.C2F745 2008          305.897'071          C2008-902951-8

DETSELIG
ENTERPRISES LTD

Detselig Enterprises Ltd.
210, 1220 Kensington Road NW
Calgary, Alberta  T2N 3P5

Phone: (403) 283-0900
Fax: (403) 283-6947
Email: temeron@telusplanet.net
www.temerondetselig.com

Support for our publishing program is recognized from the
Government of Canada through the Book Publishing Industry
Development Program (BPIDP).

Support is also acknowledged from the   Foundation for the Arts for our
publishing program.

Cover design by David J Friesen and Alvin Choong

ISBN 978-1-55059-355-6     SAN 113-0234     Printed in Canada

*To the Memory of*
*Lily and Lazarus Wesley*
*Stoney (Nakoda Sioux) First Nation*
*Morley, Alberta*

# Contents

# About the Authors

**John W. Friesen**, Ph.D., D.Min., D.R.S., is a Professor in the Graduate Division of Educational Research at the University of Calgary where he teaches courses in Aboriginal history and education. A graduate of seven colleges and universities, he is an ordained minister with the All Native Circle Conference of the United Church of Canada. He is also the recipient of three eagle feathers and author, co-author or editor of nearly 50 books including:

*The Cultural Maze: Complex Questions on Native Destiny in Western Canada* (Detselig, 1991);

*Rose of the North* (a novel), (Borealis, 1987);

*Introduction to Teaching: A Socio-Cultural Approach* (with Alice Boberg), (Kendall/Hunt, 1990);

*You Can't Get There From Here: The Mystique of North American Plains Indians Culture & Philosophy* (Kendall/Hunt, 1995);

*Pick One: A User-Friendly Guide to Religion* (Detselig, 1995);

*The Real/Riel Story: An Interpretive History of the Métis People of Canada* (Borealis, 1996);

*Perceptions of the Amish Way* (with Bruce K. Friesen) (Kendall/Hunt, 1996);

*Rediscovering the First Nations of Canada* (Detselig, 1997);

*Sayings of the Elders: An Anthology of First Nations' Wisdom* (Detselig, 1998);

*First Nations of the Plains: Creative, Adaptable and Enduring* (Detselig, 1999);

*Legends of the Elders* (Detselig, 2000);

*Aboriginal Spirituality and Biblical Theology: Closer Than You Think*, (Detselig, 2000);

*Canada in the Twenty-First Century: A Historical Sociological Approach* (with Trevor W. Harrison), (Pearson Canada, 2004);

*The Palgrave Companion to Utopian Communities in North America* (with Virginia Lyons Friesen), (Macmillan, 2004);

*Sayings of a Philosopher* (Detselig, 2005).

*What's Your Church Like? Compared with Nine New Testament Models* (with Virginia Lyons Friesen) (Xulon, 2007).

**Virginia Lyons Friesen,** M.A., Ph.D., is a Sessional Instructor in the Faculty of Communication and Culture at the University of Calgary and is a frequent instructor at Weekend University, The University of Calgary's Gifted Centre, and Old Sun College on the Blackfoot Indian Reserve at Siksika, Alberta. An Early Childhood Education Specialist, she holds a Certificate in Counselling from the Institute of Pastoral Counselling in Akron, Ohio. She has co-presented a number of papers at academic conferences and is co-author of: *Grade Expectations: A Multicultural Handbook for Teachers,* (Alberta Teachers' Association 1995), and *The Palgrave Companion to Utopian Communities in North America* (Macmillan, 2004).

She served as Director of Christian Education with the Morley United Church on the Stoney (Nakoda Sioux) Indian Reserve from 1988 to 2001, and from 2007 to the present.

John W. Friesen and Virginia Lyons Friesen have co-authored the following Detselig Titles:

*In Defense of Public Schools in North America,* 2001;

*Aboriginal Education in Canada: A Plea for Integration,* 2002;

*We Are Included: The Métis People of Canada Realize Riel's Vision,* 2004;

*More Legends of the Elders,* 2004;

*First Nations in the Twenty-First Century: Contemporary Educational Frontiers,* 2005;

*Still More Legends of the Elders,* 2005;

*Even More Legends of the Elders,* 2005;

*Teachers' Guide to Legends of the Elders,* 2005; and,

*Canadian Aboriginal Art and Spirituality: A Vital Link,* 2006.

## Cover Design

An apprenticed blacksmith, **David J Friesen** studied design at the Alberta College of Art and obtained a Bachelor of Education degree in early childhood education from the University of Calgary. He has taught elementary and art education in both public and private schools in Alberta, British Columbia, Ohio, Korea, and Japan. His interests include skateboarding, snowboarding, and web and graphic design. Some of his works may be found at http://artdesignlife.com.

# Preface

An ancient prophecy foretells that a day is coming when Indigenous people will teach other peoples and other nations the importance of life. Life in this prophecy means the sacredness of life in the whole creation, not only human life but that of other beings, the elements, forces of life in nature and in the cosmic world. This prophecy tells of a day that is coming when Indigenous people who have special knowledge of nature and Earth's ecosystems will be respected and heard by all mankind. (Chief John Snow, 2005: 242)

Canada's First Nations have faced many challenges and endured numerous times of severe testing over the generations that they have shared their lands with nonAboriginals. Surprisingly, the record will show that initial contacts between the two parties – Europeans and Indigenous peoples – were quite friendly and both Natives and nonNatives benefited from trade and commerce related to the fur trade. When that industry came to a halt, however, relations between the two parties deteriorated and Native Americans were negatively affected. Eventually First Nations were confined to reserves, where their manner of livelihood had to change drastically and economic conditions in their communities became deplorable. In addition, when the residential schools system was created, many Aboriginal children were taken from their parents and locked up in educational institutions while others attended day schools. Indian children in both institutions were informed that their traditional lifestyle was uncivilized, inferior, and spiritually decrepit, and would have to be replaced with European-inspired religious and socioeconomic values.

Generations passed, and things changed slowly so that by the end of the twentieth century, there was a glimmer of hope for a better way of life on the horizon. This happened partly because Indigenous leaders had become educated in nonNative politics and objected to the processes of colonization and assimilation that were being forced upon them. They began to demand justice and radical change. Slowly the federal government began to respond to Native American complaints and improvements were made in a number of important areas, many of which are discussed in this book.

9

We wish to begin our discussion of key issues affecting Indigenous communities by first cautioning readers that this book is essentially a work of reference. It cannot be read as a continuing story because each chapter is really an entity to itself. Now and then readers will encounter a bit of overlap in discussion content because some historical events and legal maneuvers have relevance to more than a single issue. We have tried to present as an objective analysis of each issue as possible, primarily by consulting literary sources with varying perspectives. We will readily admit that we do not entirely succeed in this endeavor, partly because of the close link we feel to the First Nations community. Over the past twenty years we have been especially blessed to have spent a great deal of time with members of the Stoney First Nation, located just west of Calgary, Alberta, and we owe them a sincere thanks for so graciously welcoming us to their community. Over the years we have learned many things from them.

Time marches on, as the saying goes, and the Indian community is no exception. In 1991 we were investigating a similar scenario in a published work, *The Cultural Maze: Complex Questions on Native Destiny in Western Canada* (Detselig, 1991). The intent of the book was to outline the dimensions of the legal and cultural maze facing First Nations in the Canadian West. A series of challenging issues were discussed in that volume including economic development, land claims, Aboriginal rights, cultural destiny, language maintenance, Native education policy, community control issues, role of elders, education, and Canadian multiculturalism. That work is now out of print.

Seventeen years have passed since that publication appeared and significant change has occurred in many First Nations communities. Several longstanding issues such as land claims, Aboriginal self-government and justice regarding residential schools remain on the order paper, but many new complex challenges have emerged. This book is a primer outlining the major challenges affecting First Nations in Western Canada as the 21st century gets underway. This publication is not intended to comprise an exhaustive treatment of those challenges, or to pose solutions. Rather the purpose is to provide basic information pertaining to the myriad of contemporary challenges faced by Western Canada's First Nations. Being informed is vital to the formulation of solutions to tough challenges. The public deserves to know. This book is committed to that purpose.

# A Note on Terminology

There are a variety of descriptive terms to choose from in writing about the original occupants of this continent, and there seems to be no frontrunner. One can choose from a long list of descriptors – Aboriginal Peoples, AmerIndians, First Nations, First Peoples, Indians, Indigenous Peoples, Native North Americans, and Native Peoples. Recently a colleague even suggested that the First Peoples in Canada be called "PreCanadians!" There are writers, Native and nonNative, who prefer a particular usage to the exclusion of all others. Currently the Government of the United States, and writers in that country, use the term Indian, or Native American while Canadians are opting for First Nations, Indigenous People, or Aboriginals.

The Government of Canada still operates a Department of Indian and Northern Affairs. Despite arguments to the contrary, a variety of these usages will be employed in the ensuing pages, partly to relieve monotony in delivery, and partially because it is difficult to know which usage might be appropriate in any given context. In some ways, it seems that the political correctness movement has temporarily stalled efforts at meaningful literary communication. As historian J. R. Miller (2004: 62) has observed; "Political correctness confines or even closes off completely the scope of investigation, ensuring that whatever 'truth' emerges will be partial at best." It should be noted that in this volume, terms to describe the First Peoples will be capitalized as a means of emphasizing the literary legitimacy of writing about them, in the same way that identities of other nationalities are capitalized.

As is both appropriate and heart-felt, we would like to thank Dr. Ted Giles and the staff of Temeron-Detselig for their support of our work. They are always prompt in meeting deadlines, helpful in making suggestions, and capable in fulfilling their duties to see that publications like this reach fruition. Publishing a book is never an individual enterprise, and we gratefully acknowledge that many people had a part in this endeavor. We only hope that the quality of the end result will justify the faith and support we received from the various parties who helped bring it to completion.

John W. Friesen
Virginia Lyons Friesen
Calgary, AB., 2008

# References

Friesen, John W. (1991). *The Cultural Maze: Complex Questions on Native Destiny in Western Canada.* Calgary, AB: Detselig Enterprises.

Miller, J.R. (2004). *Reflections on Native-Newcomer Relations: Selected Essays.* Toronto, ON: University of Toronto Press.

Snow, Chief John. (2005). *These Mountains Are Our Sacred Places: The Story of the Stoney People.* Calgary, AB: Fitzhenry and Whiteside.

# One
# Putting Things into Perspective

The popular opinion of the Indian represents him as a san-
guinary, treacherous and vindictive being, somewhat cold in his
affections, haughty and reserved toward his friends, merciless to
his enemies, fond of strife, and adverse to industry and the pur-
suits of peace. (Horatio Hale, 1883: 83)

Over the past century, the Indian people, and many white people as well, have become increasingly aware of the aura of conflict surrounding the relations between white man and red man
in Canada. The struggle has now become so intense and so emotional for so many of our people, especially our young people;
and has led to equally intense but opposite emotional response
from elements of white society. (Harold Cardinal, 1977: 7)

## Setting the Stage

Although the socio-economic status of many Canadian First
Nations communities has steadily improved over the past few
decades, they still have some ways to go in meeting national living
standards. Canadians are not generally informed about this sad
state of affairs, but as the popular media continue to include stories
of Aboriginal happenings, the situation is slowly changing.

This observation is based on many conversations we have had
with fellow Canadians about the research we have been involved in
over the past several decades. Over the years, we have been fortunate enough to have visited virtually every Native American community between Alberta/Saskatchewan and Texas and have been
severely chagrined by the nature of questions we have been asked
by our friends on our return home. Canadians generally seem to
assume that there exists a kind of pan-Indianism that can be used
to catalog every literary missile that emanates from popular media
– radio, television, Internet, newspapers, and magazines. This lack
of knowledge seems to be comprehensive, and pertains to history
and culture, legal rights, educational dimensions, and, most regret-

table of all, the spiritual base of Indian philosophy. This chapter is intended to summarize knowledge essential to understanding the situation – legally, politically, socio-economically of First Nations in Canada, and possibly clarify some of the issues with which the First Peoples have to deal on a daily basis.

My own (John) relationship with the Aboriginal people began when I first learned to read. In elementary school, in Trail, British Columbia, I came across a book relating the autobiography of an Indian woman – and I was hooked. Although born in Saskatchewan my family relocated to British Columbia when I was very young. I was still in elementary school when we returned to Saskatchewan a few years later. Here it was my privilege to attend a rural school, Lac Chavel School, with Métis children from the Duck Lake, Saskatchewan area, while Status Indian children attended the residential school in town. We often interacted with First Nations while doing business in town or when the men worked as hired hands on neighboring farms during the harvest. Years later, having completed a doctorate at the University of Kansas, where the Haskell First Nations University is located, I assumed an academic post at the University of Calgary. There, in 1968, with a colleague, we developed the university's first course on Native education. That course is still being offered, although it is now housed in the Faculty of Communication and Culture. In addition, in 1986, I was invited to serve as Minister of the Morley United Church, and did so until 2001. On request by members of the congregation, in May 2007, I came out of retirement and resumed that position. My wife Virginia has served and does serve as Director of Christian Education at Morley United Church.

My own (Virginia) perspective on Canadian First Nations was enhanced when I became aware that my great uncle, the late Alexander Calderwood and his wife Leola, donated land to the Province of Alberta to establish Head-Smashed-In Buffalo Jump in southern Alberta. My mother, Dorothy Lyons, informs me that as a child, she and her cousins often played at the site, quite unaware that their playground would eventually become so historically important. In 1988, I assumed the position of Director of Christian Education for the Morley United Church, which is located on the Stoney (Nakoda Sioux) Reserve west of Calgary. I still maintain that position although my husband John (who was minister of the church), and I did take a six-year break from the church in 2001 to 2007. Since completing a Ph.D. Degree at the University of Calgary,

I have taught in the area of Native studies through the University's Native Outreach Program at Old Sun College on the Siksika (Blackfoot) Reserve, in the University of Calgary's Gifted Centre, and through Weekend University. Course offerings we jointly teach include Canadian Native Art, Plains Indian History, and Native Education in Canada.

# Historical Perspective

It is a typically erroneous assumption that academics such as anthropologists, archaeologists, historians, and sociologists produce completely objective assessments of people, places, and cultures they study, but quite often the opposite is the case. Academics, like individuals of any other persuasion, are people – that is, they have perspectives, and opinions that have been formed throughout their life experiences. These experiences tend to color their observations and conclusions. One has only to look at the work of such writers as ethnologist, Lewis Morgan (1818-1881), who some years ago depicted Native American cultures as ". . . savages, advancing by slow, almost imperceptible steps, attained the higher condition of barbarians, by similar progressive advancement, finally attained civilization . . ." (1963: ii). Morgan, a thorough-going evolutionist, believed that the events of humankind embody themselves, independently of the efforts of humankind, in a material record that is crystallized in institutions, usages, and customs.

Morgan was not and is not alone in his naïve assessment of First Nations cultures. These kinds of negative evaluations continued into the early years of the twentieth century; for example, in a publication produced by the Hudson's Bay Company the Indian was described as ". . . still a child, literally speaking, and assimilation is slow. . . . He is still primitive in spite of all civilizing influences around" (Prest, 1922: 5-6). Several generations ago in its early days, a contemporary local newspaper offered this gem: "The Indian drives his beast [horse] at the greatest pace he can get out of him, by means of beating him constantly, up hill and down. . . . and nothing to eat unless they get a chance to rustle a bite on some vacant lot" (*Calgary Herald*, May 17, 1920).

Lischke and McNab (2005: 14) suggest that the Indian has been "described and portrayed thousand of times either as a 'noble savage' or disparaged as a 'wild Indian' who resisted the westward expansion of the [North] American frontier." Perhaps the best that

Native people can hope for today is that their own interpretations of their history and traditional lifestyle and knowledge will be paraphrased correctly by nonNatives!

Graciously, not all twentieth-century conceptualizations of First Nations were negative. In fact, the work of anthropologist Robert Lowie (1963) is remarkably objective and even praiseworthy of Native cultures. Lowie detected many similarities or "universals" among the various cultures he studied, commenting that Native Americans grappled with the same challenges of everyday living, and they employed precisely the same psychological processes of association, observations, and inference that their nonNative counterparts did. As Lowie put it, "When a Hopi Indian in Arizona raises corn where a white tiller fails . . . he is solving his everyday problems, not only competently, but with elegance" (Lowie, 1924: xvi).

One of the more obvious ethnocentric assumptions posited by historians of bygone days was that history began with nonNative activity. Anything that happened before the printed page was invented was called "prehistory," thereby giving the impression that such happenings were somehow lesser in the human scheme of things. H.H. Trevor-Roger, an Oxford professor, suggested that the recording of prehistory was "largely darkness . . . and darkness is not a subject of history" (Dickason, 2000: 12). This sense of historical arrogance haunted the writing of North American history until 1984 with the publication of Olive Dickason's monumental work, *The Myth of the Savage and the Beginnings of French Colonialism in the Americas*. After Dickason's work appeared, history books about Canadian history began to include a few paragraphs or even a whole chapter about Canada's "prehistory." Even the Bering Strait theory, the idea that Canada's Aboriginal peoples originally came from Siberia via what is now Alaska, and so long a pillar of the argument that Indians were not really Canada's first occupants, was questioned. As the late Vine Deloria Jr., once commented:

> Arriving at the University of Colorado, I was stunned to hear from my students that some of my history colleagues were beginning their courses on American history with a mindless recitation of the Bering Strait theory of the peopling of the Western Hemisphere . . . . an examination of the Bering Strait doctrine suggests that such a journey would have been nearly impossible even if there had been hordes of Paleo-Indians trying to get across the hypothetical bridge. It appears that not even animals or plants really crossed this mythical connection between Asia

and North America. The Bering Strait exists and existed only in the minds of scientists. (Deloria, 1995: 45, 107)

Much of Native American history is being rewritten these days, some of it by Aboriginal academics who naturally tend to posit a strong revisionist perspective. After all, they want to set the record straight, and no one can blame them. Having been subjected to centuries of literary subjugation and misrepresentation, they undoubtedly have that right. Some Aboriginal writers probably paint a much brighter picture of traditional ways than is merited. Battiste and Henderson (2000: 46), for example, seem to imply that traditional Indigenous knowledge is always superior to imported knowledge and in many ways. They suggest that "Historically, Indigenous peoples not only utilized the naturally occurring biodiversity of North America for food, medicine, materials, and ceremonial and cultural life, but routinely took steps to increase the biodiversity of their territories." This may have happened in many communities, but can it be declared a universal practice among all tribes? Has it been documented, and if so, where and in what form?

There can be no doubt in anyone's mind about the significant contributions made by Canada's First Peoples to this country. These contributions range from military service and justice to the arts, media, literature, education, sports, and culture. Many Aboriginals who assisted in these ventures were people who have pushed the boundaries of their communities and indeed of Canada itself (Newhouse, Voyageur, and Beavon, 2005: 9). Canadians are all better off for their efforts, and in light of the ongoing renaissance of Aboriginal traditions, will continue to benefit.

# Legal Perspective

The term "Indian" will be used throughout the discussion in this section because the federal government does not legally recognize other nomenclature – such as Aboriginal, AmerIndians, First Nations, First Peoples, Indigenous Peoples, Natives, or Native Americans.

Unlike designations used in the United States, bloodlines have little to do with who is legally an Indian in Canada. In this country the matter was settled years ago through a formal registering of Indians undertaken by federally appointed officials who were sent to Indian communities to tally the residents. The act of registration was accomplished in established Indian communities, so naturally, the people who lined up were usually full-blooded Indians, but not always. Mixed blood individuals raised in Indian communities were welcomed in the line-up, partly because the enumerator would not likely know whom to turn away. Those who stood in line, full-blooded or mixed bloods were then legally recognized as Indians, and children born to them would logically inherit legal Status.

Many Canadians are not aware that though the terms Status, Registered, and Enfranchised tend to be used interchangeably today, each term once had a specific historical meaning. To begin with, Canada as a nation was only nine years old when parliament decided to pass the *Indian Act* of 1876, the intent of which was to designate who was legally an Indian. As mentioned, enumerators were sent to Indian communities to make a register of Indians. Those who were "not in town" when the enumerator did his job, were missed and became nonStatus Indians. Status Indians were to receive health, education, and welfare benefits through federal sources. Everyone else had to rely on provincial agencies for those benefits.

With the first register more or less complete, it was the custom that children born to a Status Indian woman were registered as Indians. So far, so good, but now the waters turn murky. There are many examples of individuals who years later wanted to claim the benefits of their Status, only to find out that their ancestors did not stand in line on the day of the count and so got missed. Perhaps these individuals were out hunting, or away from home for other reasons. In any event, until 1985 there was no recourse to claiming the benefits of a lost opportunity.

In 1867, the Government of Canada was established and began making legislation. A few years later, in 1871, treaty negotiations were undertaken and the federal government began to scrutinize the list of registered Indians and shorten it. Métis names, for example, were dropped from the list as well as the names of other individuals whose heritage was dubiously regarded. There were other ways to lose Status, for example, by serving in the Canadian Armed Forces, or simply by willingly giving up one's Status.

Until 1985, when Bill C31 was passed, the situation was as follows. If a Status male married a nonStatus woman, Indian or nonIndian, that woman became by law a Status woman. The converse was not true; that is, if a Status woman married a nonStatus male, Indian or nonIndian, she immediately became classified as nonStatus. Any children born to her after that date were also classified as nonStatus. A red mark or "tick" was then attached to the women's name in the federal register, and she was labeled "a red-ticket woman." The rationale behind this state of affairs is not entirely clear, but clearly, chauvinism prevailed.

Obviously not everyone was in agreement with the rather inflexible state of affairs regarding the assignment of Status and nonStatus, so years later the federal government took steps to rectify what some thought to be a rather chauvinistic arrangement. In 1985, Bill C31 was passed, allowing those who had been passed over in the original enumeration to apply for Status. Women who had previously married out could also apply to regain Status. The process is long and cumbersome and requires legal documentation for every step along the way. Many individuals who begin the process give up because it is simply not always physically possible to locate the required papers.

The passage of Bill C-31 has not been over whelmingly endorsed by the Indian community. Some elders believe that women who married out should not be welcomed back into the fold. This belief is based on the concept that since women are the primary conveyors of spirituality, they should be very careful about preserving that status and function. Therefore, if a woman reneged on that responsibility by marrying out, she should bear the consequences of her actions and not be readmitted.

Generally speaking the Métis people have been left out of discussions pertaining to Status, but in September 2003 the Supreme Court of Canada ruled that the Métis people are indeed an Aboriginal people. However, the implications of that ruling have yet to be defined. Many observers tend to confuse Métis with nonStatus Indians, but they are not really the same. For example, the Métis emerged as a distinct cultural group in western Canada in 1869, under the leadership of Louis Riel, just before the Province of Manitoba originated. NonStatus Indians could be individuals who were omitted in the original census taking of Status Indians or those who subsequently gave up or lost their Status.

## Band Membership

Status Indians as well as many nonStatus Indians are members of one of the more than six hundred Indian bands in Canada. In Indian communities with more than one band, members even have the privilege of changing band memberships on occasion. For example, this happens on occasion on the Stoney Indian Reserve located west of Calgary, Alberta where three bands make their home – Bearspaw, Chiniki, and Wesley.

When an individual loses Status, however, he or she also loses his or her band membership. If these individuals manage to regain Status through the auspices of Bill C31, however, they may not get their band membership back. That privilege is strictly within the power domain of the band. Individuals who once lost their Status and band membership in the oil-rich Sawridge Band in Alberta, for example, very rarely have their band membership returned to them once they lose Status.

# Treaties

The Government of Canada officially began making the ten "big" treaties with Indian tribes in 1871 and continued to do so until 1899 when Treaty No. 10 was signed. Essentially treaties provide Indian nations with specified lands known as reserves. Other provisions of treaties involved the promise of schooling, certain economic benefits, and a small annual token of cash. Following British tradition, the language used in treaty-signing includes such phrases as these: "as long as the sun shines and the rivers flow," implying that the government would always look after the needs of their treaty partners. Indians, for their part, looked upon the treaties as reciprocal agreements by which they would share their lands in exchange for a guarantee that their rights would be protected (Dickason, 2000: 23). Treaty lands were assigned in most provinces, although most of Quebec and about one-third of British Columbia were unaffected by treaty-signing. In addition, one or two bands were overlooked in Alberta. Other ongoing legal entanglements pertaining to treaties have to do with Indian reserve lands that were sold, either without band knowledge or without consultation.

The end result of the foregoing discussion is that there are several different classifications of Indians now in Canada. These include: (i) Treaty-Status Indians – those individuals who belong to a band that has a signed treaty and its members have legal Status; (ii) nonTreaty-Status Indians – those whose band has no signed treaty but its members are Status individuals; (iii) Treaty-nonStatus Indians, who could be individuals whose band membership is recognized by their local band but the government does not recognize them as Status Indians; and, (iv) nonTreaty-nonStatus Indians –

individuals who have no legal Status and belong to a band that has no signed treaty. There are further complications to the legal phenomenon of being Indian in Canada, but only one will be mentioned here. It is this; when an individual such as a Red Ticket woman regains her Status via Bill C31, her children will also be regarded as having legal Status. However, "the buck stops there," and the woman's grandchildren will not be entitled to be assigned Status. Under the arrangements of Bill C31, a Status woman may now marry whomever she wishes and not risk losing her Status.

Legal recognition is very important to Canada's Indians because it is through the courts that they can access the rights and privileges spelled out in the treaties and in the Indian Act. This has become extremely important in recent years, as Native leaders have educated themselves, often through training in institutions of higher education, and therefore become more eloquent in stating their demands.

# A Cultural Perspective

It is very difficult for an individual raised in twentieth century Canada to have any concept of what it was like to live the traditional Aboriginal lifestyle. For that matter, it is very difficult for urban dwellers today to visualize what it must be like to live a rural lifestyle. The latter challenge should be a lot easier, however, because both urban and rural citizens for the most part subscribe to a competitive, capitalist somewhat free market model of living. No matter how it is described, it is a far cry from the traditional Indigenous model in major ways.

In the first instance, the original inhabitants of North America believed in living in harmony with the rhythms of nature. Their "clock" was set to follow the cycles and whims of the universe, which were set in place by the Creator. Mother Earth herself provided for the everyday needs of her children including food and medicinal provisions. Every detail of life was calibrated by natural phenomena and prayers of thanksgiving were offered for each met need. When an animal was killed for food, its spirit was offered a prayer of thanks, and a portion of the meat would be returned to the earth to honor the natural cycle of nature. When the first berry of the season was picked, a prayer of thanksgiving would be voiced for this special source of food. Various tribes had in place a variety of ceremonies that emphasized the deep spirituality the people felt for their very existence as well as for the exigencies of life.

One of the highlights of traditional First Nations lifestyle was their belief in the connectedness of all earthly phenomena, hence the Sioux saying, "all my relations," was often uttered at the end of a prayer. The expression implied an acknowledgement of the inter-relationship of all earthly things as well as their spirituality. It was believed that an individual could not interfere with one component of the universe and not expect repercussions to occur in another sphere. Thus, the various habits and life cycles of different crea-tures and plant life were deeply respected.

In days gone by, the First Nations, like many other peoples around the earth, relied on the oral tradition. This meant that beliefs and valued knowledge were passed on by word of mouth, modeling, imitation, and every day experience. Children were taught to listen to stories and legends of valued truths, but they were also expected to emulate their parents and grandparents as they observed important tribal functions being carried out. Everything learned had to be stored in one's mind because there were few if any written records. Storyrobes and winter counts (paintings on hides) were quite common among the Blackfoot, for example, the former to record important individual events and the latter to record important tribal events. Children were expected to take to heart and commit to memory the beliefs and features of their culture so when their turn came they would be able to pass them along to the next generation. The good news today is the revival of the old ways as elders are being called back into play. They are again fulfilling their roles as cultural teachers as they instruct the young. In many cases, they are ingeniously combining cultural lessons with language learning. Thus, Indigenous young-sters are being taught about their heritage in their own language and in traditional ways – storytelling, modelling and on-the-job training.

Analysis of the oral tradition will reveal that it had an element of flexibility built into it. As things changed, geographically, econom-ically, or otherwise, or if new items were added to the cultural repertoire, adjoining beliefs could also be amended. The people were not stuck to the written record even though underlying spiri-tual insights might persist. Four Guns of the Sioux First Nations once observed that "many of the white man's ways are past our understanding . . . they put a great store upon writing, there is always a paper. . . . If a white man loses his paper, he is helpless" (Friesen, 2000: 38).

The oral tradition is paralleled by another First Nations belief – being is more important than doing, and doing for its own sake is essentially meaningless. Traditionally, First Nations believed that at any given time one only has "the moment," and cannot predict whether he or she will be permitted life on earth for any period of time in the future – be it the next five minutes or fifty years. This implies that one ought to make the best use one can of "the immediate moment." Thus at any given time one only has the assurance of the present moment so that moment ought to be used to contemplate or enhance one's purpose in the universe. Any action engaged in or decided upon should then relate to the fulfillment of that purpose. The underlying belief is that each individual has an important and specific role to fulfill; furthermore, once he or she has determined what it might be, seek to live it out. The identification of that role may be assisted by contemplation, guidance from elders, experiencing a vision, or participating in spiritual ceremonies and rituals.

It is important to note that this concept will not readily be understood nor appreciated by most nonNatives. Time, which is probably the most important related factor in the process of making one's journey, becomes a relative term. At each given moment the individual must determine what kind of behavior should be undertaken that would best align with his or her purpose in life. Naturally, this makes it nearly impossible for such an individual to fit into today's clock-driven society – and therein is the rub. How can a spiritually minded Aboriginal cope with the exigencies of a society that demands adherence to its implicit and explicit mandates and expectations?

Traditionally, and even today, many individuals of First Nations affiliation prioritize family obligations above all other. In fact, they are expected to do so, for to do otherwise would run the risk of being labelled a "white man." As a result, in many First Nations communities, those who hold jobs often do not "get ahead" economically because they are expected to use their resources to help relatives who are without. The essence of sharing, however, is quite the reverse of that practiced in dominant society, because if one's relatives are without resources, they have the privilege of helping themselves to the resources of a relative who has been blessed with means. This may be translated to quite common activities like borrowing a relative's vehicle, requesting money, or taking meat out of a relative's freezer without asking. If one is asked for money and one has it, to refuse to share would be violating a sacred societal expectation. True, this kind of practice is beginning to fade in many Indian communities, but there are still places where such is the case.

One of the most admirable traits of the traditional Indigenous lifestyle is respect for the individual. Essentially a live-and-let-live society, Indian parents did not traditionally discipline their children; that responsibility was left to a relative so that the bond between parent and child could thrive on a positive note. As a child grew older, employed means by which to exercise discipline included humor, name-calling, and even ridicule, but these practices were again meted out by close friends or relatives. Children experienced a great deal of freedom in growing up; the idea being that learning by doing is the best philosophy. Naturally, if a child put itself in a harmful position, the parent would interfere, but such scenarios were rare.

Respect for individuality was also exercised in another fashion. If an individual showed promise of a particular skill or talent, and its benefit could be seen to accrue to the tribe, that individual was respected and often honored for that gift or skill. Furthermore, it was required that a particular gift or skill be exercised at any given point, the individual in question was consulted or contracted to fulfill the required activity. No one else would attempt to duplicate that particular talent unless apprenticed to do so by the one who was duly recognized. Thus, any form of competition in this particular scenario was virtually nonexistent. The bottom line, of course, was that there was consensus regarding any possible benefits of the exercise of any gift, talent, or skill. These were expected to accrue to the community.

Through the centuries of their existence, belief in the interconnectedness of all things and a reverential awe for the operations of the universe produced a deep, almost withdrawing sense of patience among First Nations. When one adds to the mix the more or less irrelevance of time, a perspective of wait-and-see results. This can be applied to the way community decisions are made. In traditional times it was important that a community made decisions by consensus. Use of this approach was important to hold the people together. Band council decisions, for example, were arrived at by consensus. People talked things through thoroughly. No decision was made until everyone present had had sufficient opportunity to express himself or herself. Then, when everyone was finally in agreement, the meeting could end. This spirit of unity is still present in many Native communities where more decisions that affect the entire community appear to be made by consensus. People seem to gravitate to a conclusion without giving the matter an open hearing. That way, if everyone demonstrates agreement, even silently, all members of the community can live in peace.

## A Spiritual Perspective

Several years ago, I (John) ventured on what I still believe to be my most important work, *Aboriginal Spirituality and Biblical Theology: Closer Than You Think* (Detselig, 2000). In the book I tried to emphasize that in light of our shrinking global reality, there is a real need for nations and religions to try to understand one another. In my own quest to do so (having been raised with a somewhat restricted interpretation of Christianity), I was fortunate enough to encounter a rich form of First Nations spirituality among the Stoney (Nakoda Sioux) people of Morley, Alberta. They have openly welcomed both of us through the years, and we are grateful to them for sharing elements of their culture with us. Above all, they have taught us that the underlying essence of the universe is spiritual, which translates to an attitude of awe, appreciation, and respect for all living things. Every act, therefore, can have spiritual implications as it relates to one's individual cosmic calling. To fulfill that calling we are invited by the Creator to become stewards of the Mother Earth, but not her master. We may be tempted to alter, rearrange, and even try to destroy elements of the universe, but this is not our calling. Instead we are to respect all elements of the world around us and bear in mind that they too are in a place of fulfilling their calling. This particularly applies to our fellow human beings. Everyone's individual journey must be permitted to be lived out, respected, supported, and even assisted whenever the opportunity presents itself.

## A Psychological Perspective

The foregoing discussion has an implicit psychological dimension; how do we regard our fellow human beings, particularly when they are affiliated with another race, creed, or culture? Do we real-

ly believe that what they believe, even though it may differ significantly from what we believe, is as important to them as our beliefs
are to us? Can we bring ourselves to accept that what they believe
is as valid in the human scheme of things as what we believe? We,
the authors, are convinced that unless this attitude is adopted there
can be no honest intercultural interaction. Any other form of interaction smacks of ethnocentrism and condescension and is probably
patronizing. The First Nations of Canada have a long history of
being regarded that way, and it is time to stop. The struggles and
challenges they face, as outlined in this book, are too much the
result of those kinds of attitudes, and the sooner they disappear, the
better. This book is a plea to all Canadians for a significant change
in mind-set. Gathering reliable information, making friends with
Indigenous peoples, and visiting their communities and participating in their public ceremonies, would be a good place to start.

# Projections

The attainment of an enriched intercultural understanding
between Canadians and members of the Indigenous community will
not likely be realized in this century. There are simply too many
complications. Canadians are generally too busy with the demands
of the competitive consumer-driven society that inveighs upon
every citizen to be completely fulfilled – biologically (by striving to
have a beautiful body), economically (by climbing up the ladder of
success), socially (by making beneficial political connections), and
psychologically (by being told by one's therapist that one is OK).
Unfortunately, this seems to be a busy enough schedule, without
having to investigate, understand, and appreciate alternative cultural and religious formats.

Native communities have similar challenges, as the various
chapters of this book will point out. These challenges are made
more complex by First Nations communities having to deal with
sometimes insensitive and uninformed government bureaucrats,
politically-minded, untrustworthy Native leaders (Adams, 1999;
Boldt, 1993; Cross, 2001; and Flanagan, 2000), and an over-
involved Canadian public. The good news is that better educated
Aboriginal youth are increasingly becoming familiar with the workings of the Canadian political bureaucracy – both at home and federally – and they will soon become leaders in their communities. In

the meantime, the challenge of educating the Canadian public remains at large.

## References

Adams, Howard. (1999). *Tortured People: The Politics of Colonization.* Revised edition. Penticton, BC: Theytus Books.

Battiste, Marie, and James (Sa'ke'j) Youngblood Henderson. (2000). *Protecting Indigenous Knowledge and Heritage.* Saskatoon, SK: Purich Publishing Ltd.

Boldt, Menno (1993). *Surviving as Indians: The Challenge of Self-Government.* Toronto, ON: University of Toronto Press.

Cardinal, Harold. (1977). *The Rebirth of Canada's Indians.* Edmonton, AB: Hurtig Publishers.

Cross, Martin. (December 17, 2001). Aboriginal Leaders Exploiting Their Own Communities. *Mennonite Reporter,* 5:24, 11.

Deloria, Jr., Vine. (1995). *Red Earth, White Lies.* New York: Scribner.

Dickason, Olive Patricia. (2000). Toward a Larger View of Canada's History: The Native Factor. *Visions of the Heart: Canadian Aboriginal Issues.* David Long and Olive Patricia Dickason, eds. Toronto, ON: Harcourt Canada, 11-30.

Dickason, Olive Patricia. (1984). *The Myth of the Savage and the Beginnings of French Colonialism in the Americas.* Edmonton, AB: University of Alberta Press.

Flanagan, Thomas. (2000). *First Nations? Second Thoughts?* Montreal, PQ: McGill-Queen's University Press.

Friesen, John W. (2000). *Aboriginal Spirituality and Biblical Theology: Closer Than You Think.* Calgary, AB: Detselig Enterprises.

Friesen, John W. (1999) *First Nations of the Plains: Creative, Adaptable, and Enduring.* Calgary, AB: Detselig Enterprises.

Hale, Horatio (1965). *The Iroquois Book of Rites.* Toronto, ON: University of Toronto Press, originally published in 1883.

Lischke, Ute, and David T. McNab. (2005). Introduction. *Walking a Tightrope: Aboriginal People and Their Representations.* Ute Lischke and David T. McNab, eds. Waterloo, ON: Wilfred Laurier University Press, 1-18.

Lowie, Robert. (1963). *Indians of the Plains.* New York: The American Museum of Natural History.

Lowie, Robert. (1924). *Primitive Religion.* New York: Grosset and Dunlap.

Morgan, Lewis H.  (1963). *Ancient Society.* Cleveland, OH: World Publishing.

Newhouse, David R., Cora J. Voyageur, and Dan Beavon. (2005). Introduction. *Contributions of Aboriginal Peoples to Canadian Identity and Culture.* David R. Newhouse, Cora J. Voyageur, and Dan Beavon, eds. Toronto, ON: University of Toronto Press, 3-13.

Prest, J. (January, 1922). Alberta Indians. *The Beaver,* 2:4, 5-6.

# Two

## The Evolution of Aboriginal Social Status

So common is this process that we might define prejudice as: an avertive or hostile attitude toward a person who belongs to a group, simply because he belongs to that group, and is therefore presumed to have the objectionable qualities ascribed to the group. (Allport, 1958: 8)

In discussions with parents, students, and staffing First Nations programs and services, students consistently report that their greatest challenge is the racism they experience. Moreover, expressions of racism escalate whenever there is a high profile conflict between First Nations and Canada, as tensions spill over into the school system. (Williams, 2000: 131)

Long before the white man over ran our vast domain, when we lived close to Nature, free to roam at will, Kisemanito, the Great Spirit, watched over the Cree speakers of the West. He had built the broad plains whereon immense herds of prairie cattle awaited us for the taking . . . (Dion, 1979: 2)

At one time in the distant past, most people around the world lived in tribal societies. Their close-knit societies provided them with a particular land-space, a strong sense of identity, and a bond of loyalty. In addition, the parameters of membership and mandated lifestyle were clearly spelled out for each individual. If one was born into a specific sib or clan or band, one's life path was fairly well delineated. Of course individual achievements either propelled by ability or spiritual vision could alter one's journey to some extent, the end result was that the local community would derive any benefits. Even this did not in any way raise questions about individual identity. Each person knew who he or she was in terms delineated by the local community.

First Nations societies as well as contemporary nonNative civilizations have a tribal background hidden somewhere in the past. They thrived in well-defined territories and used distinct dialects, and their members lived according to a well-outlined code of

29

thought and behavior. Over time they developed a strong sense of peoplehood and everyone knew their place. There was never much debate about such matters, and although new members were sometimes added through birth or by capturing members from neighboring tribes (who often became slaves), this did not affect the assignment or transmission of membership. In fact, this is the way all Native American tribes lived before being visited by Spanish and French explorers.

# Visitors Arrive

According to archaeological and historical speculations, the First Peoples of North America developed a local civilization some 12 000 to 15 000 years ago – depending on which source one consults. Before that, they may have lived somewhere else, but there is really only scant scientific proof to back that statement. Noted Métis historian, Olive Dickason, observes that many First Nations claim as North America is their land of origin, and their myths and legends metaphorically if not factually confirm that observation. Their oral history also emphasizes and underscores their fundamental attachment to the earth (Dickason, 1993: 21). The Bering Strait theory, for so long popular among historians, posits that the original inhabitants of North America migrated from Siberia along a temporary ice-free corridor, along the eastern slope of the Rocky Mountains, but research has not yet yielded the expected archaeological documentation of the theory. Historian-philosopher, the late Vine Deloria Jr., was fond of describing allusions to the Bering Strait theory:

> Basically, they were simply repeating scholarly folklore, since there is, to my knowledge, no good source that articulates the theory in any reasonable format. Indeed this "theory" has been around for so long that people no longer feel they have to explain to or defend it – they can merely refer to it. (Deloria, 1995: 45)

Deloria goes on to suggest that the Bering Strait theory is simply scientific shorthand for "I don't know, but it sounds good and no one will check" (Deloria, 1995: 81). If Deloria is correct, the primary reason for advancing the theory is simply to justify European colonization. If it can convincingly be argued that the First Peoples were also immigrants to North America at one time, they would lose their claim to being original inhabitants and with that the right of first occupancy.

The first European visitors to North America offered somewhat uninformed and negative diarized impressions of local inhabitants. Descriptors such as "ignorant, not well-informed, uncivilized, savage, and cannibals" frequented the pages of the diaries of early explorers, although a few positive notes were also included (Dickason, 1984: 5f). Christopher Columbus, for example, in a letter to the King and Queen of Spain, included this gem among his first impressions of Native North Americans.

> So tractable, so peaceful are these people that I swear to your Majesties that there is not in the world a better nation. They love their neighbors as themselves, and their discourse is ever sweet and gentle, and accompanied with a smile. . . . Their manners are so decorous and praiseworthy (Brown, 1981: 1).

Dickason (2006: 26f) makes the point that the "new world" encountered by the first Europeans who migrated here, was far from new. The Indigenous people had lived here for a long time, and built many stable societies. When the newcomers arrived, one of their main objectives was to engage in trade with local residents, particularly if they had items of interest for entrepreneurs back home. Trade was only one prong of the European overall plan, the other being to expand the land holdings of their home country. Local AmerIndians were quite eager to engage in trade, of course, because the newcomers offered items that were not locally available. Often trade negotiations include gift-giving, thereby setting the stage for the kind of diplomacy that produced amiable relations.

There is little doubt that the first European visitors soon discovered a significant cultural gap between themselves and their new acquaintances and, following the impulse ingrained in them by their own cultural affiliations over the centuries, attempted to make over the locals. While it is currently popular to depict these efforts as those of evil imperialists, the truth is that the newcomers were merely living out the mandate of their own socialization. They were not evil people by nature, and like anyone else, they adhered to the dictates of their upbringing. If anyone, like the Native North Americans, held beliefs different than their own, they felt that it was their solemn duty to dissuade them of these and prescribe a more "civilized" route. Consequently, the cultural and spiritual differences between incoming Europeans and local First Nations became increasingly pronounced.

As time went on, differences between the two parties – Aboriginal and nonAboriginal – arose in virtually every domain, particularly the way land was viewed. Local Indians perceived the land as Mother Earth who, together with the Great Spirit, their Father, provided sustenance for their children. Europeans, on the other hand, saw land as something to be seized and owned – a kind of winner takes all attitude. The Indigenous people recognized the spirit resident in all earthly phenomena and respected their workings. Hence, if game had to be killed for food, the animal spirit was approached in prayer, explaining why the killing deed was necessary. Afterwards a prayer of thanks was offered to the spirit of the animal. By contrast, Europeans simply killed animals whenever they felt the need for fresh meat.

Still another difference between the two parties had to do with the concept of sharing. The AmerIndian view was that if an individual had needed resources at his or her disposal, they had to be shared with anyone in need, particularly anyone connected to the individual's immediate family, clan, or band. As awareness of these differences intensified, the Europeans tried that much harder to convince the Indians of the errors of their ways.

## Identity Makeover

The peopling of North America was undertaken by several different European groups, each with a slightly different objective. When the North American mission was enlarged to capacity, about four distinct campaigns were launched by various European sectors (Barman, Hébert, and McCaskill, 1986). First were the fur traders who were mainly concerned with economic gain, but they were not far removed philosophically from the second group, their European counterparts, the settlers, who came to build permanent centres of French civilization in the New World. Third, were the missionaries whose stated intentions were not primarily to achieve economic gain. They intended to "Christianize, educate, and civilize" the Indians, and made no apology for it. Later it was evident that they became, somewhat inadvertently, the principal agents of European assimilation. Stoney Chief John Snow (2005: 28) calls them unwitting "advance men" for the new way of life. Basically involved in trying to make over the "uncivilized" Indians, the missionaries did try to protect their protégés from peddlers of liquor and others who tried to exploit them. In addition, there were those who fought courageously on behalf of the rights of First Nations, even though they denied the Indians the right to practice their traditional ceremonies and rituals (Jaenen, 1986; Josephy, 1968).

The fourth group of European visitors to Canadian Indian country were official representatives of the state, specifically France and Britain, but also Spain in the more southerly regions. These representatives backed missionary efforts to establish permanent centres of religion and civilization and even helped finance missionary endeavors. An indication of their working together, although not always in agreement, was the Papal Bull issued by Pope Paul III in 1537 that threatened excommunication to anyone who enslaved Indians or tried to take away their possessions. Despite some differences in philosophy, the relationship continued well into the nineteenth and twentieth centuries when the combined efforts of church and state helped sponsor schooling as the primary vehicle in the "civilization" and advancement of Canadian First Nations. As Melling (1967: 47) notes:

> Without a doubt, however, the most valuable provision of the Treaties – not written into them all, but now a regular feature of government service – was formal schooling. . . . schooling was an aspect of the total process whereby people – and in a country like Canada, especially the less developed people who were of distinctive cultural background – could come to feel at home in the wider society.

During the seventeenth and eighteenth centuries, relationships between European colonists and the different First Nations could be described as one of shifting alliances. As the exploration of North America continued, the Indigenous people were perceived to some extent in mixed ways – traders saw them as allies of sorts and missionaries and servants of the state saw them as potential converts and citizens. By the end of the eighteenth century Europeans were trading with inland tribes, building primarily on routes established during the glory days of the fur trade. It was also a period during which imported diseases took a tremendous toll on Indigenous people and many tribes lost more than half of their populations. For many First Nations it was a time of displacement and migration and a growing campaign by government officials to transform Indian culture to an agricultural base (Wilson and Urion, 1995: 55).

It has been estimated that during the nineteenth century, as many as fifty million Europeans migrated to the New World, looking for land to settle. The intensification of industrialization in Europe caused this displacement, and opportunities in North America comprised an alluring option. Canada forged its identity as a nation around the middle of the nineteenth century and promptly began negotiations with First Nations in an effort to free up land for incoming settlers. Treaty No. 1 was signed with the Peguis Band (Ojibway) in 1871 in Manitoba, and six more treaties were signed in that decade. Now First Nations were seen by many as a kind of nuisance who had to be accommodated until their numbers died out.

In 1876, perhaps realizing that they did not really have legal ground on which to proceed with treaty negotiations, the new Canadian government passed the Indian Act, primarily as a means of identifying who by law, should be awarded Indian Status. That way the government would know precisely with whom they were dealing. Although the first option was to consider blood quantum in assigning Status (Frideres and Gadacz, 2001: 25), the government soon gave up on that idea and, as outlined in the previous chapter, simply had people stand in line to be counted.

The image of Canada's First Nations at the beginning of the twentieth century was that of "poor, doomed savages," and this image did not change for some thirty years (Haycock, 1971: 1f). Based on the traditional AngloSaxon notion that every civilization is prone to follow Darwin's theory of improvement through evolution, the popular perception was that Canada's Indigenous peoples had some ways to go. No one could deny that they possessed prowess, cunning, and dignity, but they still tended to be perceived as ignorant and slothful in AngloSaxon ways.

Canada's First Nations were surprised to discover that their land holdings were not immune to fraud and confiscation. Although promises that they could keep certain lands had been made in writing via the treaties, time and time again officials of the federal government broke their word. In Manitoba, for example, the Indians were preyed upon by land speculators and dishonest or desperate settlers who tricked them into selling off parcels of reserve land which the Indians believed they held title to as individuals. Land predators also took timber from Aboriginal lands without giving compensation. The government promised that justice would be done, but did nothing. It has been estimated that during the prime ministership of Wilfred Laurier (1896-1911), some 600 000 to 700 000 acres of Indian lands were sold for an average of ten cents per acre. The reason for this action was to accommodate settlers who would make "better" use of the land (Treaty Days, 1971: 56; Friesen, 1977: 127).

After some thirty years of witnessing little progress towards adopting mainstream societal ways amidst dwindling Aboriginal populations, Canadians began to change their minds about the Indigenous people. A sense of "we ought to do better by our Indians" arose in humanitarian minded circles, and a number of help related programs were originated. In 1930, for example, Richard Finnie was commissioned to visit the north and make recommendations regarding ways to improve life among northern Aboriginals. In his report Finnie spent a great deal of space describing the dress, manner of trading, and camp life of the northern peoples, particularly deploring the negative influences of "white man's vices" such as alcohol and gambling. He noted that some Indian agents convinced Native locals to sell off their treaty rights for the sum of $50.00, thereby no longer entitling them to federal health, education, and welfare benefits. The popular press picked up on Finnie's research and a new awareness of the Indians' plight became manifest (Haycock, 1971: 33).

In the meantime, a number of church congregations and religious organizations were actively endeavoring to provide relief to members of Indian communities by distributing food and clothing, and urging youth to attend religious postsecondary schools. They were joined by a number of secular organizations, "Totemland," for example, that was begun by prominent Vancouver philanthropist, Harry Duker, with the intent of "protecting Indian art." Duker believed that to promote the objectives of Totemland one would have to understand First Nations culture. He perceived that the best way to do this was by eating authentic Indian food – baked salmon, seaweed soup and clams, and roasted Indian potatoes. By serving such food to guests at his home Duker tried to establish that not only were there Indian artists but gourmet cooks as well. His efforts even earned him an article in *Saturday Night Magazine* (Haycock, 1971: 35).

Unfortunately, during this time public perceptions of the First Nations way of life were primarily formed by the press, which was the most accessible form of public knowledge. Government documents were relatively scarce in number and academic studies, basically anthropological in nature, were usually only consulted by academics. Thus the public had to rely on the press or on personal experience to obtain information about First Nations. The press was quite negative about Indian culture and anthropologists did little better. In 1922, for example, a Methodist missionary was described in an Alberta newspaper (*The Albertan*), as having helped Indians to no longer be content to "eat the bread of idleness," but seek religious and secular education in order to learn of the white man's methods of working and civilization. That year an issue of *The Beaver,* a publication of the Hudson's Bay Company, described the Indian as "still a child, literally speaking, and assimilation is slow" (Friesen, 1977: 128).

Anthropological descriptions of Aboriginal culture were hardly more enlightening (Friesen, 1991: 27). To begin with, John McLean wrote a book entitled, *Canada's Savage Folk* (1896), George Bird Grinnell observed that "the Indian has the mind of a child in the body of an adult" (Grinnell, 1900: 8), and Ruth Benedict denounced the West Coast potlatch ceremony as ranking "low on the scale of human values" (Benedict, 1934). Robert Lowie, described Indian theological beliefs in a book entitled, *Primitive Religion* (Lowie, 1924), and Diamond Jenness portrayed Aboriginal spirituality as "crude" and "curious" (Jenness, 1977: 181-183). As time went on and social scientists became more sensitive to their inherent ethnocentrism, descriptions of the Indigenous lifestyle became more analytic. The scene changed dramatically when First Nations writers began to publish ethnological descriptions of their culture even to the point of being a bit more positive than the situation merited. Who could blame them in taking this approach after being subject to centuries of discrimination and literary misrepresentation (Friesen and Friesen, 2005: 44f)?

The civil rights movement of the 1960s drew attention to a myriad of depressed social sectors, motivated by such happenings as anti-Vietnam demonstrations, Black Power, Red Power, and student movements, and the emergence of Canadian multiculturalism. By this time a significant number of Aboriginal leaders had sufficiently familiarized themselves with the workings of mainstream Canadian institutions effectively to draw attention to a host of social injustices against First Nations. Members of the Six Nations Reserve near Brantford, Ontario, declared themselves an independent nation, a happening that led to similar events across the nation. The Six Nations had at one time been granted some 700 000 acres of land along the Grand River, but nonNatives (with government sanction), had whittled Six Nations' holdings down to only 30 000 acres. Small wonder that the people were motivated to launch a public protest.

Another front on which Canada's Indigenous peoples did not fare well was with regard to the quality of education. By now residential schools were slowly being shut down and finally the first such school was turned over to local control in 1970. That event took place in St. Paul, Alberta, after a three-month sit-in by more than one hundred local Cree residents. By 1985, about two-thirds of schools on Indian reserves were either totally or partially under the control of local Indian school boards. In the meantime, however, Native youth had to contend with daily encounters of prejudice and discrimination at the hands of those who thought them incapable of competing with their nonNative peers. Federal educational policy in the 1960s dictated that Aboriginal children be integrated in provincial schools so that, having eventually attained a worthy education, they could eventually enjoy the same privileges available to other Canadians. This policy was backed by the White Paper created by the liberal government of Pierre Elliott Trudeau with Jean Chrétien serving as Minister of Indian Affairs and Northern Development. Essentially the White Paper suggested that all Status Indians be treated the same as any other Canadian citizen with health, education, and welfare administered by the ten provincial governments. Trudeau and his colleagues believed that the best way to accomplish this objective was to abolish the *Indian Act* and the signed treaties and start negotiations from scratch with regard to Indian needs.

First Nations reactions and objections to the White Paper were swift and blunt, and no one suspected that they would emerge so quickly. Native leaders requested that the Indian Act remain and the intent of the treaties be honored. Justice would be done, they argued, by their having to deal with only one government (federal), instead of ten provincial governments. Quickly the White Paper was shelved and slow moving negotiations about Indigenous needs have been ongoing ever since. The good news is that today Aboriginal communities have in their midst a number of prominent and informed leaders who understand the workings of bureaucratic systems and are able occasionally make a dent when involved in negotiations.

As outlined in the previous chapter, Aboriginal people in Canada have the unique distinction of being segregated from their fellow citizens in many ways by federal law. This fact has undoubtedly contributed towards the way they are perceived by the Canadian public. This happened with the passing of the *Indian Act* in 1876, which established Canadian Indians as wards of the government, a not too complimentary designation that promised health, education, and welfare services to First Nations through federal auspices. Thus the First Nations deal directly or indirectly with the federal government, or its representatives, when these services are needed. Officially they have little or nothing to do with the ten provincial governments.

# The Contemporary Situation

Although the vast number of Canadians is still quite uninformed about traditional Aboriginal ways and Indigenous spirituality and knowledge, there is a glimmer of hope that the situation will gradually change for the better. Recent emphasis on Canadian multiculturalism has certainly helped, although the status of First Nations is quite dissimilar from the rest of the population. For example, the First Nations have federal treaties that guarantee them certain rights. They also have rights of first occupancy, and they are the only people in Canada not to have come from somewhere else. They are a deeply spiritual people – spiritual, not religious – in the sense that they see every human act and thought as significant in terms of their individual journeys. Religion is better defined as adherence to a certain set of expectations at certain times of the day, week, month, or year – particularly at Christmas time and during the Easter season.

It is well-known that Canada's First Nations come from a long tradition of respecting the workings of nature as opposed to exploiting its resources to the nth degree, allegedly for the betterment of society. It is gradually being recognized that Canada's First Nations are at the forefront of the environmental movement, having been good stewards of our natural resources for centuries (Dickason, 2000: 25). Battiste (2000: 201) posits that dominant society is in sore need of what Aboriginal knowledge has to offer in this regard. Perhaps it is not too late to listen to what their elders have to tell us.

Finally, it is noteworthy that many Indigenous people still believe that it is better to give than to receive, and many in their communities try to live according to that mandate. Ironically, the basis of western society allegedly rests on the Christian Gospel that prizes a spirit of humility in the act of giving. Jesus himself said, "Be careful not to do your 'acts of righteousness' before men to be seen by them. If you do, you will have no reward from your Father in heaven. . . . But when you give to the needy, do not let your left hand know what your right hand is doing, so that your giving may be in secret" (Matthew 6:1, 3-4 NIV). It would appear that many First Nations practices are quite in keeping with the Christian Gospel.

Given these significant differences in philosophical orientation and social practice, and having grounded them in several centuries of misunderstanding and colonialism, it would be unreasonable to expect very significant changes in a short period of time. However, there is some good news. The media, for example, are no longer able to publish racist new stories about Indians although some of them do manage to camouflage their underlying ethnocentrism. A number of pseudo-religious organizations have attempted to lay claim to Indigenous spirituality and even sponsored conferences on related themes. While these efforts are not entirely wrong, they often tend to be led by Aboriginal individuals who are sometimes known as "circus elders" in local Native communities. This designation originates from the fact that the New Age elders are not recognized as such in their home communities and they often sponsor public ceremonies basically for monetary gain. In traditional times elders might expect to receive a gift for conducting ceremonies, but they would not perform them as a means of seeking financial gain.

Many Indigenous communities have made significant economic gains that help them employ local people, either through direct band investment or in partnership with outside agencies (Henlin, 2006: 177f). Enrollment of Native youth in postsecondary institutions is also strong, and shows a vast increase in numbers. Over recent decades, the numbers of Aboriginal youth attending postsecondary schools doubled in the decade between 1988 and 1998 and today numbers more than 30 000 (Friesen and Friesen, 2005: 13).

There is more good news, all of it contributing to the increasingly positive image of First Nations in Canada. Native arts of various genres – architecture, painting and printmaking, ceramics, carving, sculpture, jewelry-making, mask-making, drama, film, graphic arts, basketry, music and dance, and comic performances – have become internationally recognized. Today there are more than one hundred Native artists from all across the country being formally recognized through a multiplicity of avenues. Their cultural affiliations range from the Beothuk and Mi'kmaq on the east coast across the country through the woodland, plains, and plateau regions to the land of the Haida, Tsimshian, Gitksan, and Tlinget communities on the west coast. Northern art comprises a unique genre and has established itself in its own right (Friesen and Friesen, 2006: i).

When the first portrayals of Aboriginal art by incoming Europeans appeared they were basically descriptive, and the first museums built in this country did not even bother to display them. By 1925, things had changed and the Denver Art Museum not only included Native art in its displays, but displayed it as art, not craft, as had previously been the case. Today museums all across the country include various forms of Indigenous art in their repertoires. For example, the Canadian Museum of Civilization in Hull, Quebec, has an extensive collection of Indigenous Art, much of it commissioned to Native artists, and its Grand Hall is entirely devoted to such a display.

# Projections

There is little doubt that the process of assimilating First Nations is still underway, but its impact is not longer as subtle as it once was. First Nations leaders are aware of its functioning and are developing means by which to sidetrack it. The Indian cultural renaissance that began in the 1960s has intensified and the self-image of being Indian has grown stronger. Improved education, increased emphasis on the role of traditional elders, and an intensification of cultural activities has given Aboriginal people the strength to face the onslaught of assimilation and triumph. Warry (2007: 35) points out that many social scientists, anthropologists chief among them, have for a long time tended to frame their understanding of Aboriginal culture in terms of the gradual disappearance of traditional ways and adopting of EuroCanadian values and customs. Instead, Native people, rather than adopting western ideas and practices, have adapted them to suit their own cultural purposes. This has often proven frustrating to observers because, not being Aboriginal, they have no means by which to predict what direction that adaptation will take. Warry refers to the gradual use of snowmobiles and ATVs by Native hunters, which allowed them to hunt more efficiently, but they still hunted. Many Native children trained in residential schools did not necessarily adopt western ways but returned to their home communities using the literary skills they had attained to agitate for Aboriginal rights.

Today government policies still tend towards promoting subtle forms of assimilation, but academics who are interested in First

Nations societies, are tending to perceive alternative routes for First Nations destiny. This suggests that they have been listening to Aboriginal people as the latter spell out the preferred route they wish to take in regard to their future. One thing is certain, any future plans that are to be made with regard to Indian culture and identity will have to involve a partnership among all interested parties – Aboriginals and government, and indeed all Canadians (Miller, 2000: 405). Aboriginal people are no longer willing to settle for anything less.

## References

Allport, Gordon W. (1958). *The Nature of Prejudice: A Comprehensive and Penterating Study of the Origin and Nature of Prejudice*. New York: Doubleday.

Barman, Jean, Yvonne Hébert, and Don McCaskill, eds. (1986). The Legacy of the Past: An Overview. *Indian Education in Canada,* Volume 1: *The Legacy*. Vancouver, BC: University of British Columbia Press, 1-22.

Battiste, Marie. (2000). Maintaining Aboriginal Identity, Language and Culture in Modern Socie*ty. Reclaiming Indigenous Voice and Vision*. Marie Battiste, ed. Vancouver, BC: UBC Press, 192-208.

Benedict, Ruth. (1934). *Patterns of Culture*. New York: The New American Libary.

Brown, Dee. (1981). *Bury My Heart at Wounded Knee*. New York: Holt, Rinehart & Winston.

Deloria, Vine, Jr. (1995). *Red Earth, White Lies: Native Americans and the Myth of Scientific Fact*. New York: Scribner.

Dickason, Olive Patricia. (2006). *A Concise History of Canada's First Nations*. Toronto, AB: Oxford University Press.

Dickason, Olive Patricia. (2000). Toward a Larger View of Canada's History: The Native Factor. *Visions of the Heart: Canadian Aboriginal Issues*. David Long and Olive Patricia Dickason, eds. Toronto, ON: Harcourt Canada, 11-30.

Dickason, Olive Patricia. (1993). *Canada's First Nations: A History of Founding Peoples from Earliest Times*. Toronto, ON: McClelland and Stewart.

Dickason, Olive Patricia. (1984). *The Myth of the Savage and the Beginnings of French Colonialism in the Americas*. Edmonton, AB: University of Alberta Press.

Dion, Joseph F. (1979). *My Tribe, The Crees*. Calgary, AB: Glenbow Museum.

Frideres, James S., and René R. Gadacz. (2001). *Aboriginal Peoples in Canada: Contemporary Conflicts.* Sixth edition. Toronto, ON: Pearson Canada.

Friesen, John W. (1991). Native Cultures in a Cultural Clash. *The Cultural Maze: Complex Questions on Native Destiny in Western Canada.* John W. Friesen, ed. Calgary, AB: Detselig Enterprises, 23-38.

Friesen, John W. (1977). *People, Culture & Learning.* Calgary, AB: Detselig Enterprises.

Friesen, John W., and Virginia Lyons Friesen. (2006). *Canadian Aboriginal Art and Spirituality: A Vital Link.* Calgary, AB: Detselig Enterprises.

Friesen, John W., and Virginia Lyons Friesen. (2005). *First Nations in the Twenty-First Century: Contemporary Educational Frontiers.* Calgary, AB: Detselig Enterprises.

Grinnell, George Bird. (1900). *The North American Indians of Today.* London, UK: C. Arthur Pearson, Ltd.

Haycock, Ronald G. (1971). *The Image of the Indian.* Waterloo, ON: Waterloo Lutheran University.

Henlin, Calvin. (2006). *Dances with Dependency: Indigenous Success Through Self-Reliance.* Vancouver, BC: Orca Spirit Publishing.

Jaenen, Cornelius. (1986). Education for Francisation: The Case of New France in the Seventeenth Century. *Indian Education in Canada, Volume 1: The Legacy.* Jean Barman, Yvonne Hébert, and Don McCaskill, eds. Vancouver, BC: University of British Columbia Press, 45-63.

Jenness, Diamond. (1977). *The Indians of Canada.* Seventh edition. Toronto, ON: University of Toronto Press.

Josephy, Alvin M., Jr. (1968). *The Indian Heritage of America.* New York: Alfred A. Knopf.

Lowie, Robert. (1924). *Primitive Religion.* New York: Grosset and Dunlop.

MacLean, John. (1896). *Canada's Savage Folk.* London, UK: William Briggs.

Melling, John. (1967). *Right to a Future: The Native Peoples of Canada.* Don Mills, ON: T. H. Best Printing Company.

Miller, J. R. (2000). *Skyscrapers Hide the Heavens: A History of Indian-White Relations in Canada.* Third edition. Toronto, ON: University of Toronto Press.

Snow, Chief John. (2005). *These Mountains Are Our Sacred Places: The Story of the Stoney People.* Calgary, AB: Fitzhenry and Whiteside.

Treaty Days. (1971). *Manitoba Indian Brotherhood.* Winnipeg, MB: Centennial Commemoration Historial Pageant.

Warry, Wayne. (2007). *Ending Denial: Understanding Aboriginal Issues.* Peterborough, ON: Broadview Press.

Williams, Lorna. (2000). Urban Aboriginal Education: The Vancouver Experience. *Aboriginal Education: Fulfilling the Promise.* Marlene Brant Castellano, Lynne Davis, and Louise Lahache, eds. Vancouver, BC: UBC Press. 129-146.

Wilson, C. Roderick, and Carl Urion. (1995). First Nations Prehistory and Canadian History. *Native Peoples: The Canadian Experience.* R. Bruce Morrison and C. Roderick Wilson, eds. Toronto, ON: McClelland and Stewart, 22-66.

# Three

# Cataloguing Indigenous
# Knowledge and Spirituality:
# The Pedagogical Dimension

Indigenous knowledge is different from the internal view of the ethnographic tradition in Eurocentric thought. . . . typically, rather than attempting  to understand Indigenous knowledge as a distinct knowledge system, researchers have tried to make Indigenous knowledge match the existing academic categories of Eurocentric knowledge. (Marie Battiste and James [Sa'ke'j] Youngblood Henderson, 2000: 39)

As nonAboriginal authors we are justifiably a bit hesitant to discuss traditional Indigenous knowledge, but several incidents of special encouragement have motivated us to take up the challenge, and at least offer a nonAboriginal point of view – albeit, a respectful one.

## Background Experiences

Several years ago, while preparing to conduct a workshop for teachers on the topic of Aboriginal world-view (most of them nonNative), we had opportunity to meet with a half dozen prospective participants of Cree background all of whom had been previously been enrolled in university courses which we taught. Each of them was now engaged as a schoolteacher in his or her home community.

"Something is wrong with this picture," we ventured. "This is an area with which you are much more familiar than we are. Perhaps you should be doing this session."

Almost in unison, the group voiced their disagreement. "No way," they said, "Most nonNative people will not listen to us as much as they will to you because you speak their language!" with this support, we proceeded to undertake our assignment. After the session concluded we again had opportunity to engage our friends in conversation to inquire into their reactions to our sharing their knowledge. They were most supportive and even asked us to spend some time with the nonNative principal of their school. They felt we might have something useful to share with that administrator.

A second unusual source of encouragement came from a Cree elder who is also a pipe carrier, and who had been pierced four times during Sundance ceremonies. Having read my (John) book, *You Can't Get There From Here: The Mystique of Plains Indians Culture & Philosophy* (Friesen, 1995), and listening to my lectures, he approached me with these observations:

> The title of your book is wrong. Having listened to your lectures over the past several months I now believe that it is possible for a nonNative individual to understand our ways. You have shown this through your grasp of Indigenous knowledge. You may want to change the title of your book. I believe that some nonNatives, like yourself, can get there!

Later, this individual awarded me with a teaching eagle feather accompanied by a special ritual. I was instructed that after a cleansing ceremony with sweetgrass, the feather could be held in hand and while doing so, to the best of one's knowledge, only truth would be told. This is at once a very special privilege and sacred responsibility.

A third very unique occasion of trust occurred in 2006, shortly after the death of the late Rev. Dr. John Snow, who was for many years chief of the Wesley Band of the Stoney (Nakoda Sioux) First Nation. John Snow was a close friend of ours for nearly forty years and he often spoke to our classes and at conferences we sponsored for students on the Stoney Reserve. Nationally known for his concerned political and religious involvement with First Nations organizations, John was also author of a popular book entitled, *These Mountains Are Our Sacred Places: The Story of the Stoney Indians* (Fitzhenry and Whiteside, 2005).

A few months after having been privileged to conduct John Snow's funeral, he appeared to me (John) in a dream. In the dream we were gathered at an assembly of band council where I was a visitor but invited to speak. Seated next to me was the late Lazarus Wesley, an esteemed Stoney elder. I remember hesitating, apologizing that I had no notes from which to speak, when John Snow interrupted me. "Never mind your notes, John," he stated firmly. "What you have learned and what you have to say are much more important than any notes you might have. Tell the people what you know and do not hesitate. It is important that you do so. You know many things that people need to hear!"

I awoke from the dream with a start and realized that I had been given an important mandate – one that I intend to carry out. This book constitutes part of that mandate.

## Philosophical Differences

Students of First Nations history, culture, and philosophy are gradually discovering that there are profound differences between Indigenous knowledge and that akin to European-imported ideas. The way Aboriginals traditionally used to think (and many still do), and the way members of dominant society view the world are very different. A study of pedagogical methodology, for example, reflects these differences in the way Aboriginal children used to be taught, and the way children are generally taught in today's schools. In the first instance, in traditional First Nations cultures, the teaching/learning process was not primarily undertaken in formal settings – like schools, although many First Nations did have formal structures in place in which to pass along revered spiritual and cultural knowledge (Friesen, 1993). These formal institutions, known as sodalities or religious societies, were entrusted to the leadership of respected elders who alone had the right to pass along knowledge pertaining to spiritual beliefs, medicine, or ceremonial and ritualistic practices.

Historians, archaeologists, and anthropologists seem to be generally agreed that early humans on all continents once identified sequences and repetitions in the world around them – the alternation of day and night, the coming and going of the seasons, the cycle of the tides, and the movement of the stars across the night sky. They learned how to use the patterns of migrating animals and the seasonal successions of plant life (Suzuki, 1997: 10). They designed and modified their cultural patterns in sync with the rhythms of nature. Now, looking back, it seems possible to weave together at least the rudiments of a worldview that was once common to Indigenous peoples all over the world. As certain civilizations changed, however, differences in the way the universe was viewed shifted from respect for the workings of nature toward the abilities of humankind. Enhanced technology, new ideas about change, and perceptions of the role of homosapiens in the universe convinced many to abandon ancient ways of perceiving the universe and assume a more dominating role. Soon it was believed that mankind could conquer and tame the rhythms of nature and develop a new kind of world. Many cultures, however, refused to take on a conquering stance and continued to respect the traditions of the past.

The Indigenous peoples of the Americas have tried to continue honoring the rhythms of nature, but there are signs that their way of life has also been subject to significant change. Even a superficial analysis will reveal that there are huge gaps between traditional Indigenous knowledge and knowledge getting, and the way that most many First Nations today are beginning to perceive the workings of the universe. These differences are soundly reflected in sectors of the teaching and learning milieu.

Despite having to acknowledge distinct differences between traditional Indigenous pedagogy and the contemporary EuroCanadian approach, the following discussion tries to draw parallels between aspects of the two systems of thought. After all, it would be incorrect to label contemporary North American educational thought as classically European in focus. The influence of progressive minded educators has influenced what might be called two basic homegrown systems of thought on the teaching and learning processes. These two systems of thought may be categorized into two relatively distinct systems – behaviorism and humanism. Indigenous thought can by inference more easily be compared with humanism. Informal documentation to bolster this observation will be drawn from personal research conducted in western Canada's Plains Indian configurations (Friesen, 1997; Friesen, 1999; Friesen and Friesen, 2001, 2002, and 2005a).

## Theoretical Pedagogical Framework

American philosopher John Dewey once said that the difference between educational practices that are influenced by a well thought-out philosophy and those that are not so influenced is quite clear. The former is impelled by a clear idea of the ends to be achieved while the latter is educational practice that is conducted blindly, probably under the control of unexamined customs or traditions (Archambault, 1964: 17). Dewey went on to say that it would not necessarily make any difference to the end result even if the "blind" forms of education were conducted under the guise of philosophical deliberation. Clarification and analysis of aims, objectives, and ends to be achieved are most effective when elaborated before practice is undertaken.

The First Nations of western Canada cannot be charged with proceeding pedagogically or in regard to any cultural practice without substantial theoretical backup. Granted that their philosophical backdrop was anchored in the oral tradition and shrouded in metaphysical mystery (at least it appeared so to outsiders), but their varied cultural content, which included legends, rituals, sacred ceremonies, sites, and objects comprised a massive curriculum to be appropriated by every neophyte, without benefit of written form. The underlying rationale was grounded in and derived from a series of specific philosophical assumptions backed by centuries of practice. The teaching/learning theory on which they based their methodology adheres in its presuppositions quite closely to what is sometimes called progressive education. It must be emphasized that the information in this chapter has a distinct traditional western Canadian Plains Indian bias.

It is useful at the outset of this discussion to point out that European and North American educators have long been confronted by a myriad of learning theories going back to Plato and Aristotle. In fact, there are fundamentally only two philosophical camps whose postulations underlie the teaching/learning process and they still reign – at least in North America. For lack of more sophisticated terminology (here philosophers of education might cringe), they may be labeled behaviorism and humanism.

## Modern Historical Beginnings

Fast forwarding to the modern period beginning with the sixteenth century, relevant postulations on the subject pedagogy are usually traced to the musings of one Johann Amos Comenius (1592-1670), also known as Johann Komensky, a Moravian educator. Comenius postulated that the rhythms of nature should be utilized in formulating educational methods. Among his observations was the notion that "nature observes a suitable time" (Bayles and Hood, 1966: 31) which, translated, means that children should be taught when they are ready to learn. Comenius wrote several well-known books explicating his ideas, the most popular being his *Didactica Magna* (The Great Didactic), which was to contain all the knowledge of his day. His penchant for wanting to adhere closely to the patterns of nature modeled a great many subsequent theories.

John Locke (1632-1704), an Englishman and forerunner of behaviorism, took an opposite stance to that of Comenius, and laid the foundations for faculty psychology and formal discipline. Locke believed that manipulating sensations could produce acceptable habits that would produce character. Character development, of course, was to provide the foundation for the finishing of English gentlemen, the object of Locke's undertakings. Locke advocated the enforcement of good habits through the manipulation of students' mental muscles.

Jean Jacques Rousseau (1712-1778), probably inadvertently followed up on Comenius' line of thinking by projecting the notion that education is a case of natural unfoldment, that is, "everything is good as it comes from the hands of the Creator," (Rousseau, 1911: 1). Therefore, only good can come from letting young children roam freely in the woods. In fact, children should be encouraged to unleash their natural tendencies. Rousseau denied having provided his imaginary pupil, Emile, with any form of guidance, but a closer examination of the work will reveal that Rousseau did a little manipulation of events so that Emile would come to "correct" conclusions about the workings of nature.

It was Johann Heinrich Pestalozzi (1746-1827), education's "most successful failure" (Bayles and Hood, 1966: 98), who patterned the education of his own son, Jacobli, after Rousseau's instructions. Working in Switzerland, Pestalozzi tried three times to incorporate his theory of sense impressionism into the workings of orphanages he established, but they all withered away. He even wrote a very successful novel, *Leonard and Gertrude,* to illustrate the art of sense impressionism, but before it became a success he sold the copyright for very little money. Moreover, people who read the book liked the plot, rather than appreciating its underlying educational theory. What did remain of Pestalozzi's influence motivated the formation of the child-centred movement in North American education. Educators from the United States and various parts of Europe visited Pestalozzi's experimental schools and modelled their systems accordingly. One could go so far as to say that Pestalozzi's idea framed the foundation of the progressive education movement in the United States.

Pestalozzi believed that what children see, hear, smell, taste, or touch forms the basis of their vat of knowledge. It therefore behooves educators to see that children fully experience everything around them via sense perception. One of Pestalozzi's students, Ramsauer, left a written record noting that the schools Pestalozzi started had no regular school plan nor lessons, and Pestalozzi did not limit himself to any set time when he discussed matters; he often went on with the same subject for two or three hours (Bayles and Hood, 1966: 104). Rarely did Pestalozzi examine the work of his students but let them draw whatever they felt like drawing; after all, true education burgeoned from within.

One would be remiss not to note what was happening on the behaviorist side of the fence with the work of early twentieth century psychologists Edward L. Thorndike (1874-1949) and John B. Watson (1878-1958). Thorndike's theory gave rise to such concepts as reflex-arc and psychological connectionism, implying that learning is a matter of stimulation, excitation, efferent transmission, central adjustment, and response. In short, this projected series of desired developments was soon labelled stimulus-response theory (Herrick, 1924: 121). Thorndike's contemporary, John B. Watson, set out to repudiate the introspective method in psychology and contended that the chief function of the nervous system was simply to coordinate senses with motor responses. Watson posited that the senses are not only capable of gaining knowledge of the world but are also instruments in guiding activity. Watson therefore rejected such concepts as purpose, feeling, satisfaction, and free will because he believed that they were not observable and not capable of scientific treatment or measurement (Ozmon and Craver, 2003: 204).

The efforts of Thorndike and Watson were followed up by B.F. Skinner (1904-1990), who has sometimes been called "the high priest of behaviorism." Skinner denounced philosophical approaches to psychology and argued that much error and misunderstanding about teaching and learning originated with "armchair scientists" who tried to deduce understandings of these processes by relying on *a priori* generalizations. Skinner allegedly replaced "humanistic musings" (and the notion of "self"), with scientific language that included such concepts as "conditioned" or "reinforced behavior, repertoire of behavior responses," or "operant conditioning" in regard to a specific organism known as the individual. For behaviorists, the notion of "self" or "self-concept" was too strongly tied to mental constructs and the danger exists of being misled in the direction of imputing mysterious, internal driving forces to the organism to explain "its" behavior (Ozmon and Craver, 2003: 205).

Perhaps just to create a bit of confusion, or simply to underscore the point that things are not always what they appear to be, another theorist, Johann Friedrich Herbart (1776-1841) attempted to develop a crossover theory from humanism to behaviorism. Herbart, a German professor of philosophy, visited Pestalozzi in Switzerland and was impressed by what he saw. Determined to bring "order" to Pestalozzi's learning theory, Herbart set about formulating a set-by-step explanation for what Pestalozzi was attempting. Herbart rid himself of John Locke's faculty psychology, as well as Locke's assumption that mind has the power or capacity to analyze ideas. Instead, Herbart insisted, ideas are active, and their activity accounts for the flow of mental life. The end result of Herbart's deliberations found him formulating such concepts as conscious and subconscious divisions of the mind, apperceptive mass as the vat of accumulated insights, and correlation and concentration as vital factors in remembering.

Herbart's doctrine of concentration refers to the use of "core" ideas around which subject matters are correlated, and the doctrine of correlation means that curricula should be so organized that similar or related ideas are presented together or in sequence, for such presentation promotes apperception of their relationships. Herbart also labeled broad classes of interest, that is, (i) empirical, speculative, and aesthetic, and (ii) interests directed at people – sympathetic, social, and religious. Since individuals learn best when they are interested in subject matter, it becomes the responsibility of educators to develop interest in all these areas.

Herbart, who is sometimes called "the Father of American Psychology," will perhaps best be remembered by educators for his five-step plan for teaching (which bears some resemblance to the Aboriginal model that will later be introduced). Primarily concerned about clarity in presenting new ideas as well as sequencing new information in logical order (Fain, Shostak, and Dean: 1979: 42), Herbart's approach incorporates these concerns. The five steps are: (i) preparation, which means preparing the student to receive new information by arousing interest or recalling past material or experiences; (ii) presentation, which consists of presenting new material; (iii) association, which involves helping students see the relationship between old and new ideas; (iv) generalization, that is, formulating general ideas and principles; and, (v) application, or applying new ideas or principles to new situations (Webb, Metha, and Jordan, 2000: 148).

# Progressive Education

As the twentieth century got under way new ideas about how children should be educated emerged. These ideas were formalized in the formation of the Progressive Education Association that began in 1919 and lasted a total of thirty-six years. Basic assumptions held by most adherents to the movement included viewing children as morally neutral, active in the learning process, and interactive with their social and physical environments. One of progressive education's most prominent spokespersons was philosopher and educator, John Dewey. As William Brickman once noted:

> John Dewey may not have been the world's greatest educational philosopher, but he was a pedagogue who inspired widespread rethinking of educational objectives, principles, and procedures. . . . The philosopher-educator's ideas continue to be discussed, his language to be quoted, and his books to be reprinted in English and to be translated into foreign tongues. (Brickman and Lehrer, 1961: 10)

There can be no doubt about John Dewey's (1859-1952) impact on twentieth century educational theory. Dewey believed strongly in democracy as a political system and pragmatism as a working philosophy. Like Herbart, he endorsed the value of experience in education and extended this idea to include the value of the individual's interest in seeking meaningful educational experiences as well as the development of discipline in knowledge seeking. True learning, therefore, is the accumulation of individual insight as well as the continuous reconstruction of experience.

As the progressive education movement grew it too often incorporated ideas of other educators that tended often to cloud Dewey's contributions. Much of Dewey's thinking went back to Jean Jacques Rousseau's notion of unfoldment – students should be viewed as human beings in the process of development, each of them with a unique, distinctive personality that must be understood and treated accordingly. As a result, Dewey's approach was sometimes called "child-centred education."

Dewey believed that children have a natural tendency to interact with their environment. He therefore encouraged teachers to take their students out of the lecture halls and involve them in real life experiences. The "interactive" part of the teaching/learning process referred to how teachers should listen and respond to the concerns of their students. Following Dewey, Hirst and Slavik (1990) and Little Soldier (1989) it is to be emphasized that students should be encouraged to work together cooperatively. This fits in well with a First Nations approach because Native Americans tend to be global/holistic, reflective and visual/tactile learners who achieve better in a cooperative rather than in an individual competitive setting (Knowles, Beauvais, and Medearis, 1992: 22). NonNative-derived curricula are too often organized to teach to sequential, linear, and auditory minded learners who do well in competitive settings. Many problems that Native American students encounter in schools today may be caused "by being taught to their weaknesses [growing edges] instead of their strengths" (Knowles, Beauvais, and Medearis, 1992: 22). As Jordan (1984: 62) has elaborated, "New teachers need to know about how Native children 'learn to learn' at home so that they make sure the work contexts and social interaction requirements of the classroom are made compatible with work contexts and social relationships in the culture." Dewey emphasized that students should be encouraged to develop personal perceptions of all ongoings surrounding them. Resulting insights should continuously be reconstructed in light of new experiences, with the end result that knowledge perceived and accumulated by students would be unique to them. The process of guiding experience to new perceptions should be disciplined, and when analyzed or evaluated, appropriate acknowledgement must be rendered of the fact that each student's perceptions are different than those of all others. For this reason, Dewey's approach has been variously labelled as experimentalism, Gestalt-oriented education, instrumentalism, progressivism, reconstructionism, and relativism. More recently, Dewey's theories have been warmed over and labelled constructivism.

As the "new kid on the block" of educational theory, constructivism rests on the foundation of progressive education and gives new hope for direction to twenty-first century education. Constructivists are very concerned about school reform and believe that the success of a genuine school improvement effort requires selecting and maintaining a clear, long-term focus on a few important points. Following up on Dewey's passion for democratic input, constructivists argue that all players – teachers, students, parents, and community – should be consulted in formulating these goals and they should all be involved at each stage of development (Wagner, 1998, 516). There is also some hope that the new emphasis will acknowledge and accommodate the diversity of North American society (Parkerson and Parkerson, 2001: 216).

Similar to John Dewey's approach, the philosophical underpinnings of constructivism are essentially pragmatic in nature, positing that knowledge exists in the minds of individuals only, and is constructed internally and derived from interrelation with the world (Friesen and Friesen, 2001: 76; Woolfolk, Winne, Perry, and Shapka, 2009: 343). The meanings which individuals assign to encountered phenomena depend on individual previous experiences. Thus knowledge is constructed through perception and action. The good news is that there is a vat of common knowledge "out there" that derives from a common brain and body that are part of the same universe. In terms of educational application, this means that fundamentally teachers and students can share the same perceptual knowledge that forms the basis of school curricula. Granted that the perceptions of young students may not be as "accurate" as those of trained scientists, but since they will be functioning according to their personal perceptions, these may be deemed equally valid forms of knowing. In order for these perceptions to constitute a fuller comprehension of reality, it is suggested that teachers encourage students to discuss, explain, or evaluate their ideas and procedures (Hendry, 1996). The objective is that in such a milieu, all participants may come to a fuller knowledge of "the truth." This perspective nicely parallels traditional First Nations thinking because cultural neophytes and their mentors often collaborated on discovered truths and their interpretation through discussion. Learners were encouraged steadily to develop outlooks on life by listening, observing, participating, and teaching.

## Indigenous Pedagogical Methodology

As European explorers, fur traders, and missionaries who first landed on Canada's eastern coast gradually made their way west, several First Nations followed them, no doubt lured by the unusual and appealing goods introduced by their new acquaintances. For example, although once an eastern Woodland people, the Woodland Crees migrated west, and when the fur trade economy evaporated, a number of their bands took up a buffalo-centred way of life. It is also commonly believed by linguists that the Blackfoot peoples were once a Great Lakes people who had earlier migrated west and developed a buffalo economy. Today the two Algonquian Nations exhibit similar cultural patterns since both represent cultures that respected the oral tradition. Classically, that orientation had at least one advantage – it was flexible and geared to the times. The celebration of sacred ceremonies and rituals were often observed and passed on virtually intact for centuries, but in the end even minor modifications due to a variety of factors were always a possibility. The use of legends for teaching important life skills and understanding the world around them encouraged students to become independent thinkers. Students of traditional teachers were proficient in language and problem solving, and understanding and applying the inherent message of stories was one of the primary means of teaching language and critical thinking. Most importantly, it is necessary to appreciate that First Nations pedagogy was practical – it was learning by doing. John Dewey would have been proud.

Using the foregoing as a basis, a number of distinctive parallels between progressive education and traditional Indigenous thinking can be drawn. Following the humanist convictions regarding educational theory, the traditional Aboriginal approach to learning comprised four specific steps: (i) listening; (ii) observing; (iii) participating; and, (iv) teaching. The fact that there are four steps to effective learning is not surprising since the sacred number four figures in so many Plains Indian beliefs and practices. There are, after all, four directions, four faces of the human being – the face of the child, the adolescent, the adult, and the aged. There are four kinds of things that breathe – those that crawl, those that fly, those that are two-legged, and those that are four-legged. There are four things above the earth – sun, moon, stars, and planets, and there are four parts to green things – roots, stem, leaves, and fruit (Friesen, 1995: 119).

## Detailing the Four Steps

The western Canadian Aboriginal theory of learning, like every other aspect of their manner of transmitting cultural knowledge and values, was based on the oral tradition and founded on spiritual conceptualizations of the workings of the universe (Snow, 2005: 9). This unique approach generally paralleled the "Indian ways" of other North American tribes. In fact, it could be perceived as a fairly universal early tribal teaching method. For example, Four Guns of the Oglala Sioux Nation affirmed the virtues of the oral tradition and its implicit form of teaching and learning when he stated, "The

Indian needs no writings; words that are true sink deep into this heart where they remain" (Friesen, 1998: 53). Chief Cochise of the Ciricahua Apache Nation, valued the "truth" of the oral tradition highly when he cautioned a speaker; "You must speak straight so your words go as sunlight into our hearts" (Friesen, 1998: 50). A similar orientation may be identified in the oral tradition of the ancient tribal Hebrews as expressed by King David in the Psalms; "I have hidden your word in my heart that I might not sin against you" (Psalm 119:11 NIV).

*The first step* to effective learning, adhered to by traditional Indigenous educators, is to listen and listen well – to those who know (Meili, 1991). In the ancient Aboriginal model, the major portion of teaching was done by knowledgeable individuals – grandparents and elders who were highly respected. They were teachers and mentors who told stories, offered advice, and modelled ideal forms of behavior. The respect afforded elder teachers is still observable in many tribes. Pam Red Gun (2006: 1), a university student and herself a member of the Siksika First Nation, states, "The elders are the key to survival and revival of the past."

Elders possessing varied gifts traditionally served the First Peoples of North America. First of all, there were elders who were acknowledged and consulted for their medicinal knowledge while others had earned the right to conduct sacred rituals and ceremonies. There were also elders who were simply experienced and wise individuals who were consulted as counsellors might be today (Hare, 2003: 414; MacKay, 2003: 298). Lillian Crow Chief (2006: 2), also a member of the Blackfoot community states;

> My grandmother was a medicine woman . . . I remember waking to the sound of her voice, singing her sacred songs and smelling the sweet aroma of her pipe tobacco. . . . I felt so much peace, love and compassion radiating from her and together we silently sat and watched the early morning sunrise.

Crow Chief's student colleague, Louann Solway (2006: 1) adds;

> She [my grandmother] would often say, "What are they saying?" And I would sit and listen to whatever noise I heard and often it was very peaceful and full of life . . . with all my listening and searching for new noises to hear, I have come to understand my purpose in life today.

Traditionally, many First Nations societies had esteemed elders in their villages who served as formal storytellers. Mary Muktoyuk of the Yupiaq First Nation described the attitude towards these eld-ers in this way;

> The elders, in those days, we held in great respect. Whatever they told us, we would listen very carefully, trying not to make mistakes when we listened, because we respected them so high-ly, because they knew so much more than we did. (Friesen, 1998: 9)

Parents were for the most part excluded from the responsibili-ties of child-raising since it was thought that they were mainly involved in the day to day activities of providing food and taking care of home life. Generally speaking, however, raising children was a community responsibility (Friesen and Friesen, 2005a: 128). It was traditionally considered a privilege to be taught by Native eld-ers, particularly because they were responsible for passing sacred truths. At other times they would tell stories of entertainment or moral instruction, or stories to explain why things were the way they were. Commonly known as Indian legends, the essence of these stories was often known by Indian tribes all over North America, and although storytellers might adhere to a common sto-ryline, each recognized storyteller could provide unique details as to his or her own preference (Friesen and Friesen, 2005b: 14).

Storytelling has sometimes been identified as one of the most common means of transmitting First Nations cultural values and beliefs. There was a time when all cultures relied solely on the oral tradition and there were few written forms of communication other than petroglyphs, pictograms, or storyrobes. Legends or stories shared between families and communities conveyed important belief systems, ceremonial rituals, and cultural symbols. Aboriginal bands specialized in the use of this medium.

Today's Aboriginal community is very fortunate in still being able to access legends of their heritage. Appreciation for the preserva-tion of these tales must be extended to several sectors, particular-ly elders who took upon themselves the responsibility of maintain-ing the essence of the oral tradition during times when their people were under siege to abandon traditional ways. These guardians of revered knowledge have been successful in keeping many of their valued beliefs and practices alive through very turbulent times. Adherents to the written word who first came into contact with Indigenous cultures, such as traders, missionaries, and anthropolo-gists also rendered a valuable service by committing to writing many stories they learned from their new found acquaintances.

Native legends have a unique identity. They are truly Indigenous stories, and as such they constitute the oral literature of each particular tribal cultural configuration. Indian stories are pictures of Aboriginal life verbally drawn by Indigenous storytellers, showing life from their point of view. Legends deal with spirituality, the origins of things, and various kinds of individual behavior. Legends are often entertaining and they may convey a vast range of cultural knowledge including folkways, values, and beliefs. Legends often outline the very basis of a particular cultural pattern. As might be expected, the sacred number four frequently occurs in the content of legends.

The study of Native legends can be a very rich source of learning, even for nonNatives. Traditionally, legends appear to have been told for a variety of purposes, both formal and informal. Listening to them was of utmost importance because they comprised the very essence of the oral tradition. Formal storytelling was usually connected to the occasion of deliberate moral or spiritual instruction. In fact, some legends were considered so sacred or special that their telling was restricted to the celebration of a very special event such as the Sundance. Others were told only during specific seasons. On these occasions, only recognized or designated persons could engage in their telling. Nearly anyone could engage in informal storytelling, and such legends were usually related for their entertainment or instructional value.

It is possible to classify Indian legends into four categories (with some degree of overlap), each of which has a special purpose. The four types of legends are as follows.

(i) *Entertainment legends* are often about the trickster, who is called by different names among the various tribes. Incidentally, as Grant (1993: 25) observes, the trickster figure is found in many world mythologies and his role may be interpreted in a wide variety of ways. In First Nations country the Blackfoot call him Napi, the Crees call him Wisakedjak, the Ojibway call him Nanabush, the Sioux call him îktômni, while other tribes have different names for him like Coyote, Tarantula, or Raven. Stories about the trickster are principally fictional and can be invented and amended even during the process of storytelling. There is never much difficulty in getting listeners to pay attention to trickster stories because trickster stories often involve playing tricks. Sometimes the trickster plays tricks on others and sometimes they play tricks on him.

The trickster appears to have the advantage on his unsuspecting audience, however, since he possesses supernatural powers, which he deploys on a whim to startle or to shock. He has powers to raise animals to life and he himself may even die and in four days come to life again. Aside from being amusing, trickster stories often incorporate knowledge about aspects of Aboriginal culture, buffalo hunts, natural phenomena, or rituals, or the relationship between people and animals. In this sense, trickster stories may also be instructional.

(ii) *Instructional* or *teaching legends* are basically told for the purpose of sharing information about how things work in the universe. These stories explain things. They often use animal motifs to explain why things are the way they are. For example, a child may enquire about the origin of the seasons or why the different animals behave the way they do, and a tale revolving around animal life may be told. For example, a child may ask, "Where did our people come from?" or "Why are crows' feathers black?" Stories told in response to these questions could include adventures of the trickster.

(iii) *Moral legends* are intended to teach ideal or "right" forms of behavior, and are employed to suggest to the listener that a change in attitude or action would be desirable. Since traditional Indian tribes rarely corporally punished their children, they sometimes found it useful to hint at the inappropriateness of certain behavior by telling stories. For example, the story might be about an animal that engages in inappropriate behavior and the child is expected to realize that a possible modification of his or her own behavior is the object of the telling. The onus is always on listeners to apply the lesson of the legend to themselves if deemed appropriate.

(iv) *Sacred* or *spiritual legends* should be told only by recognized elders or other tribal approved individual since their telling is considered a form of worship. It is possible to find spiritual legends in written form (tribal origin stories, for example), but some elders consider this to be inappropriate. In precontact days, spiritually significant stories were never told to just anyone who asked, nor were they told by just anyone. Among some tribes, particular versions of sacred legends were considered property and thus their transmission from generation to generation was carefully safeguarded. First, selected individuals learned a legend by careful listening; then, on mastering the story, passed it on to succeeding generations, with the liberty (or implied liberty) of perhaps changing aspects of the story to suit their own tastes. The amendments would centre on a different choice of animals or sites referred to in the story and preferred by the teller.

Legends comprised only a part of a tribe's spiritual structure, which also included ceremonies, rituals, songs, and dances. Physical objects such as fetishes, pipes, painted teepee designs, medicine bundles, and shrines of sorts, supplemented these. Familiarity with these components comprised sacred knowledge, and everything learned was committed to memory. Viewed together these entries represented spiritual connections between people and the universe which, with appropriate care, resulted in a lifestyle of assured food supply, physical well-being and satisfying the needs and wants of the society.

*The second step* of the traditional Indigenous teaching and learning scenario occurred when an elder considered a youthful listener ready to observe the practice of certain cultural customs or even more sacred ceremonies and rituals. If deemed ready, an elder might invite a youth to observe the proceedings. Observers of a Cree Sundance, for example, had to follow a strict protocol. The most inner circle of four of the Sundance would be reserved for the centre lodge in which revered ceremonies, such as the opening of sacred medicine bundles might take place. The second circle from the centre would be reserved for the dancers, and the third circle for observers. The fourth or most outer circle would be regarded as a place for more social kinds of interaction. We have several times been invited to observe the enactment of spiritually significant ceremonies and rituals, and have always respected the required protocol.

If a parallel may be made to the world of travel, one might say that it would be better to first read up on a place before taking a trip to a particular destination. Being informed beforehand, one would know better what to expect on arrival. People who participate in field trips, for example, always return better informed if they are properly briefed or primed beforehand. This step nicely parallels Herbart's notion of preparation, namely to ready students to encounter new data.

In traditional Indigenous cultures observations of many kinds occurred, from the simple daily activities having to do with sustenance, to those held in highest regard. In summer, for example, when Saskatoon berries ripened, a Blackfoot child might observe an elder being presented with the first berry picked. The berry would be held in the air, and a prayer of thanksgiving would be uttered. The berry was then put into the ground as an offering to the Creator, as an expression of thanksgiving, and as an affirmation of communion with Mother Earth. Hungry Wolf (2001: 77), a member of the Blackfoot Confederacy, states that she could remember when healing plants were picked a similar ceremony would take place, her grandmother putting a pinch of tobacco into the ground and offering a prayer of thanksgiving. Nothing was taken for granted; everything was considered a gift from the Creator.

*The third step* to effective learning in an Aboriginal setting is participation or, as the common expression has it, "learning by doing." It was probably Jean Jacques Rousseau who first emphasized the need to "get out there and let your senses go to work," but Johann Heinrich Pestalozzi actually applied the principle to the education of his five year-old son, Jacobli. Johann Herbart formalized related procedures, and John Dewey brought educators to the realization that the end result must be centred on the individual. According to Dewey, each person functions according to his or her accumulated perceptions or, in Aboriginal terms, has his or her own journey to travel.

Traditionally, elders from many Plains tribes insisted that children must learn their culture by accessing traditional forms of education on the land. A sense of connectedness to the natural world, as well as to people in it, was developed through extended experiences on the land, either in the company of an elder or alone (Ward and Bouvier, 2001: 8). When a youth was given the privilege of participating in a specific ceremony it was always under the supervision of a responsible individual. Participating in a sacred ritual or ceremony requires use of all five senses, encompassed in an attitude of spirituality. This, in Native terms, implies adding a sixth sense – namely spiritual awareness. Participating in a sweat-lodge ceremony, for example, would itself verify the readiness of the participant. If the lodge was entered with negative thoughts, the individual might afterwards experience uneasiness or even illness. If the participant had the right attitude, he or she would feel spiritually refreshed after having taken part in the ceremony.

*Fourth,* and finally, Indigenous-learning theory posits that there is no better way to affirm one's success in learning than by trying to teach others. Many beginning academics can no doubt testify to this. We probably learn a great deal more about a subject by first teaching it, even if we have already attained a doctorate in the field. It requires a great deal more study to be ready to explain a theory than merely repeating its essence on an examination. Fortunately, one's fears generally do subside as one continues in teaching and becomes more familiar with the specifics of the related subject matter.

This would not necessarily be the case with regard to the experience of the Algonquian cultural initiate who might be assigned his or her first teaching charge. In the first instance, by now initiates would be more mature adults, and would be likely be dealing with spiritual subject matter and procedures of a more sacred nature. In addition, their "subjects" would likely be just as familiar with (or more so) than they were with the significance and procedure of the particular enactment. No doubt they would have put into their hearts the sacredness of what they were about to do and they would be adequately prepared to undertake the task. The slogan, "learning by doing" would have special meaning in this scenario.

It is important to acknowledge the more formal procedures of Indigenous educational theory, and these were in the charge of formal societies. Anthropologists have described the function of the various Blackfoot secret societies or sodalities by such names as Mosquitos, Buffalo Bulls, Horns, Crazy Dogs, Brave Dogs, or Pigeons. In many tribes sodalities functioned in a serving as well as preserving capacity, and were committed to passing along sacred knowledge and traditions to succeeding generations. Each sodality had its own special knowledge that was carefully and formally passed on to initiates following the four steps outlined in this paper.

# Projections

Many First Nations of the plains, like the Blackfoot and Crees, believe that the end result of all human experience and learning is for the good of the community. True, each individual has his or her own journey to travel, and elders can be of great assistance in this pursuit, but the end result of that fulfillment must be for the benefit of the community.

It is a concept that could no doubt be appropriated by our generation of educators with great benefit.

# References

Archambault, Reginald, ed. (1964). *John Dewey on Education: Selected Writings.* New York: The Modern Library.

Battiste, Marie, and James (Sa'ke'j) Youngblood Henderson. (2000). *Protecting Indigenous Knowledge and Heritage: A Global Challenge.* Saskatoon, SK: Purich Publishing Company.

Bayles, Ernest E., and Bruce L. Hood. (1966). *Growth of American Educational Thought and Practice.* New York: Harper & Row.

Brickman, William W., and Stanley Lehrer. (1961). *John Dewey: Master Educator.* New York: Atherton Press.

Couture, Joseph E. (1991). Explorations in Native Knowing. *The Cultural Maze: Complex Questions on Native Destiny in Western Canada.* John W. Friesen, ed. Calgary, AB: Detselig Enterprises, 53-73.

Crow Chief, Lillian. (2006). Indigenous Ideas on Instruction. Calgary, AB: University of Calgary, Unpublished paper. Faculty of Communication and Culture. 3pp.

Fain, Stephen M., Robert Shostak, and John F. Dean. (1979). *Teaching in America.* Glenview, IL: Scott, Foresman and Company.

Friesen, John W. (1999). *First Nations of the Plains: Creative, Adaptable and Enduring.* Calgary, AB: Detselig Enterprises.

Friesen, John W. (1998). *Sayings of the Elders: An Anthology of First Nations Wisdom.* Calgary, AB: Detselig Enterprises.

Friesen, John W. (1997). *Rediscovering the First Nations of Canada.* Calgary, AB: Detselig Enterprises.

Friesen, John W. (1995). *You Can't Get There From Here: The Mystique of North American Plains Indians' Culture & Philosophy.* Dubuque, IA: Kendall/Hunt.

Friesen, John W. (1993). Formal Schooling Among the Ancient Ones: The Mystique of the Kiva. *American Indian Culture and Research Journal,* 17:4, 55-68.

Friesen, John W., and Virginia Lyons Friesen. (2005a). *First Nations in the Twenty-First Century.* Calgary, AB: Detselig Enterprises.

Friesen, John W., and Virginia Lyons Friesen (2002). *Aboriginal Education in Canada: A Plea for Integration.* Calgary, AB: Detselig Enterprises.

Friesen, John W., and Virginia Lyons Friesen. (2001). *In Defense of Public Schools in North America.* Calgary, AB: Detselig Enterprises.

Friesen, Virginia Lyons, and John W. Friesen. (2005b). *Legends of the Elders Handbook for Teachers, Homeschoolers, and Parents.* Calgary, AB: Detselig Enterprises.

Grant, Agnes. (1993). *Our Bit of Truth: An Anthology of Canadian Native Literature.* Winnipeg, MB: Pemmican Publications.

Hare, Jan. (2003). Aboriginal Families and Aboriginal Education: Coming Full Circle. *Children, Teachers, and Schools in the History of British Columbia.* Jean Barman and Mona Gleason, eds., *411-430.* Calgary, AB: Detselig Enterprises.

Hendry, Graham D. (April, 1996). Constructivism and Educational Practice. *Australian Journal of Education,* 40:1, 19-45.

Herrick, C.J. (1924). *Neurological Foundations of Animal Behavior.* New York: Holt, Rinehart and Winston.

Hirst, L., and C. Slavik. (1990). Cooperative Approaches to Language Learning. In J. Reyhner (Ed.), *Effective Language Education Practices and Native Language Survival.* Choctaw, OK: Native American Language Issues. Proceedings of the Ninth Annual International Native American Language Issues Institute, 133-142. (ERIC Document Reproduction Service No. ED 342), 512.

Hungry Wolf, Beverly. (2001). Life in Harmony with Nature. *Women of the First Nations: Power, Wisdom, and Strength.* Christine Miller and Patricia Chuchryk, editors. Winnipeg, MB: The University of Manitoba Press, 77-82.

Jordan, C. (1984). Cultural Compatibility and the Education of Hawaiian Children: Implications for Mainland Educators. *Educational Research Quarterly,* 8:4, 59-71.

Knowles, T., J. Gill, A. Beauvais, and C. Medearis. (1992). *Teacher Education and the Rosebud Tribal Education Code.* Tribal College, 4:2, 21-23.

Little Soldier, L. (1989). Cooperative Learning and the Native American Student. *Phi Delta Kappan,* 7:2, 161-163.

MacKay, Eva. (2003). If they read what you are writing, this is the teachings, this is some of the teachings that we want them to read about. *In the Words of Elders.* Peter Kulchyski, Don McCaskill, and David Newhouse, editors. Toronto, ON: University of Toronto Press, 289-310.

Meili, Diane. (1991). *Those Who Know: Profiles of Alberta Elders.* Edmonton, AB: NeWest.

Ozmon, Howard A., and Samuel M. Craver. (2003). *Philosophical Foundations of Education.* Upper Saddle River, NJ: Merrill Prentice-Hall.

Parkerson, Donald H., and Jo Ann Parkerson. (2001). *Transitions in American Education: A Social History of Teaching.* New York: Routledge-Falmer.

Red Gun, Pam. (2006). The Teachings in Blackfoot Stories Through Our Elders. Unpublished paper. Calgary, AB: University of Calgary, Faculty of Communication and Culture. 3pp.

Rousseau, Jean Jacques. (1911). *Emile*. Translated by Barbara Foxley. New York: Dutton.

Snow, Chief John. (2005). *These Mountains are Our Sacred Places: The Story of the Stoney People*. Calgary, AB: Fitzhenry and Whiteside.

Solway, Louann. (2006). Indigenous Ideas on Instruction. Calgary, AB: Unpublished Paper. University of Calgary, Faculty of Communication and Culture. 3pp.

Suzuki, David, with Amanda McConnell. (1997). *The Sacred Balance: Rediscovering our Place in Nature*. Vancouver, BC: Douglas & McIntyre.

Wagner, Tony. (March, 1998). Change as Collaborative Inquiry: A Constructivist Methodology for Reinventing Schools. *Phi Delta Kappan,* 79:7, 512-517.

Ward, Angela, and Rita Bouvier. (2001). Introduction. *Resting Lightly on Mother Earth: The Aboriginal Experience in Urban Educational Settings.* Calgary, AB: Detselig Enterprises, 5-16.

Webb, L. Dean, Arlene Metha, and K. Forbis Jordan. (2000). *Foundations of American Education.* Third edition. Upper Saddle River, NJ: Merrill Prentice Hall.

Woolfolk, Anita E., Philip H. Winne, Nancy E. Perry, and Jennifer Shapka. (2009). *Educational Psychology.* Fourth Canadian Edition. Toronto, ON: Pearson Canada.

# Four
## The Challenge of Urban Adjustment

A final theme of considerable importance for some Aboriginal women and youth living in urban environments is the need to expand and strengthen the meaning of Aboriginal identity. . . . Sometimes they give accounts of Aboriginal persons who feel hopelessly strung between two cultures and psychologically at home in neither. Witnesses identify many in this predicament as falling "into patterns of despair, listlessness and self-destruction." They carry a heavy burden or pain and self-doubt that undermines their cultural identity. Witnesses also report, however, that some are able to "see across this great divide." (Schouls, 2003: 95)

Although the exact number is not known, the majority of Status Indians in Canada now live off reserve and the trend toward urban migration is continuing (Indian Affairs and Northern Development website). The average age of Aboriginals in Canada is 25 years of age, a fact that weighs heavily on urban migration. Native youth who live on reserves soon realize that economic opportunities are limited, so they head off to the city in search of employment or education. Those who seek a new life in the city are also culturally diverse. In Vancouver, for example, one can identify Indian dwellers who represent eleven distinct tribal affiliations, and similar situations occur in other larger urban centres (Todd, 2001: 100).

Despite the development of a variety of government and tribal programs over the last several decades, economic opportunities on most Indian reserves are limited, thus forcing young people to seek their fortunes elsewhere. Many Native youth pursuing postsecondary education have already located to nearby towns and cities, making employment there after graduation a logical choice. Cities like Edmonton, Regina, Saskatoon, Toronto, Vancouver, and Winnipeg are home to large populations of First Nations, thereby creating unfamiliar challenges for the new immigrants. In many instances the new urbanites have banded together to encourage significant policy change on the part of the federal Indian Affairs Branch. Their position is that Canada's urban Indians have been abandoned by both Native and nonNative politicians. Certainly, the creation of urban Indian reserves represents some kind of official response to the needs of Indian city migrants, but that development has influenced fresh needs such as the need for increased public awareness and improved access to financial and cultural services.

## How it All Began

The creation of urban Indian reserves is a post World War II phenomenon, partially bolstered by the rapidly increasing Native population in Canada. After WW II Native populations in Canada revealed unprecedented growth and government officials were challenged to do something about it. Native population growth has continued, and even today population projections from 1997 to 2005 indicate that on reserve Aboriginal population will grow by 2.3% compared with the national Canadian rate of 1.1%. It has been estimated that by the year 2045, for example, Aboriginal people in Saskatchewan will make up more than one-third of the total population (Barron and Garcea, 1999: 7).

When World War II came to a close, many nonNative farmers prepared to expand their holdings. They began to buy more land and bigger machinery, and thus changed the face of prairie farming. Farmers who were equipped to do so rented Indian lands, a trend partially influenced by the fact that Indian farmers were not able to expand their industry. For a long time, Indian farmers were not even allowed to own farm machinery that would enable them to commercialize production. Officials feared that they might be able to compete successfully with nonNative farmers if they let that happen. As a result reserve farming began to decline as did the demand for wage workers on nonNative farms. This form of employment could accommodate only a fraction of Indian workers at the best of times which meant that the rest of them had nowhere to go except to urban centres (Buckley, 1993: 67-71). When they did so, the welcome they received was significantly less than warm.

Although often motivated by economic factors, Nagler (1973: 9f) found that reasons for Aboriginal urban migration were somewhat varied. Following patterns set by nonNative youth, some

Indian migrants simply wearied of reserve life and sought a more technologically-enriched lifestyle in the city. The 1950s witnessed a wider availability of radio and television as well as other forms of media (to say nothing of better medical facilities), and the city was the place to find these. Professional training was more readily available in the city as well, and the concept developed that in cities the streets were paved with gold. Once exposed to these pleasures, there was no way that Canadian youth, Native or nonNative, wanted to return to rural areas. Besides, with the size of farms increasing thanks to increased prosperity and larger, more efficient machinery, there was little need for their help.

Prior to the 1960s, Native people in western Canada had little work experience. Buckley (1993: 93) notes: "Although they foraged far and wide in search of employment, they mainly got it on farms or roads, on construction projects or in the forest industry." This reality motivated a significant relocation to urban areas. In the 1960s, barely ten percent of Aboriginal people living in Manitoba were living in urban areas and this number rose to twenty-five percent by the 1970s. A similar trend was evident in Alberta and Saskatchewan. Reserve life had virtually become unbearable. The choice was clear – either develop a way of life centred on social assistance or migrate to the unfriendly city to seek an alternative means of livelihood. Those who left were lured and or motivated by a variety of factors such as seeking escape from personal problems and poverty, or simply to pursue a more rewarding lifestyle. A number of young people had dreams of obtaining postsecondary forms of education, quite mindful of the popular slogan of the 1960s, "Stay in school and make more money!" Nagler (1973: 44) notes that some Indigenous youth were able to fulfill their dreams of enrolling in postsecondary institutions because the federal integration program of the 1960s made educational grants available to Native youth, as part of a larger plan to integrate Aboriginal people into mainstream society. Although a number of Native youth enrolled in postsecondary programs, because of a variety of factors, many did not complete their training. Having to undergo a significant change in lifestyle, coupled with having to face discrimination, prejudice, and racism, proved to be too much for many of them and they returned to reserve life. Others simply missed home and went back to live among their friends and relatives.

The first Aboriginal urban migrants who basically sought employment in the city, were confronted by a variety of negative experiences including discrimination, the inability to find desirable forms of employment, or finding suitable housing. Lack of education prepared them for only very menial kinds of jobs with inadequate pay. This was a real hardship, particularly for individuals with family responsibilities. Meanwhile, those who stayed on reserves fell victim to a welfare society and basically lived far below any statistically devised poverty line. In 1972, for example, seventy-eight percent of the reserve population in Manitoba was receiving social assistance, seventy-six percent in Saskatchewan, and seventy-three percent in Alberta (Buckley, 1993: 77). The stage was set for significant change.

# Urban Reserves

Lands set aside in urban areas specifically for Native use are known as urban Indian reserves, and their birthplace was Saskatchewan. The main purpose in building these communities was to provide central urban locations for Aboriginal businesses. In 1992, the Saskatchewan Government, through the *Saskatchewan Treaty Land Entitlement Framework Agreement,* set aside $446 million to purchase land on which to develop urban reserves. Twenty-eight of Saskatchewan's seventy Indian bands signed on, and twenty-eight urban reserves were created, nine of them in larger centres (Steckley and Cummins, 2008: 141).

Barron and Garcea (1999: 24) suggest that the creation of urban Indian reserves is directly related to treaties and treaty land entitlement. When the treaties were signed, particularly those in the 1870s, it was soon established that, compared with the rest of Canadians, Indians were land poor. A hundred years later, they comprised a full three percent of Canada's population, but possessed only 0.02 percent of available land. Their rapid population growth could only make matters worse, so many Aboriginal leaders began to approach government about this discrepancy.

When Treaties Nos. 4, 6, and 7 were drawn up, the conditions were basically that every family of five would be awarded a full section of land. Often the federal government failed to live up to this arrangement and simply short-changed the Indigenous people. Even when bands did receive full entitlement of land, government often failed to live up to its commitment. Finally, in Saskatchewan at least, in 1976, the federal government, the provincial government, and Native leaders signed an agreement known as the

Saskatchewan Formula, through which land equity would be worked out. In the meantime the Conservative party came to power in both provincial and federal elections and abandoned the deal. In 1992, however, they signed the Saskatchewan Treaty Land Entitlement Framework Agreement that gave twenty-seven bands some 446 million dollars in compensation (Barron and Garcea, 1999: 15).

The necessity of creating urban reserves is based on a number of important considerations. In the first instance, the concept of a bonded community offers strong encouragement for economic development. When this objective is pursued, it becomes necessary for the players to formulate some kind of self-government. After all, any reserve, even an urban reserve is comprised of people who form a community. They should have the right to govern themselves, at least in matters that pertain exclusively to their locale. Changing demographics, namely a rapidly growing community, virtually motivated the need for some form of self-government. Increasing numbers of people necessitated the formulation of rules for living, respect for others, and setting of goals for the community.

The social scenario of urban reserve life becomes a bit complicated when the varying lifestyles of those who frequent these communities is studied. Essentially there are three groups of affiliates, the first group being those who live on the urban reserve and work either on the reserve or nearby. Their social ties are obviously localized. The second group comprises those who live outside the particular town or city where an urban reserve is located, and work in town, but have relatives or close friends on the urban reserve. Thus some of their socializing will occur within the bounds of the urban reserve. The third group are Native people who live on a rural reserve, or at least outside the city, but come to urban centres to work. Their social life is entirely based outside the urban area. By law, the federal government has responsibilities towards all three groups and its officials must walk a very fine line in determining who is in most need of financial assistance.

When matters of governance are discussed it appears obvious that the Canadian federal government has been quite willing to abdicate its responsibilities towards First Nations and turn governance matters over to the provinces. Provincial governments, on the other hand, seem determined to hand over control of Native programs and service funds to Native people. Bobiwash (1997: 91) suggests that in Saskatchewan, for example, the provincial govern-

ment identified up to $550 million a year in the areas of health, edu-
cation, justice and social services that could eventually be transferred to band administration. Bobiwash (1997) observes that such
a move may have commendable features, but it too easily allows
the federal government to shirk its responsibilities toward First
Nations communities. In fact, the legality of whether provinces even
have authority to negotiate agreements with Aboriginal governments is another question. As Bobiwash (1997: 91) notes:

> Among the arguments used by the federal government in
> regards to provision of social services for off-reserve Native peo-
> ple has been that if provinces are the main beneficiaries for lands
> and resources under Lands and Resources Transfer Agreements
> and Acts (by which the provinces also became parties to later
> treaties such as the Williams Treaty of 1923), then some of those
> benefits ought to go to off-reserve Native People.

Urban reserves were not created without opposition. At first
politicians from all levels of government were opposed to the idea.
They argued that any form of reserve government could establish
rules and laws that might contradict those passed by city council.
They worried about money, jurisdictional matters, and the effect
that the establishment of a different kind of neighborhood would
have on federal and provincial grants to cities and towns. They also
voiced concerns about the development of what might turn out to
be potential ethnic ghettos. Without a doubt, the establishment of
Canada's first urban reserves was not without its fair share of prejudice and discrimination. These were not all objections framed in
caring concerns.

Governance of urban reserves is what might be called a heretofore un-named phenomenon. If a reserve is created, will compensation be paid for lost municipal property taxes and school levies?
What arrangements will be made for payment of municipal taxes?
How will municipal bylaws be applied and enforced? Will there be,
or should there be a joint consultative process that involves the various levels of government, which might be affected in the event of
dispute? These and other legitimately arising questions indicate the
complexity of the venture, but on the positive side, new concepts
have a way of bringing various parties together, and often the
exchange of ideas fosters good will. As Makela (1999: 89) suggests,
"The development of urban reserves presents great opportunities
for both Aboriginal and nonAboriginal people . . . with the issues at
stake reaching beyond matters of tax-loss compensation or bylaw
compatibility." Above all, the idea is about sharing wealth and power

in the pursuit of providing equal opportunity for education, employment, adequate housing and other social benefits.

## Urban Reserve Specifics

A specific example of a successful rural to urban move includes action by the Saskatchewan Peter Ballantyne Cree First Nation in 1979 when, in cooperation with government, they purchased forty-one acres of federal land in the midst of a residential neighborhood in the City of Prince Albert, Saskatchewan. The land had previously been used to house northern Indian youth who had relocated to the city. By a government Order-in-Council the reserve was named the Opawakoscikan Reserve

Another successful development of a Saskatchewan urban reserve was undertaken by the Muskeg Lake Cree First Nation in 1984. Comprised of 1 200 members, most of them living away from their reserve, the leaders of the Muskeg Cree First Nation decided to make their move. In 1984 the Saskatchewan government arranged for them to purchase 33 acres of land in the City of Saskatoon. In 1988 the reserve was named the McKnight Commercial Centre in honor of the minister of Indian Affairs who expedited the matter. In 1993, the band signed a service agreement with the city that involved an annual payment to the city for municipal services such as snow and garbage removal, electricity and water. Today some 300 Native employees work for local businesses on the reserve, many of them wholly or partially Aboriginal owned (Steckley and Cummins, 2008: 141).

In 1988 the Starblanket Band in Saskatchewan selected seven town lots in downtown Fort Qu'Appelle, where the post office had previously been located, so the land had been assigned surplus status by the federal government. Relying on an unfulfilled claim dating back to the 1880s, the Starblanket Band insisted that although the land could be considered partial payment for past losses, they were still entitled to back payments. Accordingly, the band was awarded some four million dollars over twelve years and the Qu'Appelle Reserve attained official status in June 1994 (Barron and Garcea, 1999: 26).

In 1996 the Sakimay Band rejoiced at the official recognition of their urban reserve in Yorkton, Saskatchewan. They had previously been able to purchase land based on a 1907 unfulfilled agreement that awarded them a total of almost four million dollars. They used the money to purchase the Tribal Council's Education Centre in Yorkton. Plans were to use the land for educational and band administrative purposes. Historical details reveal that in 1907 the Little Bone Band was dissolved by government action and the few remaining members were absorbed into the Sakimay Band. This fact obligated the federal government to undertake compensation.

## Operational Details

Relocating to a new environment always poses difficult challenges, some of them quite complex. Moving from a rural or small town to a large urban area is particularly challenging for any youthful individual regardless of ethnic affiliation. For Native youth, however, this kind of relocation may be classified as comprising a unique genre. Descriptors such as poverty, ignorance, poor education and no urban know-how, and lack of familiarity with sophisticated employment practices, all figure in the equation. The familiar attitudes of discrimination, prejudice, and racism will consistently be encountered.

Aware of these realities, in 1962 the Aboriginal community in Toronto began to prepare for the Indian exodus from nearby reserves. A number of forward-looking innovators founded the Native Canadian Centre of Toronto as a place which incoming Native people could frequent and receive a warm welcome. The centre also played the role of an ambassador to nonNative people and provided a place for all individuals from all backgrounds to learn from Aboriginal people. The staff worked hard to promote equitable relationships between Native and nonNative people as well as promoting public awareness (Obonsawin and Howard-Bobiwash, 1997: 25).

The idea for the Native Canadian Centre of Toronto emerged in 1950 when a group of individuals from the central YMCA formed the Toronto Indian Club aimed at arranging for or providing cultural activities for the Toronto community. At that time, only a few hundred Native people lived in Toronto, but the group felt the need to promote public awareness of First Nations culture. It was a difficult time for Native people in Toronto and as many as were able, tried to "pass" for white in order to avoid becoming targets of discrimination and racism. Others, not so fortunate, encountered these attitudes of a daily basis. Members of the Toronto Indian Club saw the need to do more than provide cultural programs, so in 1963 they established a location for a new Native Canadian Centre of Toronto and expanded their areas of concern to include providing urban migrants with assistance with finding housing and employment.

The first of three locations for the Native Canadian Centre of Toronto was a house on Church Street with low rent, but despite this generosity of the owner, the staff was kept busy trying to raise funds for the centre's operation. The concept caught on immediately. The centre's logbook revealed that in its first year of operation, 6 000 people passed through its doors. By 1964 this number rose to 10 000 people and 16 000 the following year. The staff soon found itself undertaking hospital visitations as well as providing social services such as courtwork assistance, alcohol abuse seminars, personal counseling, housing assistance, and welcoming newcomers to city life. The centre also maintained contact with some thirty-five social service agencies in the city and with some eighty-nine reserves in the province of Ontario (Obonsawin and Howard-Bobiwash, 1997: 34).

The second location of the Native Canadian Centre of Toronto at 210 Beverly Street was larger and offered facilities that visitors could utilize for more leisurely activities. The centre essentially became a meeting place and referral centre for Native people who were served by a newly renovated library and craft sales room, a monthly Native newspaper, and a volunteer speakers' bureau. As activities and responsibilities continue to increase it became necessary a third time to search for larger quarters. These were found by purchasing the facilities of the Ontario Bible College at 10-16 Spadina Street. By now some 25 000 people were annually frequenting the centre, and a number of spin-off agencies were founded, for example, the Migrating Native Peoples Program and the Wigwamen Housing Corporation. The centre also served as a stimulus for other such institutions in cities across the nation. Centres began to be established in numerous Canadian cities, many times in conjunction with work already in progress in friendship centres. As the Native population in urban centres continues to grow there will no doubt be a need for this kind of institution to flourish and expand.

Because of expanding urban migrant numbers, in 1996 the Royal Commission on Aboriginal Peoples identified urban Aboriginals as an important emphasis in their research. To date there has been very little literature available documenting the personal experiences of Aboriginals who relocate to urban centres.

Most of it has been produced by nonNative academics, consultants, and researchers. An exception to this trend was documented in 1997 by the Native Canadian Centre in Toronto. The final chapter of their book, *The Meeting Place: Aboriginal Life in Toronto,* which commemorates thirty-five years of operation, includes interview data from eight Native migrants who offer personal testimony regarding their migrations. The interviews for the profiles were conducted in 1997 and offer perspectives on the experience of being strangers in one's own country, the importance of language maintenance, the politics of relocating community, and the role of education.

## Aboriginal People in Urban Life.

Observations regarding moving to an urban community made by the eight interviewees include Jim Mason's comments. Describing himself as "the beginning of a new breed: the urban Indians" (Mason, 1997: 97), Mason laments that many Indians who come to the city, do so out of unfortunate circumstances. His parents left the reserve years earlier and were disenfranchised. Thus they were no longer entitled to return to their reserve. Essentially a forward-looking individual, Jim says he is always learning and believes that good learning sources are conversations with young people. He believes that a good education is essential to experiencing success in contemporary society, but it does not have to be attained at the expense of losing one's culture.

Another interviewee, Frances Sanderson concurs, emphasizing that a good formal education provides opportunities for Aboriginal youth that they could not otherwise attain. As she elaborates, getting a good education is like fighting fire with fire. Having done well in school, as well as experiencing success in the corporate world, Sanderson has managed to live her philosophy – a good example for youth to follow.

In his interview, Bob Crawford emphasizes that all the needs of the circle of life must be met if unity among the various facets of life is to be accomplished. This implies that one's social, intellectual, physical and spiritual needs must be met if wholeness is to be realized.

Harvey Manning, who for 21 years has regularly moved in and out of the city, suggests that a firm grip on one's identity as an Aboriginal person will not only provide self-discovery, but contribute to building a strong and healthy community in the city. Ivy Chaske can testify to that. A Dakota Indian by heritage and a residential school survivor, Ivy earned a degree in social work from the University of Manitoba and spent her life in that profession in the city. Now, facing retirement, her dream is to return to the land of her Indigenous teachings and work with elders. She believes that spending time on the land (reserve) helps one to gain strength and keep their spiritual fires burning. Andrew McConnell sums up the challenge of rural to urban move by offering this gem, "To know where you are going, you have to know where you've been" (McConnell, 1997: 149).

Although the fear of cultural loss in the city is real, Warry (2007: 111) believes that it is a myth that Aboriginals who relocate to urban areas have to abandon their culture. Warry notes that this kind of thinking is being promoted by the neoconservative right and has no support in research. He argues that Aboriginal culture is not necessarily tied to the land, and many First Nations who do migrate to the city manage to keep their identity very well. Warry is some-what in disagreement with the observations of the Royal Commission on Aboriginal People (1996) when it states:

> The requirements of survival in the city frequently force Aboriginal people to change their way of life and reshape the way they express their beliefs and values. The resulting adaptations run a complete range, from maintenance of a strong Aboriginal identity based on traditional Aboriginal culture to assimilation into the pervasive non-Aboriginal culture. (Todd, 2001: 106)

Warry identifies social scientists as those who have perpetuated the myth of cultural loss, and suggests that too much research has concentrated on the "have-nots" of Indian society, and successful middle class migrants have been left out of the picture. Warry's concern is that the latter have basically been represented as assimilated, and what little research there is does suggest that issues of culture and Aboriginal identity are important to them.

One of the institutions that has worked well for urban Aboriginal cultural maintenance is the Indian friendship centre, a 1950s phenomenon. At first friendship centres functioned as get-together agencies, but soon expanded to foster a wide variety of services, many of then through networking with other agencies. In 1972 the federal government formally recognized the National Association of Friendship Centres and implemented the Migrating Native Peoples' Program (MNPP) to help individuals of First Nations background in adapting to urban life. Funding, which became permanent in 1988, was offered to eighty such centers through the federal Secretary of State. Currently the Canadian National Association of Friendship Centres includes 99 core-funded and 15 non-core funded friendship centres, as well as seven Provincial Territorial Associations across Canada (Warry, 2007: 113).

Essentially friendship centres have become more or less "official" starting places for migrating First Nations. These centers offer helpful connections to urban newcomers in such vital areas as housing, employment, and education. A relatively new phenomenon, urban elders, has come into being, some of them formally connected to local friendship centres where they make themselves available for consultation, for prayer, and conducting spiritual ceremonies and rituals.

The role of the government in assisting urban Indian migrants has not always been particularly supportive. During the 1980s the federal government established a "twelve month rule" which implied that anyone who had lived in an urban area for at least that period of time was no longer a responsibility of the federal government. Instead, municipal and provincial governments were to take over that responsibility (Buckley, 1993: 115). Support for friendship centres from government sources was not without its political underpinnings. In fact, when governments did provide financial backing, the underlying intent was to foster assimilation. The plan backfired when Indian leaders who managed friendship centres became aware of the government's intent and deliberately set about establishing programs that would encourage cultural pride and identity. As time went on friendship centres became important cultural agencies that not only offered social services, but cultural and spiritual opportunities as well. Some even assumed a role as research centres and advocates for government policy changes (Warry, 2007: 114).

Many Native elders and political leaders urge their young people to pursue education, particularly postsecondary education. However, as Calliou (1997: 230-243) points out, this is easier said than done. Calliou likens a postsecondary institution to a fabled house built for a giraffe. An elephant visits the giraffe and cannot fit into the door. He also discovers that the stairs in the house are not built for his weight. Regretfully, the two never do meet on equal ground.

Aboriginal students often sense that postsecondary institutions are not modelled to accommodate Indigenous ways of thinking and behaving. They frequently encounter ethnocentric and uninformed professors who provide false or misleading information about First Nations and design multiple-choice exams that force students to think in restrictive ways. Other obstacles to Aboriginal students feeling at home on postsecondary campuses include an alienating curriculum designed with no Aboriginal input, faculty performance criteria that emphasize research to the detriment of teaching, and the use of out-dated textbooks that portray Indians in demeaning ways. These textbooks perpetuate false myths about First Nations cultures, and professors who are already mis-informed tend to shy away from incorporating relevant labor-intensive teaching and assessment techniques that Aboriginal students need. Aboriginal students who already feel unwelcome in universities and colleges also have to contend with the fact that there are very few Aboriginal professors and staff members in many of Canada's postsecondary institutions. Calliou does admit to seeing some positive signs. For example, when uninformed or biased professors are confronted with their ethnocentrism, they tend to be very cooperative. In addition, the development of Native student centres on campuses has provided commendable services to incoming students. Not only do they provide counselling and referrals, but they tend to provide a comfort zone for students – a home away from home (Calliou, 1997: 132-133).

# Projections

While urban First Nations struggle to make their way in the city, there are inequities that must be addressed if they are to be successful. Improved education alone will not make the difference because there are serious financial concerns. There is a real need for economic development, more appropriate services, changes in government policies and jurisdiction, and a voice in governance and decision-making (Peters, 2000: 261). Henlin (2006: 175) draws attention to the financial imbalance that exists between reserve communities and those organized in urban centres. At present, 90 percent of federal government transfer payments go to rural communities while the larger, off-reserve population receives only 3.5% of this assistance. Obviously, urban dwellers have similar needs to those of their rural relatives, but the monies to meet them are not available. Henlin recommends that two separate strategies be formulated, one for rural communities and one for urban communities. Both policies must marry education to economic well-being, and not merely concern themselves with academic skills and insights. The reality is that the Aboriginal business sector is expanding dramatically and, in fact, increasing at an annual rate of 30.7 percent. This is a rate nine times faster that that for self-employed Canadians overall. Now the challenge will be for First Nations to blend valuable historical culture elements (including spirituality), into their emerging capitalistic configuration.

## References

Barron, F. Laurie, and Joseph Garcea, eds. (1999). Introduction. *Urban Indian Reserves: Forging New Relationships in Saskatchewan.* Saskatoon, SK: Purich Publishing.

Barron, F. Laurie, and Joseph Garcea. (1999). The Genesis of Urban Reserves. *Urban Indian Reserves: Forging New Relationships in Saskatchewan.* F. Laurie Barron, and Joseph Garcea, eds. Saskatoon, SK: Purich Publishing, 22-52.

Bobiwash, A. Rodney. (1997). Native Urban Self-Government in Toronto and the Politics of Self Determination. *The Meeting Place: Aboriginal Life in Toronto.* Frances Sanderson & Heather Howard-Bobiwash, eds. Toronto, ON: Native Canadian Centre of Toronto, 84-94.

Buckley, Helen. (1993). *From Wooden Ploughs to Welfare: Why Indian Policy Failed in the Prairie Provinces.* Montreal, PQ: McGill-Queen's University Press.

Calliou, George D. (1997) Urban Indians: Reflections on Participation of First Nation Individuals in the Institutions of the Larger Society. *First Nations in Canada: Perspectives on Opportunity, Empowerment, and Self-Determination.* J. Rick Ponting, ed. Toronto, ON: McGraw-Hill Ryerson, 222-244.

Henlin, Calvin. (2006). *Dances with Dependency: Indigenous Success Through Self-Reliance.* Vancouver, BC: Orca Spirit Publishing & Communications.

Makela, Kathleen. (1999). Legal and Jurisdictional Issues of Urban Reserves. *Urban Indian Reserves: Forging New Relationships in Saskatchewan.* Barron F. Laurie, and Joseph Garcea, eds. Saskatoon, SK: Purich Publishing, 78-95.

Mason, Jim (1997). The kind of reward you put into your heart. *The Meeting Place: Aboriginal Life in Toronto.* Frances Sanderson & Heather

Howard-Bobiwash, eds. Toronto, ON: Native Canadian Centre of Toronto, 97-105.

McConnell, Andrew. (1997). To know where you are going, you have to know where you've been. *The Meeting Place: Aboriginal Life in Toronto.* Frances Sanderson & Heather Howard-Bobiwash, eds. Toronto, ON: Native Canadian Centre of Toronto, 149-155.

Nagler, Mark. (1973). *Indians in the City: A Study of the Urbanization of Indians in Toronto.* Ottawa, ON: Canadian Research Centre for Anthropology, Saint Paul University.

Obonsawin, Roger, and Heather Howard-Bobiwash. (1997). The Native Canadian Centre of Toronto: The Meeting Place for the Aboriginal Community for 35 Years. *The Meeting Place: Aboriginal Life in Toronto.* Frances Sanderson & Heather Howard-Bobiwash, eds. Toronto. ON: The Native Canadian Centre of Toronto, 25-59.

Peters, Evelyn. (2000). Aboriginal People in Urban Areas. *Visions of the Heart: Canadian Aboriginal Issues.* Second edition. David Long and Olive Patricia Dickason, eds. Toronto, ON: Harcourt Brace, 237-270.

Schouls, Tim. (2003). *Shifting Boundaries: Aboriginal Identity, Pluralist Theory, and the Politics of Self-Government.* Vancouver, BC: UBC Press.

Steckley, John I., and Bryan D. Cummins. (2008). *Full Circle: Canada's First Nations.* Second edition. Toronto, ON: Pearson Education Canada.

Todd, Roy. (2001). Aboriginal People in the City. *Aboriginal People and Other Canadians: Shaping New Relationships.* Martin Thornton and Roy Todd, eds. Ottawa, ON: University of Ottawa, 93-130.

Warry, Wayne. (2007). *Ending Denial: Understanding Aboriginal Issues.* Peterborough, ON: Broadview Press

# Five

## In Pursuit of Quality Health, Education, and Welfare Services

> Aboriginal education has made great strides. Increased educational options for Aboriginal children mean children living on-reserve often attend a school operated by their own community. Other on-reserve families may choose to send their children to provincial or private schools. Most Aboriginal children living in urban settings now attend school alongside their non-Aboriginal contemporaries almost as a matter of course. (Hare, 2003: 426)

> From a positive perspective, initiatives have been implemented to increase the participation of Aboriginal people in the design, management and delivery of health care. A considerable boost has been given to traditional medicine and healing, and progress has been made in introducing accessible and appropriate services, and generally re-shaping the mainstream health and social welfare provision. (Mercer, 2001: 156)

The history of Aboriginal health, education, and welfare since the time of European contact is not a particularly positive narrative, but things are getting better. The beginning of the story is pleasant enough if one goes back a few centuries before European contact. Then the sky turns darker shades and the record shows many Native tribes suffering from a variety of inflicted ills. In fact, for many generations, beginning shortly after the fur trade originated to the 1980s, the negative aspects of Aboriginal health, education, and welfare outweigh the positive. Today the overall scene of better health, more education, and increased concerns about welfare has improved, but there is much more to be done. Life expectancy for Indigenous people is up, employment in Indian communities is rising, and more Native young people are being educated in elementary and high schools with increasing numbers of them enrolled in postsecondary institutions. In the mid 1960s there were about 200 Status Indian students enrolled in Canadian colleges and universities. As the twenty-first century emerged on the horizon, more than 27 000 were enrolled in postsecondary institutions. Since then that number has risen slowly to include more than thirty thousand students. The expansion of Aboriginal studies in postsecondary institutions has also been enhanced. Both Aboriginal and nonAboriginal students can major in Native studies at many colleges and universities, particularly Trent University, the University of Alberta, the University of British Columbia, the University of Manitoba, the University of Saskatchewan, and the First Nations University of Canada which is connected to the University of Regina. The University of Calgary offers an undergraduate degree in International Indigenous Studies. Early inception of these programs began with the University of Saskatchewan in 1960 with selected courses, and the more formalized approach resulted in the formation of the First Nations University of Canada in 1976. Since then the First Nations University has developed branch offices in Prince Albert and Saskatoon as well as providing learning opportunities in various other communities. The university currently offers both undergraduate and graduate degree programs.

As indicated in a previous chapter, many First Nations bands have built and are operating cultural centres that are open to both Aboriginal and nonAboriginal. Hopefully, the latter will avail themselves of the opportunity to learn more about the history and culture of Canada's First Peoples. Finally, it is exciting to note that the economic picture of Canada's First Nations is brighter as band councils begin to involve themselves in negotiations with resource companies for local industrial development (Friesen and Friesen, 2002: 16-17).

## A Look Back

Various contemporary Native writers have sketched quite positive aspects of their tribal lifestyle before the Europeans came, and that in a very forthright manner. Steckley and Cummins (2008: 187) point out that it is often erroneously assumed that the First Nations of North America had no diseases and no health problems before European contact. Aboriginal people did suffer from disorders such as arthritis, and eye problems caused by too much smoke in enclosed places. However, big-killer communicable diseases like measles, mumps, smallpox, tuberculosis, and whooping cough were not a problem. These diseases were imported.

Native writers have tended to portray their traditional lifestyle as quite idyllic. For example, Chief Dan George (1974: 36-37) had this to say about his experiences growing up in West Coast Indian culture:

> In houses like these, throughout the tribe, people learned to live with one another; learned to serve one another; learned to respect the rights of one another. And children shared thoughts of the adult world and found themselves surrounded by aunts and uncles and cousins who loved them and did not threaten them. My father was born in such a house and learned from infancy how to love people and be at home with them.

Chief John Snow of the Stoney (Nakoda Sioux) First Nation near Calgary, Alberta, echoes Chief Dan George's description of a pleasant upbringing by pointing out that the Stoney people did not have locks on the doors of their houses, and they did not have jails. There were no atheists among them. They did not have senior citizens' homes in which to place the elderly because elders were highly respected and often provided with the best that the tribe had to give. In Chief Snow's (2005: 8) words:

> Human kindness was imprinted in our hearts, and the law of the Great Spirit, the Creator, was the only law we observed. Our society was built around the concept that the Creator is the Supreme Being, the Great Mystery, recognizing Him as the One who provides all things was the very first step and the beginning of our tribal society. The recognition of the Creator in all of life was essential for our survival here on earth. The recognition of the Creator in all of life was essential for our survival here on earth and in the hereafter.

Chief Snow goes on to emphasize how much children were valued in Stoney society. It was a very important responsibility of tribal members to pass along valued historical and spiritual knowledge to their children and grandchildren. Parents, grandparents, and elders often told and retold legends that contained tribal beliefs to the children in teepees, by campfires, on hillsides, and in forests. Instruction was based on the approach later popularized by progressivist educators like American philosopher, John Dewey – learning by doing.

Assiniboine Chief Dan Kennedy (Ochankugahe) (1972: 55) reiterates Chief John Snow's recollections by recalling the happy events prior to the "coming of the White man." Somewhat wistfully, Kennedy laments being robbed of his Assiniboine name in residential school and having a "White" name tacked on to him. However, he also emphasizes the need to go with the times. Kennedy notes that in the Assiniboine language there were no profane words. In fact Indians had to break the Christian commandment – "You shall not misuse the name of the Lord your God . . ." (Exodus 20:7a NIV) – in order to learn the white man's language. Kennedy concurs that missionaries brought Christianity to the Assinboines, but, he states, ". . . may we ask who brought blasphemy?" (Kennedy, 1972: 55).

Mike Mountain Horse of the Blood (Kainai) First Nation in southern Alberta makes mention of a deliberate belligerent attitude on the part of the Bloods when they were first informed by incoming missionaries that the Bloods did not believe in God. "The Indians also believed for ages in the existence of a Supreme Being. . . . We pray earnestly and sincerely to whatever spirit we wish to supplicate for assistance in bestowing a special favor" (Mountain Horse, 1989: 54, 57). Mountain Horse emphasizes other positive characteristics of the society in which he was raised, particularly the respect that people had for one another. Hospitality was instinctive among the Bloods. No tribesman ever visited a teepee without being certain of a warm welcome. No Blood was ever "down and out" so that he needed to ask for assistance in providing for his needs or those of his family (Mountain Horse, 1989: 76). Also a member of the Blood tribe, Beverly Hungry Wolf (1982: 110) emphasizes the respected role of women in traditional Blackfoot society:

> Let me just say that in the culture of my people the work of the women was generally respected and honored, for the men knew very well that they could not live without them. The people of the past thought it a great honor that the women should bear and rear the children, ensuring that there would be people in the future. Equally honorable was the women's work of creating lodges that made the homes, taking them up and down when camp moved, heating them, and providing the bedding and clothing for the household members.

Hungry Wolf seems to pine for the "good old days" when she recalls the help and friendship she received from her peers while growing up and eventually establishing her own home. In her words:

> How else would I know that one of the finest rewards for being an old women comes from going outside the camp circle early each morning, to face the rising sun and call out the names of all the children, grandchildren, great-grandchildren, and friends, during a prayer that shows the old woman's thankfulness and humbleness before the Creator, and brings cheerful tears into the eyes of all those in the camp who can hear? (Hungry Wolf, 1980: 110-111)

Joseph Dion, a Cree Elder is easily the most complimentary of traditional Native culture before European contact. He extols virtually every aspect of the old ways, and although he admits that the traditional ways of the Cree were difficult and there were many inconveniences, disappointments, and hardships, it was a good life. Dion says that the Crees of old were healthy and strong. Their constant roving in quest of good hunting grounds, and their steady diet of fresh meat, together with clean living gave them superb bodies and clean alert minds. He continues:

> He was seldom sick and the great outdoors provided him with dependable remedies for his few ailments. He learned to appreciate every achievement and derived much pleasure in even the little things which tended to make others happy. The tidbits from his kill, such as the kidney of the deer or moose which he would very much like to eat in the raw, he wrapped in a clean birch bark to bring home to his little son or grandchild. (Dion, 1979: 5)

If it may be acknowledged that these writers may have exaggerated the high quality of traditional Indian culture in some ways, but that would surely be their privilege. It is never a particularly positive experience for any people to be victimized by oppressive colonialism and have their culture taken from them. It may be true that some of the incoming Europeans had the best interests of the First Peoples at heart, but the devastating effects that their various conquests had on the health, education, and welfare are deeply lamentable.

# Downward Spiral

Allies during the glory days of the fur trade, everything changed between trading partners – Europeans and First Nations, during the years 1790 and 1830. Suddenly viewed as irrelevant, unfortunates, or as a nuisance, and robbed of their traditional hunting grounds, the Native people fell prey to extremely difficult times. Imported diseases took their toll, and many individuals yielded to the effects of alcohol addiction. The effects of influenza, measles, and whooping cough depleted the population of the Blood Tribe from 2 488 in 1878 to 1 776 in 1885, and then down to only 1 111 in 1920 (Dempsey, 1997: 30). Devastated by smallpox, the Sarcee or Tsuu T'ina Band population of over a thousand was reduced to 245 by a smallpox epidemic. By the late 1860s, the population had risen to 420, but another onslaught of smallpox reduced them to less than 100 (Dempsey, 1997: 43). The Keehiwin Cree Band was reduced from 211 members in 1876 to 145 by 1908. In later years, however, with improved health and welfare programs, the population rose to 1 367 in 1996 (Dempsey, 1997: 62). Other tribes suffered similar losses.

Eventually reduced to living on reserves, Canada's First Nations continued to suffer loss of identity and limits of resources. Previously they had access to the open spaces that provided them with everything they needed to survive. Now they were required to change their ways of making a living and that on what many considered to be very small plots of land. Even then, in many cases Indian lands were sold off because their populations were decreasing and government officials judged that they needed even less land than they had been allotted.

William Wuttunee, a Saskatchewan born Cree and the first Aboriginal lawyer in western Canada, suggests that Indians were herded onto reserves like buffalo and kept in place by the Northwest Mounted Police (Wuttunee, 1971: 111). He goes on to describe reserve life in these words:

> The Indians suffered quietly from malnutrition and disease in the primeval silence, and turned the reservations into permanent havens away from the white man. In the quiet of the hinterland the old people taught their grandchildren of the glories of the past and of their struggles with enemy tribes. . . . The people learned to subsist on a meager diet of bannock, lard and tea and occasionally potatoes and rabbit. The first generation to be fenced in by reserves had participated freely in the glories of the hunt; the second generation could only listen to the stories of the past while they watched their people die like snow before the sun; the third and fourth generations could only dimly picture a glorious past . . . (Wuttunee, 1971: 112)

The late Harold Cardinal, a northern Cree and former president of the Indian Association of Alberta quoted a young Indian chief to observe:

> Years ago our people were self-reliant. We made our living by trapping and from whatever nature was able to provide for us. Our life was hard. It was not an easy life – we had to use our minds continually to try and find means and ways by which to survive. But we lived like men. Then the government came and offered welfare to our people. . . . For a few years they provided welfare. During those years, our minds went to sleep, for we did not have to use them in order to survive. Our minds went to sleep. (Cardinal, 1969: 62)

According to Wuttunee (1971: 113), the exile imposed on Aboriginal peoples eventually became a voluntary exile – a safe haven of sorts. Reserves became the last bastion of safety where cultural practices could be maintained if not directly forbidden by the local Indian agent. Some tribes, like the Bloods of Alberta, continued to practice the Sundance even though it was expressly forbidden by federal law. Parenthetically, the American Crow First Nation continued to practice the Sundance, but did so on the fourth of July. They convinced the Indian agent that they were in fact celebrating the Fourth of July in traditional style.

Beyond a doubt, one of the most often discussed dimensions of Indian life in the past half century is the residential school phenomenon. The rules of dormitory life at residential schools were demanding and patronizing. Aboriginal children were forbidden to speak their Native languages, and they were told that their traditional religion was wrong. Also, the transition from trap-line and woodland living to dormitory life was simply too much for many students who often ran away and were punished severely for it. Boys and girls were divided from each other so that family members of the opposite sex were often not able to converse.

Oddly enough, not every Indian child attended residential schools. In 1900 there were 2 229 children enrolled in federally-run residential schools, and another 1 612 in industrial schools. Two hundred and forty-one day schools accounted for another 6 784 students. The total number of Indians between the ages of six and fifteen numbered 19 528. This meant that residential schools were providing education for 19.7 percent or one-fifth of Indian students. The residential school system grew slowly after that and school attendance for Indian children was made compulsory in 1920. By 1927 one-third of Indian students were in residential schools. At their most numerous point of growth, when some eighty residential schools were in operation, these schools never educated more than one-third of the potential population of Native youth (Miller, 1997: 142).

The concept of boarding students on site was not a particularly North American idea since it was fairly common in various parts of Europe. The first known boarding school for Native youth was built in 1620 under the auspices of Récollect priests near a settlement on the St. Lawrence River (Miller, 1997: 39). Reasons for starting such schools varied. Some initiators believed that children could not be educated while their nomadic parents roamed at will. Others wanted to rid the children of their traditional ways and socialize them to European religion, culture, and civilization. Besides, educating Indian children apart from their parents made the job easier.

Negative stories of life in residential schools abound (Cooper, 1999; Dyck, 1997; Furniss, 1995; Grant, 1993; Haig-Brown, 1993; Knockwood, 1994; and Schissel and Wotherspoon, 2003). Many former residential school dwellers have told and retold horrific stories about being hungry, abused (physically, emotionally, and often sexually), and mistreated, and told that their heritage was inadequate to cope with changing times. Many former residential school students have been diagnosed as suffering from Post-Traumatic Disorder which exhibits symptoms like panic attacks, eating disorders, insomnia, uncontrollable anger, alcohol and drug abuse, sexual inadequacy, or addiction. Many find it difficult to form long lasting or intimate relationships (Steckley, and Cummins, 2008: 195). Many teachers in residential schools were ill-equipped to teach, and while some of them may have been knowledgeable about Christianity, they knew little about educational philosophy or pedagogy. As late as 1957, fifty percent of school teachers working in residential schools were legally unqualified. This number was reduced to 10 percent by 1962 (Milloy, 1999: 227). The importance of having properly qualified teachers cannot be easily overlooked. Craig (1992) notes that teachers are in a position to have significant impact on the cognitive profiles of students who do not fit the middle class stereotype. There is a rich body of research on instruction in cognitive strategies that can assist students to become empowered to deal with tough academic challenges. Strategy instruction highlights those characteristics of the learning environment that are most critical to completing tasks. Only properly trained teachers will know what these strategies are and how to access them.

The demise of the residential school was not necessarily caused by any inadequacy in the system. Rather, it was a trend of the times toward secularism that ended the missionary era, and religious leaders were sometimes shocked to see their schools taken over by government bureaucrats. The takeover was designed by government officials, with some pressure from lobbyists, and then secularized without much consultation with Native parents. The move was typical of previous dealings with First Nations on the notion that "we must do the best we can for them – and we do know best."

The move to close down residential schools paralleled the federal government's policy to move towards integrating Indian children into provincial school systems. The federal system was failing Aboriginal children badly, particularly with reference to grades one and four. Things got so bad that it could be stated with a high degree of accuracy that "An Indian child who enters school at age 7, fails grade one and four, is of legal age to leave school at grade 6" (Buckley, 1993: 98). The few students that did continue to attend school soon dropped out because they did not feel comfortable attending school with nonNative children who were much younger than they were. On a parallel note, In December, 2001, Canada.comNews announced that 45 percent of Aboriginal children in Saskatchewan schools were dropping out even after local bands took charge of education. One reason for the high rate of dropouts was because bands took over educational jurisdiction without appropriate planning. The Manitoba dropout rate was even higher, possibly as high as 75 percent, and this in a province with the highest Native population (Palliser, 2003).

Educators were not the only ones responsible for training children away from their parents, even though for a long time residential schools served informally as the government's child welfare services. As the field of social work advanced, their professionals were also being charged with additional responsibilities in relation to the Native community. Their involvement had deep historical roots in the general policy of the Department of Indian Affairs and Northern Development. Duncan Campbell Scott, who was deputy superintendent general of Indian Affairs made this statement to the House of Commons in 1920: "Our object is to continue until there is not a single Indian in Canada who has not been absorbed into the body politic and there is no Indian question, and no Indian department, that is the whole object of this bill" (Walmsley, 2005: 9). By the 1950s social workers were actively involved in removing children from their parents' homes if the latter were in any way judged to be unfit parents. As a result, Aboriginal children were significantly overrepresented in Canadian child welfare systems.

By the 1960s, Aboriginal parents were becoming better informed as to their rights and protested about their children being removed too quickly from their homes. For example, most of the children from the Spallumcheen Indian Band in British Columbia were in the care of the provincial Human Resources Department and placed in nonNative homes. The protest was so successful, that by the 1970s, many of the children had been returned to their family homes; however, some had died and others were in distress

(Strong-Boag, 2005: 152-15). On this basis, Native parents reached the conclusion that there was no such thing as a good nonNative adoption situation or foster home. However, research showed that this was indeed not the case. There were adoptees who reported very positive experiences in having been adopted by nonNative parents. This kind of result compelled Aboriginal leaders to search for distinctive and innovative approaches to child welfare practices. Eventually the Government of British Columbia established a Native Child Welfare Advisory Committee. One of the new requirements was that foster and adoptive parents of Indian children be required to keep adoptees in touch with their home communities.

Walmsley (2005: 3f) concurs that Indian children were often too quickly removed from their homes and placed in government care. Since the field of social work was in a developing stage, social workers often made decisions without a solid scientific knowledge base by which to decide whether or not to remove children from their parents. If that indeed was the case, making a decision constituted fundamentally a moral action. As the field of social work has matured, now backed by more solid research, it has become obvious that children's needs are best met within the context of family – even if family life in any specific case is judged to be less than healthy. After all, "it takes a whole community to raise a child" (Walmsley, 2005: 5). This is particularly true in high context cultures that emphasize participation in extended family relationships. First Nations cultures have always emphasized the role of elders as teachers, caregivers, and purveyors of cultural and spiritual knowledge. It is important to recognize the spiritual dimension of Aboriginal culture for it is the foundation of all teaching and learning.

It is gratifying to report that over the past two decades child adoption practices in Canada have greatly improved. However, the approach to child welfare practice of the first half of the twentieth century has left unfortunate circumstances in its wake. Many individuals continue to suffer from the discriminate and unjust treatment they received from an inadequate system initiated and approved by government. As Strong-Boag (2005: 156) notes, reconnecting with the past makes it more difficult to ignore ongoing relations of disadvantage and advantage that underpins so many exchanges of children in Canada.

# Towards a Better Deal

What are the characteristics of an education for citizenship in a democracy where legitimacy resides with individual citizens? . . . *First,* an education for citizenship must be distributed in such a way that no child is . . . prevented from eventual participation in a democracy of individual citizens. *Second,* it seems clear that an education must be democratically organized and *third,* the content and the means by which such an education is taught and learned is critical to an education for a democracy of individual citizens. (Stockden, 2005: 87, italics ours)

Education for citizenship rests on the foundation of having good health and being treated fairly. Hence, Stockden's point about equal distribution of services, which has certainly not been the case for Canada's First Nations. What is making a difference today is the return of Aboriginal traditions, including ancient medical practices that are having a very positive effect on debilitating health conditions. Alcohol addiction, for example, has been successfully treated by such Native-run institutions as Poundmaker's Lodge and the Nechi Institute. Stockden emphasizes the input from all societal sectors can only happen in a truly democratic setup, and this is happening when Aboriginal people are treated as full partners when health, education, and welfare considerations are on the table. Walmsley (2005: 138) emphasizes that health, education, and welfare agencies must adopt flexibility if they want to be effective in delivery. Thus, when Aboriginal representatives strive for different approaches to be considered, they must be taken seriously. In a truly democratic system, all input must be regarded as having equal value. Aboriginal organizations and their representatives continue to assert that the child protection needs of their communities are different than the needs of dominant society, and therefore those needs require different policies and practices.

A similar situation exists with regard to the administration of elementary and secondary schooling, which has been turned over to local control. In fact, the good news is that ninety-eight percent of schools on reserves are administered by First Nations themselves. This means that the school programs can be tailored to meet local needs. On November 23, 2006, Bill C-34 was passed by the House of Commons and ratified by the Senate. It received Royal Assent on December 12, 2006. Essentially the bill endorses the lifelong learning philosophy promoted by First Nations and is now in the process of phasing in jurisdictional control to local Native communities. Areas that have been negotiated include teacher certification, accrediting of schools, and structures and roles of community education authorities. This development will provide local schools with the power to create and amend programs to suit the needs and learning style of their students. Local interest has been high. In December, 2005, the Minister of Indian Affairs announced that seventeen Treaty Six chiefs had sent in proposals on how to improve education in their jurisdictions.

Two decades ago, when learning styles research became popular, researchers discovered that First Nations children had different educational needs than their nonNative peers (Hodgson-Smith, 2000: 160). *First* of all, Aboriginal children entered the foreign environments of nonNative schools with low self-esteem, and lacked confidence in their academic abilities. *Second,* they showed a strong preference for more precisely spelled-out assignments. *Third,* they indicated a need for a greater variety of classroom interaction patterns. *Fourth,* they preferred more teacher-student interaction – possibly for assurance. *Fifth,* they possibly were more peer oriented than their nonAboriginal counterparts. *Sixth,* they were more positively oriented toward collaborative learning and enjoyed small group tasks. Adjusting to these preferences would most certainly require both sensitivity and flexibility on the part of educators.

One of the more positive happenings in First Nations communities in Canada has been the establishment of cultural centres. The Cultural/Educational Centres Program was begun in 1971 and consolidated under the memorandum of understanding with the Department of Indian Affairs and Northern Development and the Treasury Board respecting Increased Ministerial Authority and Accountability. The objective of the program has been to help First Nations communities establish and operate cultural/educational centres for the purpose of enlightening locals and visitors about Indian history, culture, and spirituality. Some of the objectives of cultural centres include: to revive and develop traditional and contemporary cultural skills of First Nations and Inuit people; to conduct and/or facilitate research in First Nations/Inuit heritage and culture; to develop First Nations/Inuit linguistic resources; and, to develop and test culturally-oriented educational curricula, methods, and materials for use by established and other programs. Staffs of the centres are committed to promoting cross cultural awareness and develop accurate information about First Nations/Inuit heritage. They hope to improve opportunities for the public to become knowledgeable about as well as develop sensitivity to the historic and current role of the First Nations and Inuit peoples of Canada. There are currently more than one hundred cultural centres in Canada.

# Projections

Having witnessed recent dramatic improvements in Aboriginal health, education, and welfare does not mean that equality has been attained. The statistics are there; positive changes have been made in all of these areas. However, there are still huge pockets of inequality in many communities. Despite some progress, in British Columbia, almost half of Aboriginal students in grade seven failed to meet provincial standards on reading tests. Only four of every ten male students enrolled in high school graduate (*Times Colonist,* January 17, 2008). According to Aboriginal parents, lack of education on reserves is the most serious problem facing their children. The website of the Society for the Advancement of Excellence in Education documents that only 37 percent of the 117 000 Aboriginal students living on reserves in Canada will complete high school. Some 20 percent of reserve children eligible to attend elementary and high school are not enrolled. In the meantime, the population of reserve Aboriginals is growing rapidly and it will be difficult to keep up with their educational needs – to say nothing of playing catch up. The challenge to improving what has already become a much better situation is threefold; governments must take it upon themselves to provide equality in health, education and welfare to all citizens. Local leaders must lay aside petty politics and like their chiefs of old, really care for their people. Finally, a democracy can only function well if every citizen becomes concerned about the welfare of others by becoming informed, campaigning for justice to be done, and mounting a willingness to offer personal participation and assistance where needed.

# References

Buckley, Helen. (1993). *From Wooden Ploughs to Welfare: Why Indian Policy Failed in the Prairie Provinces.* Montreal, PQ: McGill-Queen's University Press.

Cardinal, Harold. (1969). *The Unjust Society: The Tragedy of Canada's Indians.* Edmonton, AB: M.G. Hurtig.

Chief Dan George. (1974). *My Heart Soars.* Toronto, ON: Hancock House Publishers.

Cooper, Michael L. (1999). *Indian School: Teaching the White Man's Way.* New York: Clarion Books.

Craig, Susan E.   (September, 1992). The Educational Needs of Children Living with Violence. *Phi Delta Kappan,* 24.1, 67-71.

Dempsey, Hugh A. (1997). *Indian Tribes of Alberta.* Calgary, AB: Glenbow Museum.

Dion, Joseph F. (1979). *My Tribe The Crees.*  Calgary, AB: Glenbow Museum.

Dyck, Noel. (1997). *Differing Visions: Administering Indian Residential Schooling in Prince Albert, 1867-1995.* Halifax, NS: Fernwood Publishing and Prince Albert, SK: The Prince Albert Grand Council.

Friesen, John W., and Virginia Lyons Friesen. (2002). *Aboriginal Education in Canada: A Plea for Integration.* Calgary, AB: Detselig Enterprises.

Furniss, Elizabeth. (1995). *Victims of Benevolence: The Dark Legacy of the Williams Lake Residential School.* Vancouver, BC: Arsenal Pulp Press.

Grant, Agnes. (1993). *Our Bit of Truth: An Anthology of Canadian Native Literature.* Winnipeg, MB: Pemmican Publications.

Haig-Brown, Celia. (1993). *Resistance and Renewal: Surviving the Indian Residential School.* Vancouver, BC: Tillacum Books.

Hare, Jan. (2003). Aboriginal Families and Aboriginal Education: Coming Full Circle. *Children, Teachers and Schools in the History of British Columbia.* Second edition. Jean Barman and Mona Gleason, eds. Calgary, AB: Detselig Enterprises, 411-430.

Hodgson-Smith. (2000). Issues of Pedagogy in Aboriginal Education. *Aboriginal Education: Fulfilling the Promise.* Marlene Brant Castellano, Lynne Davis, and Louise Lahache, eds. Vancouver, BC: UBC Press, 156-170

Hungry Wolf, Beverly. (1982). *The Ways of My Grandmothers.* New York: Quill.

Kennedy, Dan (Ochankugahe). (1972). *Recollections of an Assiniboine Chief.* Toronto, ON: McClelland and Stewart.

Knockwood, Isabelle. (1994). *Out of the Depths: The Experiences of Mi'kmaw Children at the Indian Residential School at Shubenacadie, Nova Scotia.* Lockeport, NS: Roseway Publishing.

Mercer, Geoffrey. (2001). Aboriginal Peoples: Health and Healing. *Aboriginal People and Other Canadians.* Martin Thornton and Roy Todd, eds. Ottawa, ON: University of Ottawa Press, 131-160.

Miller, J. R. (1997). *Shingwauk's Vision: A History of Native Residential Schools.* Toronto, ON: University of Toronto Press.

Milloy, John S. (1999). *A National Crime: The Canadian Government and the Residential School System, 1879 to 1986.* Winnipeg, MB: University of Manitoba Press.

Mountain Horse, Mike. (1989). *My People, The Bloods.* Calgary, AB: Glenbow Museum.

Palliser, Brian. (September 8, 2003). Canadian Aboriginal Policy: Where to From Here? *The Carberry News.*

Schissel, Bernard, and Terry Wotherspoon. (2003). *The Legacy of School for Aboriginal People.* Don Mills, ON: Oxford University Press.

Snow, Chief John. (2005). *These Mountains Are Our Sacred Places: The Story of the Stoney People.* Calgary, AB: Fitzhenry & Whiteside Company.

Steckley, John I., and Bryan D. Cummins. (2008). *Full Circle: Canada's First Nations.* Second edition. Toronto, ON: Pearson Education Canada.

Stockden, Eric W. (2005) Pluralism, Corporatism, and Educating Citizens. *Educating Citizens for a Pluralistic Society.* Rosa Bruno-Jofré and Natalia Aponiuk, eds. Calgary, AB: Canadian Ethnic Studies, 71-93.

Strong-Boag, Veronica. (2005). Interrupted Relations: The Adoption of Children in Twentieth Century British Columbia. *Child and Family Welfare in British Columbia: A History.* Diane Purvey and Christopher Walmsley, ed. Calgary, AB: Detselig Enterprises, 139-164.

Walmsley, Christopher. (2005). *Protecting Aboriginal Children.* Vancouver, BC: UBC Press.

Wuttunee, William, I.C. (1971). *Ruffled Feathers: Indians in Canadian Society.* Calgary, AB: Bell Books.

## Six

## *It Wasn't All Bad:*
## *A Different Perspective on Residential*
## *Schools from Those Who Know*

Attitudes about residential schools are diverse. One of Shirley's relatives actually got high marks and seemed to enjoy the residential school. Shirley speculates that she may have enjoyed her experience at the school because she had so many childcare responsibilities at home. (Grant, 2004: 95)

Not all residential school experiences, of course, were bad. They can be credited with producing band managers, advocates, and political leaders with the skills necessary to effectively negotiate with, and oppose, government actions. But the abuses that did take place are well-documented. (Warry, 2007: 61)

"I honestly don't know what the fuss is all about," a male Aboriginal elder told our university class. "I had a great deal of fun in residential school. We secretly used to date the girls in school and once in a while we would even stage a panty raid in the girls' dormitory. I had a lot of fun in residential school."

Naturally, the class was somewhat taken aback by this testimony since it flew in the face of much of which has been written about the horrors of life in Canada's residential schools. Indeed, there are hundreds of men and women who were incarcerated in residential schools who can testify to having been abused, culturally deprived, made fun of, and often left to go hungry. Was this man's testimony the voice of a lone wolf from the pack?

## The Residential School Phenomenon

By now most Canadians will be familiar with the phenomenon of Indian residential schools as a blight on Canadian history. It is commonly believed that most Indian children were at one time incarcerated in residential schools, but the truth is that only about 30-35 percent of Aboriginal children attended residential schools. In 1900, for example, of the roughly 20 000 Status Indians of school age, only 3 285 were in 22 industrial schools and 39 residential schools, while another 6 349 attended day schools (Steckley and Cummins, 2008: 191). It must be emphasized, however, that efforts to downplay traditional Native beliefs and practices and assimilate Aboriginal youngsters constituted equally as strong a campaign in day schools as it did in residential schools.

Numbers aside, accounts cataloguing the atrocities that took place in residential schools may be found in the daily press, and contained in academic studies, and government documents. Generally considered an ineffective tool of assimilation processed by well-meaning religious and civil innovators, residential schools have most recently been portrayed as institutions that forcibly contained children and provided them with inadequate nourishment and poor health care. Children were told to renounce their spiritual beliefs, abandon their migratory lifestyle, and take up Christianity. Missionaries of various denominations worked hand in hand with government officials to try to control Canada's First Nations in every way – spiritually, physically, mentally, and in terms of lifestyle (Berger, Epp, and Møller, 2006: 182f). What transpired in terms of the teaching/learning process in residential schools could hardly be called adequate education. Teachers, many of them with strong religious connections, were poorly trained by today's standards, and often knew nothing about the rudiments of sound pedagogy (Schissel and Wotherspoon, 2003: 53). They were mostly concerned that their pupils would be inculcated with the rudimentary elements of the fourth "R" namely, religious instruction. Most students fared poorly, mainly because of the consequences of dealing with the rift between the traditional Indian way of teaching and learning and that imported from Europe. In addition, the approach to teaching was for the most part alien to Native students who were accustomed to learning by observation and participation, storytelling, and mentoring. In addition, the curriculum content was quite unfamiliar to them, concentrating as it did on European interpretations of the Christian faith.

Language was another cultural issue in residential education. Native children were expected to abandon their Native tongues and take up French (and later English). The European newcomers who first arranged for pedagogical instruction for Aboriginal children assumed that learning French or English was necessary to the spiritual development of their young charges. Some of these early educators thought that teaching had to be done in European languages so that the spiritual undercurrents of their message would remain intact. To their credit, however, many missionaries did learn Native languages and use them as vehicles of instruction. Cree and Mi'kmaq were taught, for example, and in 1836 the Reverend James Evans developed a Cree syllabic orthography that is still used today. The Mohawk of Tyendinga appreciated the fact that their children were being instructed in their Native tongue that they petitioned Bishop Strachan of the Anglican Church to build a school where both Mohawk and English would be taught. They even offered to pay for the cost of printing books to be used in the school. Unfortunately, the Superintendent of Indian Affairs, Captain Anderson, disapproved of the use of books printed in Indian languages because he perceived the future of First Nations to be involved with the nonNative world. Therefore teaching Indian languages would be "time and effort lost" (Anderson, 1863).

## Chronology

The story of Canadian Native residential schools goes back to the beginning of the seventeenth century when the Récollets arrived in New France to establish missions among the First Nations. They initiated their work among the Hurons of Georgian Bay in 1615, then turned their attention to the Mi'kmaq. The Jesuits who followed them built the first residential school for Huron children at Quebec City in the 1630s. The Jesuits also established a mission and encouraged the nearby Montagnais to settle into agricultural villages (Furniss, 1995: 17). By 1667, the Jesuits began day schools on permanently settled Montaganais and Algonkian reserves initially known as "reductions." These reserves were close to French settlements, but separate in organization and administration. The plan was to educate the Indians but also to keep them from negative influences such as alcohol, syphilis, and smallpox. Each reserve contained a mission house and a church operated by missionaries. The educational program consisted of religious studies, agriculture, and manual trades, the latter intended to ignite a working ethic in Indian children (Jaenen, 1986: 45f).

Mission work among the Indians by various male religious orders was paralleled by the efforts of Sister Marguerite Bourgeoys who initiated the first uncloistered order of sisters. Bourgeoys arrived in the tiny settlement of Ville Marie in the mid 1600s, motivated by a vision she had back in France. It took several years before she was able to start a school for Aboriginal children. Its purpose was four fold: to teach Christianity, social graces, the three "R's," and house-wifely skills. When she experienced a measure of success, in 1658 she returned to France to seek additional help. She returned with three colleagues and eventually arranged for formal status as a religious order (Chalmers, 1974: 4f). This was achieved in 1676, and the work eventually expanded into the west and into most other parts of Canada. The order of Ursulines has prevailed to this day, albeit operating in accordance with amended objectives.

As the nineteenth century got underway, new European occupied settlements were developed in the new land. Roman Catholic missionaries were accompanied by Protestant groups (Anglicans and Methodists) with the same objectives – Christianize, educate, and civilize the Indians. When the government of Upper Canada saw the need to develop a form of public education Governor Metcalfe appointed Egerton Ryerson Assistant Superintendent of Education and Ryerson quickly ascended to the position of Superintendent of Education for Upper Canada (McNeill, 1974: 118f). In 1847 the new government published a report on educational policy based on Ryerson's ideas. In it he advanced the idea that Indian children should be educated by federal government arrangements "to raise them to the level of the whites" (Haig-Brown, 1993: 29). Aboriginal parents had little say in the matter, principally because it was perceived that Native parents exercised little control over their children and basically let them do as they pleased. A few years later the Department of Indian Affairs devised a plan to allot private property to encourage Aboriginals in industry, but the plan was rejected by band councils. Chiefs and band councils did favor public education, however, and new reserve schools were established.

In 1860 responsibility for Indian matters was transferred to the then Province of Canada, and the *British North America Act* (BNA Act) of 1867 mandated that First Nations education become the responsibility of the federal government. Indian day schools now became the responsibility of the federal Department of Indian Affairs and somewhat spelled out in the *Indian Act* of 1876. In 1879, the Davin Report (prepared by lawyer Nicolas F. Davin), urged the establishment of residential schools following the pattern set in the United States. Thus, during the 1880s the Canadian government shifted its Indian education policy from the creation of additional day schools to residential schools. In 1884 the *BNA Act* was amended to mandate compulsory education for Indian children up to the age of sixteen. The following year the government introduced the concept of industrial schools and by 1900 there were 22 industrial schools in operation supplemented by 34 residential (boarding) schools and 225 day schools. Four decades later authorities realized that residential schools were not working. They were not accomplishing the department's objectives. Despite this realization, by 1939 the number of residential schools operating in Canada had grown to seventy-nine, enrolling 9 027 children (Milloy, 1999: xii)

In the meantime, a number of reforms were instituted including the recommendation of the Indian Affairs Branch that provincial curricula be used in Indian Day schools. The emphasis in residential schools was primarily to be on vocational training. Then, in 1944 the Director of Indian Affairs appeared before a Special Committee on Reconstruction and Re-Establishment to argue for a shift from residential schools to day schools.

# Industrial Schools

It might be appropriate at this point to explain the nature of industrial schools. Back in 1830 when the administration of Indian Affairs was transferred from military to civil authority, the new administration committed itself to taking the Indian "from a state of barbarism . . . to the industrious and peaceful habits of civilized life" (Scott, 1914). To this end the government established a series of slightly different boarding schools that were committed to introducing specific skills. Indian boys, for example, were taught shoemaking, carpentry, blacksmithing, and tailoring. Girls were taught sewing, knitting, proper laundry practices, and cooking. The decline of the fur trade and the rapidly increasing European population caused growing concern among church leaders as well as within government circles, and it was decided that the First Nations needed to make drastic economic changes. In addition to emphasizing manual trades, the curriculum of industrial schools promoted the same values as the residential schools did, namely European Christian values. The role of the church in "civilizing" the Indians was supported by government officials such as Major General Darling, a superintendent of Indian Affairs, who stated that Indians must ". . . embrace Christianity and civilization" (Brookes, 1991: 67).

By 1858 the "handwriting was on the wall;" industrial schools were not accomplishing the purpose for which they had been constructed. The commissioners saw little evidence that students were applying the skills acquired in school upon returning home. Government evaluations did not blame church societies that managed the schools for their failure. Basic problems outlined in the evaluation included late enrollment of pupils, and consequently short periods of attendance; parental prejudice against the schools (parents justifiably feared that school leaders were intent on seducing their children culturally); and lack of funds to establish "graduates" on the land. Despite this negative report, industrial schools continued to operate in Canada well into the twentieth century.

## Educational Integration

The push for assimilation on Canada's First Nations has never really left the order paper of Indian Affairs. In 1948 policy makers began to use the term "integration," which meant that Indian children should now attend schools along with nonNative children (Friesen, 1983: 48). In 1951 the Indian Affairs Branch replaced the previous half-day attendance policy with a full day policy and the old residential system began to show signs of loosening its grip on Native education. Some observers perceived that the federal government was finally paying attention to the educational needs of First Nations communities and in a five-year period ending in 1957 the number of teachers of Aboriginal background increased from 42 to 81. It was also realized that residential schools had exhausted their usefulness and were only necessary in some instances as places for day students to live. Thus the operation of day schools persisted and by 1958, 7 330 Indian students were attending integrated schools.

On March 15, 1967, the Honorable Arthur Laing, Minister of Indian Affairs and Northern Development, announced a seven-point integration program for Indian education. The plan was to work hand in hand with provincial governments in integrating Aboriginal children into provincial schools. Laing promised a measure of consultation with Indian parents about the plan, inviting them to sit on school boards in districts where a significant number of children were enrolled (Burns, 1998: 53f). That same year a memorandum sent to regional school superintendents made recommendations about including Indian cultural activities in residential schools because there were signs that Native people had begun taking an active interest in the education of their children. Many of them were weary of being ignored in these matters or being invited to sit on ineffective and virtually powerless advisory boards. They wanted to play a more active role in the education of their young. In 1958, a government sponsored study of school textbooks showed that their content was inappropriate for use in Native communities.

The move for more involvement of Indian parents in the education of their children produced another response from government. During the 1960s, control of Indian schools by religious orders was taken over by the Indian Affairs Branch – both day schools and residential schools, and church connected school staff were replaced with secularly trained teachers. By this time, sixty percent of Native children were enrolled in provincial schools.

In 1969 the Trudeau government issued a White Paper urging full integration of Indian people into the Canadian mainstream via ten provincial jurisdictions – including education. Indian response was quick, with the first opposition paper, the *Red Paper*, originating with the forty-four Indian chiefs of Alberta. They stated that they had no particular desire to have to work with ten individual provincial governments when working with one government office (federal) was difficult enough. The educational implications of the White Paper were addressed by the National Indian Brotherhood who stressed the importance of local control of education by Indian bands, more effectively educated teachers, relevant curriculum, and better school facilities.

Perhaps motivated by the after effects of the Red-Paper – White Paper phenomenon, in 1970 an event of significant proportions occurred in St. Paul, Alberta, when a group of Cree educators and parents took over the Blue Quills Residential School and demanded that its control be turned over to them. Modeled on a similar happening by Navajo Indians at Rough Rock, Arizona, the protestors demanded a say in school on goings, particularly with respect to hiring teachers, determining school curricula, and setting school policy. After a ninety-day sit-in, the government finally gave in and Blue Quills became the first locally controlled school in a Native community in Canada (Friesen and Friesen, 2005: 82). By 1985, two-thirds of some 620 Indian bands controlled all or part of their local school programs. A spin-off from these deliberations mandated that nonNative teachers in First Nations schools be required to take courses in intercultural education to prepare them for their task.

In the meantime, residential schools continued to be closed down, although some of them continued under local Indian administration. The last federally run residential school, the Gordon Residential School in Saskatchewan, closed in 1996, and the last band-operated residential school closed its doors in 1998.

# Damages

A significant of books and articles have recently been published documenting the harm that residential education inflicted on unsuspecting children (Bull, 1991; Dyck, 1997; Furniss, 1995; Grant, 1996; Haig-Brown, 1993; Hookimaw-Witt, 1998; Knockwood, 1994; Miller, 1997; Milloy, 1999; Steckley and Cummins, 2008; Schissel and Wotherspoon, 2003; and Warry, 2007). Descriptions of residential education is basically negative, a sample of which includes these perceptions.

> Children who resided in these educational institutions experienced severe cultural discontinuities. Some initial discontinuities on entering school were as follows: learning to speak a foreign language, food, rules, a whole new pattern to adopt and to adapt to in terms of life in an institutional setting. Serious academic problems resulted from linguistic complications. (Bull, 1991: 17-18)

> This continuing practice created a situation in which the standard of residential schooling provided to Indian children in Prince Albert was systematically kept beneath acceptable levels. (Dyck, 1997: 126)

> While the sexual charges against Oblates have caused St. Joseph's to be one of the most-publicized and notorious residential schools in Canada, concerns with the negative impact of the residential school system are shared by Native people across the country, from the grassroots level to the highest national political organizations. (Furniss, 1995: 115)

> Canadians must not pass these schools without pausing to hear the muffled cries of little children in the night or the screams of children who were being beaten unmercifully. One feels the fluttering spirits of children who died alone and unloved, away from family. They lie, quietly buried by school officials, in soil foreign to their ancestors. The dreaded killer tuberculosis was rampant in all Native communities, but the anguish of parents who did know whether their children were dying alone cannot be comprehended today. (Grant, 1996: 21)

Although there was some change over time, Indian culture was never accepted by the school as a real, living culture. Rather, it was seen as something archaic and undesirable, something to be annihilated. . . . An examination of daily life accents these claims and demonstrates clearly the systematic destruction of culture was attempted. (Haig-Brown, 1993: 58-59)

A lot of problems that Native people have today came out of the Residential School; psychological problems. And we passed our problems to our children. (Hookimaw-Witt, 1998: 226)

The majority of the nineteen boys who were flogged are now dead, as are many of their 1934 classmates. In any case, what remains in the survivors' minds is the memory of the beating itself. As children they knew nothing of the political machinery which led to a public hearing and then to the dismissal of all allegations against Father Mackey. (Knockwood, 1994:152)

For the people who operated missions and schools, it was simply taken as a "scientific fact" that the Aboriginal people to whom they ministered were inferior to them culturally, morally, and economically. (Miller, 1997:  414)

Badly built and ill-maintained, they were both the cause and the context of a dreadful crisis in sanitation and health. Throughout the industrial school era, children in the schools had been dying in unbelievable numbers. In that conjunction of the condition of the schools and the health of the children lay, as Dr. P.H. Bryce termed it in 1922, the "national crime." (Milloy, 1999: 75)

Most clearly, our arguments are based on the contention that the history of the relations between Aboriginal peoples and formal education is largely a history of cultural genocide. (Schissel and Wotherspoon, 2003: 35)

Even war seldom shows as large a percentage of fatalities as does the educational system we have imposed upon our Indian wards. (statement made by Doctor P.H. Bryce in 1907 in Steckley and Cummins, 2008: 191)

The reality, of course, is that the negative impacts of the residential experience, particularly on families, are well-documented and have been for over 20 years. (Warry, 2007: 61)

Warry (2007: 61) points out that not all residential school experiences were negative. The schools can be credited with producing band managers, advocates, and political leaders possessing the necessary skills to deal effectively in government negotiations. There are also instances where individual students forged lasting friendships with their peers, however necessary they may have been to personal survival (Slobodin, 1966: 14). This is not to say that abuses did not take place for they did – emotional, physical, and sexual abuse, as well as enforced loneliness. To date, however, the government has rejected claims for general damages such as language or cultural loss, but upheld compensation for cases of physical or sexual abuse.

# Settlement

For many years, survivors of residential schools have sought compensation for abuses they suffered in their educational experience, but to date only a few have been successful (Friesen and Friesen, 2002: 115). Many times their awards have been severely diminished by legal costs. For example, on July 12, 2001, the Supreme Court of Canada authorized an award of half a million dollars to six Aboriginal litigants for damages suffered during their stay in residential schools. Originally the litigants asked for five million dollars in damages, but when their bills were paid, it was doubtful that the litigants would receive any money. Their lawyers required forty percent of the total amount awarded, and court costs took most of the rest. As one observer noted, the prosecutors would see "hardly a dime of the awards" (*Calgary Herald,* April 14, 2001).

Things have gradually changed for the better. On April 5, 2007 the Canadian courts approved the awarding of financial settlements to those Indigenous people who once spent time in residential schools. The fund of 1.9 billion dollars will be used to make payments to former students of these schools on the basis of $10 000 for the first year spent at such an institution and $3 000 (or part thereof) for each additional year. Applicants had until August 20, 2007 to submit the appropriate forms that would entitle them to payment. Anyone not wishing to be part of the program had to sign an opt-out form and forward it to the appropriate federal office. Thereafter they were free to launch a legal case against the government on their own and at their own cost (*Eagle Feather News,* May, 2007: 7).

# A Unique Perspective

People often wonder how survivors of residential schools, many of them in their middle and senior years and many of them respected elders in their communities, can still remain loyal to the respective church denominations which operated residential schools.

These individuals are active in local congregations and some of them serve as clergy or lay people in the very denomination that contributed to their suffering. The answer to this question lies veiled in mystery. Have these kind folk forgotten how they suffered, have they blacked out these unfortunate experiences, or are they just naturally forgiving individuals? Perhaps all Native elders are naturally positive thinking individuals, or acceptance and forgiveness come with the office of elder. As the Kainai study will point out, however, some children learned in and enjoyed residential education. Their words indicate this, and that cannot and must not be taken away from them.

The view that Native elders tend to view the world positively is anchored in many writings by both Aboriginal and nonAboriginal writers. Three examples containing exemplary elder quotes are Karie Garnier's, *Your Elders Speak: A Tribute to Native Elders* (1990), Dianne Meili's, *Those Who Know: Profiles of Alberta's Native Elders* (1991), and Harold Cardinal and Walter Hildebrandt's, *Treaty Elders of Saskatchewan* (2000). Garnier's collection of interviews with twenty-six west coast elders includes a photograph of and a short statement by each elder interviewed. In the book, Celina August (Sto:lo) is quoted as saying, "My heart is real good today because all my life I loved helping old people" (p. 22). Amy Natrall (Squamish) states; "In my lifetime I've known all nationalities and found they are all good people" (p. 26). Lena Jacobs (Squamish) adds, "Love and respect for people and nature will bring you to the Great Spirit" (p. 44).

Meili's (1991) interviews with Alberta elders produced the same reactions. Russell Wright (Siksika) offers this advice; "I believe Native people could contribute to the concept of Canadian community, if we ever get that far. That's what our ancestors had – common unity, community spirit. That's how they survived" (p. 56). Adam Salopree (Dene Tha') suggests, "You are doing a good thing by visiting elders. I tell you always remember the Creator and that He sees everything you do. . . . always remember the Creator" (p. 131). Arnold Orr (Cree) adds, "Love is what you have to hold onto, just hang on to that. Don't let it slide from person to person, keep it steady" (p. 215).

The contributions of Saskatchewan elders lend support to the thesis that elders tend to think positively (Cardinal and Hildebrandt, 2000) include these examples. Victor Echodh, Acting Chief of the Black Lake Denesuline Nation said, ". . . we basically have developed ways of working with each other and sharing with each other, we respect the land, we respect the wildlife, we respect each other" (p. 6). Jacob Bill (Cree) states, "It was the will of the Creator that the White man would come here to live with us, among us, to share our lives together with him and we also both of us collectively to benefit from the bounty of Mother Earth for all time to come" (p. 7). Simon Kytwayhat (Cree) adds, "When our cousins, the White man, first came to peacefully live on these lands . . . with the Indigenous people, as far as I can remember, Elders have referred to them as kiciwâminawak as our first cousins" (p. 33).

## Kainai Study

Realizing the value of the wisdom of their elders, and wishing to preserve them for posterity in written form, in 1992 the Board of Education of the Kainai (Blood) First Nation in southern Alberta, decided to gather the stories of their elders and publish them. A total of 200 elders were interviewed and three years later their stories were published in a three volume set (Zaharia, and Fox, 1995). A fourth volume consisting of an additional 72 interviews with elders was published in 2003 (Zaharia, Fox, and Fox, 2003). A major undertaking, this project is one of the largest of its kind in Canada and underscores the extent of appreciation that the Kainai have for their elders.

When interviewed, most of the Kainai elders described their residential school experiences and offered personal analyses of them. Many of the memories they share in these publications are positive and uplifting, influencing readers to come to the conclusion that they must have had good times in school. To be fair, many of the students did not enjoy their stay at residential school. They complained that they did not attain many academic skills, they stole food from the kitchen, and they were often lonely. However, amidst the regrets and complaints, readers will encounter a host of positive evaluations. Many of the statements made by elders are brief, but as Akan (1992: 193) cautions;

> An Elder's talk sometimes consists of words or partial words within a phrase that at first seem like an incomplete thought, or an unfinished sentence, but that structure actually works to empower or strengthen the whole with meaning. . . . Teaching actually becomes more like preaching.

The following are representative positive quotations from the four volumes, *Kitomahkitapiiminnooniks: Stories from our Elders*, subdivided into the following categories: domestic and life skills, faith, recreation, vocational training, and enjoyment.

### Domestic and Life Skills

Finally at the age of about nine years of age, I was placed at the old Roman Catholic Mission School in Standoff. I didn't mind being in school. I was taught to work and cook there and was well taken care of. Since our residence was close to the river, we went swimming every day during the warm weather. (Annette Russell, I: 31)

In 1924, the new St. Paul's Anglican Indian Residential School was completed and we were all transferred there. Upon my arrival there, I thought I was in heaven. The building was warm, had electricity, indoor plumbing and good food. Besides school work we learned how to sew, crochet, clean, cook, and bake. Every day after school we were given chores such as scrubbing floors and other cleaning that had to be done. (Bertha Davis, 1:52)

I have always taken great pride in my school. I appreciate the manners I was taught there. I was taught to be tidy and clean, to have good manners, to cook, sew, do first aid, and keep a clean house. I learned skills which stayed with me all of my life. (Josephine Soop, I: 78)

I went to the St. Paul's Anglican Residential School where I worked half a day and attended half-day classes. . . . At school I learned some good life skills such as cooking, baking, sewing and home nursing. (Beatrice Goodstriker, II: 18)

I was seven years of age when I started my formal education at St. Mary's Roman Catholic Residential School. The nuns taught me some good life skills which I still utilize to this day. (Angeline Standing Alone, III: 57)

I received my education at St. Mary's Roman Catholic Residential School starting at age six. My academic education was overshadowed by the life skills emphasis. I learned how to cook, sew and use other general housekeeping techniques. I also learned how to pray. (Irene Small Eyes, III: 60)

I entered St. Paul's Anglican Residential School at age seven. Besides academic education, I also learned good housekeeping skills which I have used throughout my life. I never heard of, nor knew about, any abuse of students at St. Paul's. (Rosella Black Plume, III: 71)

My formal education was at St. Paul's Anglican Residential School where I was placed at age eight. There I learned to cook and to sew. I learned other life skills which are helpful to me. . . . The supervisors were very strict which was good for our character building. (Annie Heavy Head, III: 78)

I was only eighteen weeks old when my mother put me at St. Mary's Roman Catholic Indian Residential School. I was raised by nuns. I have good and happy memories of my school life. The nuns were very good to me and my good friend Elsie (nee Sweet Grass) First Rider. The nuns taught me household skills which were of great use to me in later life. (Bridget Many Grey Horses, IV: 21)

I am glad that I attended St. Mary's. even though the nuns were very strict with us, they taught us many things such as cooking, baking, sewing, knitting, embroidering and how to do household chores. (Theresa Devine, IV: 33)

At age seven I went to St. Paul's Anglican Residential School. I was one of the lucky ones who attended classes all day, every-day and didn't have to work half days like many of my classmates did. I also learned how to play piano, household chores such as cleaning, sewing, cooking and other duties. (Georgina Williams-Freeman, IV: 57)

I started my formal education at St. Mary's Roman Catholic Indian Residential School at age eight. The nuns were kind and treated me well. I learned all about the Catholic religion, sewing, cooking and good housekeeping skills. . . . the nuns were strict and that was all right with me. (Mary Standing Alone, IV: 112)

## Faith

I was born in 1917 and went to the Roman Catholic Residential School when I was ten years old. It was not too bad. I was taught to be a good Catholic and to live an exemplary life. (Margaret Fox, I: 112)

When the new St. Mary's Roman Catholic Residential School was completed, we were all transferred there by wagon. What a nice place awaited us – indoor plumbing, electricity, and much more heat . . . Besides the classroom schooling we learned to pray and work. (Eva Mills, II: 10)

Agnes [as interviewed] attended the St. Paul's Residential School from 1926 to 1935. Work and religion were a major part of Agnes's life. She strongly encouraged her children to follow this way of life. Agnes was a very devout Catholic seldom missing church during Lent, first Fridays and Sundays. (Agnes Shade, II: 16)

We went to mass every morning and prayed often. I didn't mind this because I like to pray. (Annie Cotton, II: 79)

I didn't go to school until I was twelve years old. We wore uniforms at the St. Mary's Roman Catholic Residential School. After class and after church we always changed into our play clothes. This is a practice I still carry to this day. (Margaret Hindman, II: 41)

I went to St. Mary's Roman Catholic Residential School in 1929. I didn't mind the school at all. The nuns were very good to me. They taught me how to bake, cook, sew and clean. I was taught how to pray and be respectful. (Maggie Eaglespeaker, II: 56)

I was seven years old when my formal education started at St. Mary's Roman Catholic Residential School. I was taught to respect religion. (Bernard Tall Man, III: 34)

One of the teachings I received at the residential school is my religion, which is very important in my life. It has guided me to live a better life. (Harriet Wells, IV: 45)

I attended St. Mary's Roman Catholic Residential School from 1939-1947. The residence was all right except the food was no good. I did learn good discipline and how to pray. (Jim Twigg, IV: 62)

I started my schooling at age nine at St. Mary's Roman Catholic Indian Residential School where I learned to pray. I also learned housekeeping skills I enjoyed the time I spent there and really have no complaints. (Alberta Vielle, IV: 135)

## Recreation

In spite of all this we had good times too. We played football and baseball. Since our school was close to the river we often went swimming and fishing. We brought the fish we caught to the kitchen where it was cooked for us. (Sam Red Crow, I: 50)

I was eleven years old when I went to the old Roman Catholic Mission School in Standoff. . . . About a year later we moved to the new St. Mary's Roman Catholic Residential School. It was good to be at a clean, new place with indoor plumbing. We enjoyed sports such as hockey, football and baseball at school. (Frank Manyfingers, I: 95)

I went to St. Paul's Anglican Residential School when I was six years old and remained there until I was sixteen. . . . I worked in the kitchen, bakery, dining room, laundry and sewing room. I really learned about housekeeping. I liked the school and was well treated. I always had clean clothes and good meals. We had dances every Friday, wedding dances, reunions, school parties and Halloween dances. All in all I enjoyed my stay at St. Paul's and did not see nor witness any abuse as we saw in the movie *Where the Spirit Lives.* (Winnie Panther Bone, II: 93)

Another early recollection I have of St. Paul's were the "straw ticks." In the fall, the staff and some of the senior girls would make straw ticks to fit all the beds in the dormitories. When the threshing of the grain was done the men from the school would fill the ticks with fresh straw. It was much fun for us children to crawl up on top of our high beds. By spring the straw ticks were flat and worn down to the springs of our beds. (Jennie Neilson, III: 23)

I started my education at St. Paul's Anglican Residential School at age seven. School was good. At times we were taken to different places to play ball. I joined the Anglican choir and received such awards as the General Stewart Award. I was also a Girl Guide leader. (Helen Chief Moon Rogers, III: 62)

I was placed at St. Paul's Anglican Residential School in 1936 at age seven. I don't regret the time I spent at this residential school because I learned to adjust to my new surroundings/environment. I learned to sew, cook and do all the necessary chores needed to keep a clean house. We also had social activities like dances. They were very enjoyable. (Irene Tailfeathers, III: 74)

I entered St. Mary's Roman Catholic Residential School at age seven. I liked the training that I received: life skills such as cooking, sewing and general housekeeping. I enjoyed being with my friends Mary, Stella, Pauline and others. . . . We did some exciting things like play baseball. It was especially fun against teams from Fort Macleod, Aakoahkiimiisksi, Glenwood and St. Paul's. (Forence Red Crow, III: 95)

I went to school at St. Mary's Roman Catholic Indian Residential School in December, 1938 just before my seventh birthday. Life at St. Mary's was not too bad. I went up to grade seven. In sports, we had skating, football, softball and basketball. (Everett John Bruised Head, IV: 60)

I went to school at St. Mary's Roman Catholic Indian Residential School in 1941, and adjusted quickly to the routine of the day. . . . the nuns were good to me and I really cannot complain about them at all. . . . Frances Heavy Head, one of my friends, and I had fun telling stories. We played football and softball. (Roger Across the Mountain, IV: 73)

I was six years old when I went to school at Ninaistako, St. Paul's Anglican Indian Residential School. I enjoyed sports, football, baseball and boxing. After my discharge, I went to the States where I learned more boxing. (Gus Calf Robe, IV: 138)

## Vocational Training

I was placed at the old St. Paul's Anglican Mission School when I was ten years old. While there I got sick and was sent home where I finally got better. I was sent back to school and had a good time there. If I had been smart I would be an air pilot today, Ninastako put me in the cadets where I learned how to use a gun. (Joe Hunt, I: 16)

In spite of all this, I have some fond memories of my carefree school days. . . . That's where I learned how to raise chickens. After I was married, I raised chickens and turkeys and made good use of what Sister Fafard had taught me. (Kate Shade, I: 19)

During my fourth and last year there [St. Paul's] we moved to our new school. It was a nice warm building. . . . I milked the cows and went by sleigh to get hay for the horses. I was also taught to build granaries. The boys were all taught practically the same things. . . . During the last year I was also taught farming and how to work with farm implements. (Pete Weasel Moccasin, I: 63)

In 1931 after my seventh birthday I was placed at St. Paul's Anglican Residential School. Today as I think back, I see that we were taught good, useful things which I have utilized all my life. These were things such as good manners and life skills (Rosie Day Rider, I: 83).

[they] . . . placed me at St. Paul's Anglican Residential School. I didn't mind the place at all. As a matter of fact I rather enjoyed it. I learned many useful things which stayed with me all my life. I learned how to clean house, cook, bake bread and cook-ies. . . . I still bake my own bread. (Adeline Singer, I: 116)

The new residential school was very nice so I did not mind being kept there year around. I tried my best to do well and I was one of the privileged ones to be given piano lessons. To this day I still play the organ in church. (Annie Bare Shin Bone, II: 12)

I was educated at St. Mary's Roman Catholic Residential School from 1930 to 1938. During my first year there all I did was play. . . . After a few years in the classroom, I started working outside under Brother Tom where I learned practical skills such as milking cows, cleaning the barns and milking the cows. (Leo Hairy Bull, II: 37)

I was nine years old when I arrived at St. Paul's Anglican Residential School. . . . I did learn discipline because I had to follow strict rules. I also learned about farming, milking cows and other useful work skills. (Eddie Soop, II: 45)

While at school, our teachers were very strict. They insisted on good behavior, acceptable table manners and excellence in our everyday manners. These manners included how to talk to people. I learned to speak English and developed other practical skills such as farming with horses and tractors, how to plant and maintain trees and other good gardening methods. (Charlie Bull Shields, II: 69)

I was placed at St. Mary's Roman Catholic Residential School in 1931 at the age of seven. I did not learn much academically, although I did learn about farming when I worked at the school. In 1939, at the age of fifteen I left residential school to work on my dad's farm, because his health was failing. (Phillip Aberdeen, II: 89)

When my parents separated, I was placed at the St. Paul's Anglican Residential School. I was very young. . . . I attended classes half a day. The other half day I worked on the farm and ranch. I also learned gardening and carpentry. What I learned in those days I still use today. (Orton Eagle Speaker, II: 103)

I started my formal education at St. Paul's Anglican Residential School. I liked the school and was rather attached to it. I worked half the day and went to classes the other half-day. My education there was not too bad. I was taught to work properly and I acquired good life skills which I still use today. (Jean Healy, III: 9)

I was placed at St. Mary's Roman Catholic Residential School at age seven. . . . School life was strict and so I learned self-discipline, respect and good work skills which were of great help to me in later years. (Isaac Crow Chief, III: 15)

At age seven I entered St. Mary's Roman Catholic Residential School. In a way it was good because I learned to work on the farm. I learned how to drive tractor and take care of cattle, pigs and chickens. I also learned how to milk cows. (Francis Vielle, III: 63)

At age nine I was placed at St. Paul's Anglican Indian Residential School. I didn't mind being there since my friends were there too. I attended classes in the morning and I worked on the farm in the afternoon . . . My experience in working with farm equipment was a great help to me during later years and made it easier for me to get jobs. (John Small Eyes, IV: 5)

At the age of seven I was placed in St. Paul's Anglican Residential School. During the eight years I spent there I learned to work outside, to take care of livestock, and to farm. All this I found very useful to me. (Donald No Runner, IV: 162)

## Enjoyment

We were all transferred to the new St. Paul's Anglican Mission School when it opened in 1924. What a change from the old school. The new school was bright and warm and the food was much better. For the next two years I worked at the school supervising little boys, working as kitchen help, and at times helping in the classroom with youngsters who couldn't speak English at all. (Josephine Fox, I: 22)

The new St. Paul's Anglican Residential School was ready in 1924. I was so happy and surprised to find such a nice, warm and bright new school. During this time the older girls were kept at school during the holidays. I didn't mind at all because we got to go camping in the mountains. (Helen Cochrane, I: 40)

Before long I was placed at that school [St. Paul's] which had many children there. Mr. McHugh was my first teacher. He gave us chances to be at the blackboard. We would be given some small colored squares to erase with and we made beautiful designs. If the teachers liked our work, we would get a star. I worked hard to get my stars. (Kitty Wadsworth, I: 44)

I was placed at the St. Paul's Anglican Residential School when I was six years old. I liked the school because I was with my friends, some of whom are still around today. I listened carefully to what I was being taught and did my best to learn quickly. (Rosaline Shot Both Sides, I: 55)

Since our school was located close to the river we sometimes caught fish which was later cooked for us. . . . in April 20, 1926 we moved to our new school, St. Mary's Roman Catholic Residential School. Wow? I Thought I was in heaven. It was like a dream – no more chopping wood, no more carrying water, and no more outhouses! We had electricity. While at school I neither witnessed, nor heard about, child molesting. (Edward Little Bear, I:104)

I left the residence in 1936. It was strange how I felt lonesome. I missed the residential school and my friends. I didn't have any worries at school. (Margaret Young Pine, II: 3)

I attended the St. Paul's Anglican Residential School after I turned seven. The school was alright. Everyone was good to me. I attended classes every day until I was eleven years old. (May Weasel Fat, II: 24)

I was taken to the St. Paul's Anglican Residential School in 1930. I learned to clean house, scrub pans, iron clothes and cook. . . .

When I think back on my school days, I realize now that they were really the best and happiest days of my life. (Emma Many Feathers, II: 61)

I have good memories of St. Paul's. We were disciplined when necessary. . . . Otherwise our teachers and supervisors were good to us. Canon Middleton was an outstanding missionary and was very well-liked by all who knew him. . . . I was accepted into the army and spent four and a half years overseas. I was decorated with six medals and came back to Aakaohkiimiiksi on September 29, 1945. I had no home so I went to St. Paul's where Cannon Middleton helped me out. (Steven Mistaken Chief, II: 66)

My school years started at age ten at St. Mary's Roman Catholic Residential School as far as I can remember, the school took good care of me and I was happy there. I was discharged from the residence after I turned sixteen. (Mary Rose Low Horn, II: 85)

I went to St. Paul's Anglican Residential School when I was nine years old. I learned good working skills such as farming, gardening and carpentry. We also had social activities such as dances. I have good memories about my school days. (Harold Healy, III: 7)

I arrived at St. Mary's Roman Catholic Residential School at age seven. I liked it there though I found it very difficult at first because I couldn't understand English. . . . I learned to cook and sew and many other good life skills which I used later in my life. I can truthfully say that my school days were the happiest days of my life. (Rita Tall Man, III: 36)

My early formal education started at St. Paul's Anglican Residential School. . . . I really didn't learn much since I spent much time playing and coloring. The experience was good. The nuns took good care of us and I really enjoyed my stay there. (Tom White Man, III: 39)

I was really happy when at age seven, it was my turn to pack my little suitcase and join my brothers and sisters as mom and dad took us to the residential school. . . . I enjoyed going to classes and being with my friends. . . . A happy time was Christmas Eve when there were very few cars in Kainaissksahkoyi and our parents came to sleep at the school in order to attend Midnight Mass.... The other happy time was at the end of June when there were promotions, awards and the beginning of our two months' holiday. (Flora Zaharia, III: 43)

At age ten, I was taken to St. Mary's Roman Catholic Residential School to join the other children from Kainaissksahkoyi. I tried my best to do what I was asked and to obey all the rules and regulations of the school. I was rewarded by the priest and nuns at the time of my discharge from the school. They gave me gifts in appreciation for my good behavior. (Rita Calf Robe, III: 67)

I was placed at St. Paul's Anglican Residential School At the tender age of four or five to join my sisters Nora and Doreen . . . One of the nicest teachers I ever had was Laura Mustard. She was not only an excellent teacher but mixed well with us and was a very nice person. I thoroughly enjoyed her. Jean Webster was another excellent teacher. (Pauline Dempsey, III: 79)

At seven years of age I went to St. Paul's Indian Residential School. I didn't learn very much academically. However, I learned to cook, and how to do various household chores. . . . I consider my days at St. Paul's as the best days of my life where I had no worries of any kind. (Dorothy Boutland, IV: 75)

I was still very young when I started school at St. Mary's Roman Catholic Indian Residential School. . . . As I became accustomed to my surroundings, met relatives, made new friends and started learning the English language, my classes and life at the residential school became more tolerable and even enjoyable. (Lena Russell, IV: 120)

I attended Crowfoot Roman Catholic Indian Residential School as a day student. I was treated well there and cannot criticize the school at all. It hurts me to hear other people say unkind things about the priests and nuns. I learned to sew, do household chores and keep a clean house. (Mary Ann Wells, IV: 141)

Healing

There can be no doubt about the need for healing on the part of those individuals who suffered through the residential school experience. However, as effective counselors do when they deal therapeutically with painful memories, it is necessary to recognize that even negative experiences are not necessarily always harmful. Positive growth can occur even through painful analysis if individuals are willing to proceed through them with professional assistance. In the First Nations context, elders with good medicine have traditionally fulfilled the role of healers by helping individuals to see the need to take risks and follow new visions.

Today there is a real need to consult elders who have good medicine.

# References

Akan, Linda. (1992). Pimosatamowin Sikaw Kakeequaywin: Walking and Talking: An Asaukteaux Elder's View of Native Education. *Canadian Journal of Native Education,* 19:2, 191-214.

Anderson, T.G. (1863). *General Tuition Agreement.* Edmonton, AB: Department of Indian Affairs and Northern Development, Alberta Region.

Berger, Paul, Juanita Ross Epp, and Helle Møller. (2006). The Predictable Influences of Culture Clash, Current Practice, and Colonialism on Punctuality, Attendance, and Achievement in Nunavut Schools. *Canadian Journal of Native Education,* 29:2, 182-205.

Brookes, Sonia. (1991). The Persistence of Native Education Policy in Canada. *The Cultural Maze: Complex Questions on Native Destiny in Western Canada.* John W. Friesen, ed. Calgary, AB: Detselig Enterprises, 163-180.

Bull, Linda R. (1991). Indian Residential Schooling: The Native Perspective. *Canadian Journal of Native Education,* 18:Supplement, 1-64.

Burns, George F. (1998). Factors and Themes in Native Education and School Boards/First Nations Tuition Negotiations and Tuition Agreement Schooling. *Canadian Journal of Native Education,* 22:1, 53-66.

Cardinal, Harold, and Walter Hildebrandt. (2000). *Treaty Elders of Saskatchewan.* Calgary, AB: University of Calgary Press.

Chalmers, John W. (1974). Marguerite Bourgeoys, Preceptress of New France. *Profiles of Canadian Educators.* Robert S. Patterson, John W. Chalmers, and John W. Friesen, eds. Toronto, ON: D. C. Heath Canada, Ltd., 4-20.

Dyck, Noel. (1997). *Differing Visions: Administering Indian Residential Schooling in Prince Albert, 1867-1995.* Halifax, NS: Fernwood Publishing and Prince Albert, SK: The Prince Albert Grand Council.

Friesen, John W. (1983). *Schools With a Purpose.* Calgary, AB: Detselig Enterprises.

Friesen, John W., and Virginia Lyons Friesen. (2005). *First Nations in the Twenty-First Century: Contemporary Educational Frontiers.* Calgary, AB: Detselig Enterprises.

Friesen, John W., and Virginia Lyons Friesen. (2002). *Aboriginal Education in Canada: A Plea for Integration.* Calgary, AB: Detselig Enterprises.

Furniss, Elizabeth. (1995). *Victims of Benevolence: The Dark Legacy of the Williams Lake Residential School.* Vancouver, BC: Arsenal Pulp Press.

Garnier, Karie. (1990). *Your Elders Speak: A Tribute to Native Elders.* Volume One. White Rock, BC: Published by Karie Garnier.

Grant, Agnes, ed. (2004). Shirley Sterling. *Finding My Talk: How Fourteen Native Women Reclaimed Their Lives after Residential School.* Calgary, AB: Fitzhenry and Whiteside, 87-100.

Grant, Agnes. (1996). *No End of Grief: Indian Residential Schools in Canada.* Winnipeg, MB: Pemmican Publications.

Haig-Brown, Celia. (1993). *Resistance and Renewal: Surviving the Indian Residential School.* Vancouver, BC: Tillacum Library

Hookimaw-Witt, J. (1998). Keenabonoh Keemoshominook Kaeshge Peemishishik Odaskiwakh [we stand on the graves of our ancestors]: Native interpretations of Treaty #9 with Attawapiskat Elders. Unpublished Master's Thesis. Peterborough, ON: Trent University

Jaenen, Cornelius J. (1986). Education for Francization: The Case of New France in the Seventeenth Century. *Indian Education in Canada, Volume 1: The Legacy.* Jean Barman, Yvonne Hébert, and Don McCaskill, eds. Vancouver, BC: University of British Columbia Press, 45-63.

Knockwood, Isabelle. (1994). *Out of the Depths: The Experiences of Mi'kmaw Children at the Indian Residential School at Shuberacadie, Nova Scotia.* Lockeport, NS: Roseway Publishing.

McNeill, John L. (1974). Egerton Ryerson, Founder of (English-Speaking) Education. *Profiles of Canadian Educators.* Robert S. Patterson, John W. Chalmers, and John W. Friesen, eds. Toronto, ON: D. C. Heath Canada, Ltd., 118-140.

Meili, Dianne. (1991). *Those Who Know: Profiles of Alberta's Native Elders* (1991). Edmonton, AB: NeWest Press.

Miller, J. R. (1997). *Shingwauk's Vision: A History of Native Residential Schools.* Toronto, ON: University of Toronto Press.

Milloy, John S. (1999). *A National Crime: The Canadian Government and the Residential School System, 1879 to 1986.* Winnipeg, MB: University of Manitoba Press.

Schissel, Bernard, and Terry Wotherspoon. (2003). *The Legacy of School for Aboriginal People.* Don Mills, ON: Oxford University Press.

Scott, Duncan C. (1914). Indian Affairs. *Canada and Its Provinces.* Volume Four in Adam Short and Arthur Doughty. Toronto, ON: Brook and Company, 714-715.

Slobodin, Richard. (1966). *Métis of the MacKenzie District.* Ottawa, ON: Centre Canadien de Reserches en Anthropologie, Universite Saint-Paul.

Steckley, John I., and Bryan D. Cummins. (2008). *Full Circle: Canada's First Nations.* Toronto, ON: Pearson Prentice-Hall.

Warry, Wayne. (2007). *Ending Denial: Understanding Aboriginal Issues.* Peterborough, ON: Broadview Press.

Zaharia, Sikotan Flora, and Makai'sto Leo Fox. (1995). *Kitomahkitapiiminnooniks: Stories from our Elders.* Three volumes. Standoff, AB: Kainaiwa Board of Education.

Zaharia, Sikotan Flora, Makai'sto Leo Fox, and Omahksipiitaa Marvin Fox. (2003). *Kitomahkitapiiminnooniks: Stories from our Elders.* Volume Four. Standoff, AB: Kainaiwa Board of Education.

# Seven

# The Challenge of Cultural Identity and Positive Self-Image

Children have the right to know that they are worthy beings. They have the right to value themselves for whatever they are and whatever they do. (Iris Tiedt in Tiedt and Tiedt, 1986: 23)

Several months ago, while conducting a workshop on Aboriginal legends and cultural identify, we shared the classic story of the Comanche horse race with the workshop participants. The reaction of one young woman in the audience was especially memorable.

We must, however, begin at the beginning. According to reliable sources, members of the Comanche Nation were among the most expert horsemen on the continent. Not only were their warriors expert riders, but the Comanches also bred and trained particularly outstanding ponies. Horse stealing and capturing wild horses were also a good source for Comanche ponies.

A typical Comanche warrior could ride his horse at top speed with his legs wrapped around the horse's neck and still fire arrows at his enemy from beneath the horse's stomach. Training horses was another Comanche specialty and they devised a number of very effective ways to influence horses to yield to their commands. One way was to fire an arrow at a horse's head at a certain place near the ear, and render the animal unconscious. When the horse awoke it would find itself tethered to an old trained mare and in the process of being broke by an able horseman. Being bound in this fashion restricted the untrained animal from enjoying too much freedom and thus the horse soon found itself putty in the hands of a Comanche warrior.

When the United States Army eventually invaded Comanche territory, not all exchanges between the two parties were necessarily negative. One of the activities both army soldiers and Comanche warriors enjoyed was horse racing. Apparently this sport often took place and bounties were high. Before the race, both soldiers and warriors piled up bounties for the eventual winner consisting of robes, hides, rifles and other horse related paraphernalia. The end result of such a contest – winner takes all.

In one particular instance, Colonel Dodge of Fort Chadburne and his troops were involved in a horse race with the Comanches. When preparations of the race were completed, Dodge's troops brought out a very fine looking steed with great height and good grooming. The Comanches, amid giggles, brought out a short, dubious looking animal with an unkempt mane and its tail dragging on the ground. Naturally, the army men felt quite secure about their choice, but when the race was over, the small Comanche horse was one head length ahead of the army horse. The challenge was repeated, "Would you like to try race again?" the army spokesman queried. The Comanches agreed and army officers scurried into their barn to produce an even taller, more promising animal than the first one. The Comanches decided to stay with their first choice and their scruffy-looking horse remained on duty, much to the surprise of the army men. With hope in their hearts, the stakes were raised; more hides and rifles and other items were added to the prospective prize. Once again, the winner would take all.

The race began and at first it looked like a close competition. After a short time, however, the Comanche horse took the lead, and when the race ended, their steed was a full three lengths ahead of the army horse. Moreover, the rider was seated backwards on the animal, urging the army horse to go faster! Later the army learned that the Comanches had used the same animal to dupe the Kickapoo Indians out of 600 ponies.

After our workshop ended the young woman who appeared very interested in the story identified herself as a member of the Comanche nation. She also stated how happy she was to hear the story being told and how much it made her proud to belong to the Comanche Nation. A few weeks later she sent an e-mail requesting information as to a written source for the story. The story appears in a book entitled, *The Comanches: Lords of the Southern Plains* by Ernest Wallace and anthropologist E. Adamson Hoebel (1986: 49f).

# Introduction

Studies of the importance of self-esteem as a primary factor in academic achievement have flourished in recent decades. Emphasis on the importance of classroom discipline, for example, has given way to the realization that a misbehaving child may be an unhealthy child, and the encouragement of positive self-esteem may be viewed as a more effective approach to discipline. It has also been established that a teacher who possesses a healthy sense of well-being, exhibits such positive characteristics as emotional stability, buoyancy, attractiveness, and cooperativeness (Ornstein, 1990: 547). Naturally, this sense of wellbeing is passed on to students who in turn will feel better about themselves and hence achieve better if they are taught by a teacher with a positive self-image.

One of the components of a healthy self-concept has to do with cultural background, and if the picture is to be complete, students should be encouraged to accept themselves as they really are – physically, socially, culturally, and spiritually. Students should be encouraged to accept their peers as they are, and to see their own unique selves and those of their peers as assets, not liabilities. In this way it may be possible to achieve two pedagogical goals: (i) to enhance personal self-esteem, and (ii) to bring students to a fuller appreciation of the pluralist nature of Canadian society and be better prepared to contribute toward it from their own unique value orientation and personality.

Although the ethnic mix of North American population has changed dramatically over the past century, many Europeans still view the continent as a former colony. As a result, many ethnic minority cultures have long been neglected in school curricula, media content, and in literature generally. Fleras and Elliott (2007: 320) point out that when minorities are included, they are many times misrepresented as a result of misinformation, personal prejudice, or discrimination. Even sensitive presentations, however, must grapple with such challenges as knowing how to portray accurately subcultures whose value systems are somewhat at odds with fundamental democratic principles. Writers and producers must also decide if only positive features of a particular cultural group are to be presented, or should every aspect of each configuration be described. If cultural differences are portrayed or even highlighted, there is always a danger that they may reinforce stereotypes and polarize the situation into an "us versus them" situation. Either way, it's a tough call.

# Aboriginal Portrayals

First Nations in Canada have never been particularly positively described since the days of European contact and the development of the fur trade. At first the Native peoples were regarded as allies in the accumulation of wealth in the form of trade goods, but as the need for furs diminished in Europe, the locals were increasingly viewed as interlopers in the development of a new Canada. It is possible to trace a series of stages about Aboriginal acceptance by Canadians generally.

The twentieth century experience of Canadian Indians did not have a very positive beginning (Haycock, 1971). In the first stage, which lasted from 1900 to 1930, the Indian was portrayed as "poor doomed savage," sentenced to assimilation by the incursion of AngloSaxon paternalism. Promulgated by the national media, the themes of religion, customs and manners, travelog, popular history and contemporary Indian affairs were utilized as a framework for this thesis. Most analysts viewed Aboriginal people as unable to ward off the impending influences of assimilation, while some envisaged First Nations as noble savages, children of nature who had prowess, cunning, and dignity, but ignorant and slothful in AngloSaxon eyes. A few more sympathetic observers blamed nonNatives for corrupting Native culture when they should have been fulfilling their moral responsibility to raise Aboriginals to a new kind of civilization fashioned on the European model.

Perceptions of Canadian First Nations changed somewhat from 1930 to 1960 when a theme of social humanitarianism coupled with guilt emerged, sympathetic observers now emphasized the "plight of the Indian" and declared themselves willing to assist in the elevation of First Nations culture to European levels. Literature of the time emphasized the debased socioeconomic status of Indians and a spirit of humanitarianism gradually replaced the attitude of rabid individualism that had preceded it. This approach was followed up by or paralleled the civil rights movement that featured anti-Vietnam demonstrations in the United States, and the emergence of Black Power and Red Power movements. The 1960s were highlighted by a formation of a series of anti-institutional organizations that emphasized an enhanced participation by ordinary people in decision-making. The status of Native people was not greatly enhanced through these developments, and when overtures were made to their communities, they were always accompanied by an underlying assimilative bent. It is true that Native people were encouraged to take a more substantive role in Canadian society, but always on terms dictated by dominant society.

In 1971 the Canadian government adopted a multicultural policy which included these statements in its content.

> The Government of Canada will support all of Canada's cultures and will seek to assist, resources permitting, the development of those cultural groups which have demonstrated a desire and effort to continue to develop, a capacity to grow and contribute to Canada, as well as a clear need for assistance. The Government of Canada will assist members of all cultural groups to overcome cultural barriers to full participation in Canadian society. (Friesen, 1993: 8)

The policy naturally led to non-governmental discussions about the nature of First Nations participation in such a society, and some analysts were quick to point out that the policy really did not fit their situation on several counts (Berry 1981: 214f). First, only First Nations in Canada have the right of first occupancy. Second, their geographic specialty is that they originated on a continent different than that of all other Canadians; they alone came from here – not from anywhere else. Third, their culture is unique in the way that its participants tend to view nature and indeed the universe. They respect the rhythms of nature to the extent of wanting to work with them, not harness or conquer them. This perspective is still deeply engrained in Native philosophy and many bands in Canada wrestle daily with bridging the gap between their traditional ways and those of dominant society.

First Nations have a unique legal identity in Canada in that they are the only cultural group to have special legal rights via the *Indian Act* and the signed treaties. These documents originated around the time of the birth of Canada, and they were signed in good faith by both government and Indian leaders. These documents set the Native people apart from the rest of society. These documents need to be respected, and when negotiations regarding them get underway, both parties are to be perceived as having equal status. Finally, it is reality that First Nations in Canada occupy the lower rungs of the country's socioeconomic ladder. Their income levels and access to education, health care, and welfare benefits are considerably more restricted than they are for other Canadians, partly because they live in outlying areas. Politicians frequently refer to this reality, and although some improvement has been made over recent decades, it is still true that Canada's First Nations are hard done by in comparison with their nonNative neighbors.

Canada's multicultural policies (federal and provincial) were initiated without consultation and without reference to the First Nations community. This has historically been the case with regard to Indian affairs since matters concerning the First Peoples have officially been the concern of the federal Indian Affairs Branch of the Department of Indian Affairs and Northern Development. In the past government officials were not used to doing much consulting when it came making First Nations policy, so the origination of a multicultural policy without Indian input was not be too surprising. This was again the case when the federal government issued its White Paper of 1969, which outlined the government's attitude toward assimilating Canada's Indian people without asking them about it. In the paper the government proposed to abolish the *Indian Act*, ignore the signed treaties, turn control of Indian lands (reserves) directly over to Indian communities, and provide health, education, and welfare services through the auspices of the ten provincial governments. No one, particularly government leaders expected the strong reaction they received from Native leaders all across the country, and the government was forced to abandon completely the proposals in the White Paper.

The federal government learned something from their 1969 experience with the White Paper. In 1996, the federal government released the report of the Royal Commission on Aboriginal Peoples, which had been five years in the making – much of it in consultation with Aboriginal people in many Indian communities across the nation. Consisting of 4 000 pages and 440 recommendations, the report addressed virtually every aspect of Native affairs, and most Canadians eagerly awaited the announcement that the report had been completed (Steckley and Cummins, 2008: 130). The report contained many important recommendations, including a call for the creation of what would essentially be a third order of government, an Aboriginal parliament, and an independent tribunal to decide on land claims and more money to be spent to improve housing, health, education and employment.

The Royal Commission began with the acknowledgement that First Nations had made a significant contribution to Canada over past centuries and this needed to be advertised. The report suggested that greater awareness of Aboriginal contributions be encouraged through celebrations, ceremonies, and recognition of special days. Second, the Royal Commission recommended that an ombudsman be appointed to work with various appropriate government departments to resolve issues of Aboriginal veterans' benefits as well as the matter of land claims.

The Royal Commission specifically emphasized the government's intentions to implement an array of measures dealing with employment, training, and economic development. One such institution to be established was the Aboriginal Healing Foundation which implemented a series of practices such as healing circles and community group processes for residential school survivors across the country. The report also triggered court actions against religious denominations and the government, which resulted in public apologies issued by mainstream churches for their role in residential school abuses (Warry, 2007: 61).

There are indications that government officials are gradually learning to regard First Nations affairs as a vital, but different part of the Canadian mosaic. Still, the process is slow. Ten years after the report was published, the AFN (Assembly of First Nations – formerly the National Indian Brotherhood), offered a report card of the government's progress in implementing the report's recommendations. Of the 66 recommendations evaluated by the Assembly of First Nations the federal government received 37 Fs, 11 Ds, and two D minuses. It scored only one A (establishing a National Aboriginal Day) and one B+ (creating an Aboriginal Sports Council). The report card also stated that despite the release of the commission, First Nations communities continue to face ongoing poverty and an increasing gap in living conditions compared with other Canadians. It also stated there has been no sustained investment by government in meeting their basic needs.

The Assembly of First Nations also identified a series of recommended projects that have not been implemented. These include the formation of a national framework to guide treaty discussions, an Aboriginal Nations Recognition and Governance Act that would recognize Aboriginal governments as one of three orders of governance in Canada, an independent administrative tribunal of land and treaties, long-term economic development agreements, and a network of healing centres. The AFN report card suggested that the federal response to the Royal Commission has been limited in scope to a narrow range of recommendations. Because of government inaction, there has been a shortfall of nearly $8 billion in funding to Aboriginal communities since 1997.

First Nations communities continue to face ongoing poverty and an increasing gap in living conditions with other Canadians because there has been no sustained investment in meeting their basic needs. To date there has been no further progress on the part of the federal government in implementing the recommendations of the Royal Commission on Aboriginal Peoples.

# Impact

What happens to students who encounter only negative descriptions of their cultural history in school curricula? What happens to students who are raised by parents who have little knowledge of or regard for their cultural past? Will these students think less of themselves because they have been taught that their cultural heritage matters little on the national or human landscape? For many years educators have been asking and answering these questions through careful research. The results are clear; children who feel good about themselves will project this feeling of worth to others. They will perform better in class and they will have a clearer perception of what they want to do with their lives. Some thirty years ago, when the field of multiculturalism began to bloom, Margaret Gibson (1976) emphasized how important it was for schools to begin to teach about varying cultural lifestyles so that students could understand and appreciate them.

Canada's multicultural mix was highlighted around the turn of the nineteenth century when the nation's population skyrocketed by 43 percent, resulting in the immigration population rise by 22 percent of the nation's whole. By World War I the intensification of assimilative forces reached new heights as hyphenated Canadians like Dutch-Canadians, German-Canadians, or Japanese-Canadians were ferreted out for discrimination. German-speaking immigrants were forbidden to speak their language and a series of negative stereotypes targeting Asian immigrants evolved. Although Canadians in the various regions reacted a bit differently to this scenario, a particular pattern could be identified in the west. As Palmer noted (1981: 180), it was only after the First World War that each province saw the growth of greater tolerance generated by new social, economic, and intellectual conditions. After that war it took the nation a few decades to untangle its identity. The arrival of many intellectuals among the postwar refugees from Eastern Europe, coupled with an enhanced motivation for upward mobility among second and third generation resident AngloCanadians, forced the issue of inequality out into the open. Thus the "quiet cultural revolution" of the 1950s laid the base for the campaign to increase government recognition of incoming cultural groups.

As mentioned earlier, the 1960s could be described as a decade of unrest in various social sectors, mostly involving youth. The Royal Commission on Bilingualism and Biculturalism revealed its own inadequacy by missing out on the reality of Canada's pluralist make-up. True, it seemed to be feasible to establish only two official languages, but the country's cultural reality was much broader than that. This led inevitably to the formation of Canada's multicultural policy that was announced on October 8, 1971. Several provinces announced similar legislation soon thereafter. Suddenly it became the mandate of public schools to operationalize multicultural policies in the classroom, thereby setting an example for the rest of the community. As usual, the business world was slow to respond to the challenge but eventually several major companies did formulate relevant hiring and operational policies. A survey of fifty major companies in Calgary in 1989 revealed that twenty-four companies laid claim to having paid attention to the announcement of the federal multicultural policy in 1971 and implemented related changes in policy. Several company officials responded to indicate that their existing policies already incorporated multicultural concerns and several others indicated that they saw no need for such a policy in the first place (Friesen, 1989).

Recent emphasis on multicultural concerns have now been subsumed under the rubric of global education on grounds that effective intercultural relations involve a great deal more than cultural understanding. In fact, the enlarged scope of emphasis incorporates concerns about geographic abuse and resource mismanagement as well as spiritual themes that affect planet earth. There are even scientists like David Suzuki who insist that the rapid and catastrophic degradation of the planetary biosphere has been the main catalyst for a radical reassessment of the power and limits of scientific insight and application (Suzuki, 1992: xxxiii). First Nations societies on all continents including North America traditionally respected and honored Mother Earth, and utilized her benefits only to the extent that they were needed for the maintenance of human life. Suzuki argues that if members of the scientific community will take a hard look at the ecological crisis and examine traditional Native regard for the workings of nature, they may want to incorporate those aspects of Native thinking into their future plans. For example, the fact is that the speed of global warming is currently proceeding at a much faster rate than previously thought. There may be a solution to this situation embedded within traditional First Nations philosophy, but it will need to be investigated, appreciated and implemented before it has any effect on the current global situation.

## Towards a Global Outlook

Aboriginal children who attend today's schools fare a bit better than their parents and grandparents did when they encounter the subject matter of school curricula. Many provincial courses of study now include content pertaining to First Nations history and culture, and teachers occasionally invite Native spokespersons into their classrooms to share aspects of their traditional way of life. These developments can be relevant for Native children who are sometimes even admired for their unique cultural attachments. After all, they are descendants of the First Peoples of this continent.

Information itself, however, is not enough. Scholars who have lauded cross-cultural appreciation as a means of promoting national good will are also quick to point out that additional steps are needed (Fleras and Elliott, 2007; Garcia, 1994; Gollnick and Chinn, 1986; Ghosh, 1996; Tiedt and Tiedt, 1990). It is true that reliable and accurate information is a good starting point; children do need to have opportunity to read positive descriptions of their background. However, other people are also involved in the process. School children also need to have opportunity to gain insights about cultural perspectives other than their own, but new facts cannot remain in an intellectual vacuum; they must be applied in some way.

Having access to reliable information about cultural backgrounds other than one's own may be a good starting point, but such information must be presented in a sensitive, pedagogically sound atmosphere. A grounding belief would be the realization that everyone, regardless of cultural affiliation, possesses a measure of appreciation for the cultural configuration in which they have been raised. What is it about their culture that they appreciate, admire, or want to cling to? Can outsiders understand it enough to appreciate it? What are the steps to be taken to gain cultural appreciation? The following discussion may help answer these queries.

The foundation of successful intercultural understanding rests on two important points. The first is to realize that members of cultures other than our own believe that their values and customs are as important to them as ours are to us. Anyone who can grasp and appropriate that axiom has passed the first mark of being truly a multicultural individual. The second realization it to be able to come to the point of believing that others have the right to believe that their values are as significant in the scheme of things as those of others – including our own. Undoubtedly, few Canadians can make that claim, but our schools are hard at work trying to make this a reality.

A recent survey by the Montreal-based Institute for Research on Public policy discovered, among other things, that Canada's claim to be a tolerant nation should be reviewed. When interviewees across the country were challenged with this statement, "it is reasonable to accommodate religious and cultural minorities," only 17 percent of those aged 55-64 said, "yes," while 24 percent of those aged 25-34 said "yes." In addition, only 24 percent of those with a university education answered in the affirmative (*MacLean's*, October 22-29, 2007; 19-20). When the national policy on multiculturalism was first announced, national surveys showed a mild form of tolerance for differing cultural beliefs. Studies undertaken a decade later revealed that Canadians had grown a little more tolerant. Now, however, it may be time to re-examine the benefits of the national policy. Perhaps Canadian attitudes towards minorities have not become more positive as the decades since have passed.

The literature which fosters cross-cultural appreciation as a means of promoting national good will reveals that the process is not uncomplicated (Fleras and Elliott, 2004; Garcia, 1994: Gollnick and Chinn, 1986; Ghosh, 1996). It is necessary to begin with the premise that no one can help being born who they are. No one chooses his or her physical shape or size, race, belief system or culture, or personal identity. These characteristics are accidents of birth and no one should rightly ever be blamed or credited for having them.

A second necessary condition to grasping a global outlook is to believe that most everyone gains some measure of appreciation for their heritage and background as they grow up, and this is understandable. The challenge will be for outsiders to try to understand the importance of those beliefs on the part of the one who belongs to the culture in question. Essentially the process will involve five steps. A breakdown of this model may be elaborated in a crescendo of intensity featuring five steps, targeting the school milieu: (i) tolerance, (ii) understanding, (iii) acceptance, (iv) appreciation, and (v) affirmation.

## (i) Tolerance

The road of least effort in so far as attempting to understand culture configurations other than one's own is merely to put up with them. This is the meaning of tolerance. This stance requires no energy other than awareness, which of itself could happen accidentally. There is no requirement to accommodate anyone; at best, the effort is simply a form of tokenism (Baruth and Manning, 1992; Miller-Lauchmann and Taylor, 1995). Tolerance can be patronizing, and often emanates from a strong feeling of ethnocentrism because it implies a position of superiority on the part of those doing the tolerating (Fleras and Elliott, 2007). Tolerance per se implies no obligation for adjustment and no need for further learning. It is a dead-end street and does not even deserve a passing grade in terms of strengthening any links of human communication. Any school program can teach tolerance in the sense that the existence of other cultures and belief systems is acknowledged. There is no further effort or movement to learn anything about these configurations with a possible view to appreciating their distinctiveness.

## (ii) Understanding

A slightly deeper level of cultural sensitivity emanates from the effort to understand, to cognitively become aware of different meanings, or varying interpretations of the workings of the universe, for example. With this stance energy is devoted to understanding perspectives; why do people behave the way they do? Why do certain ethnocultural groups believe so strongly in their unique religious enactments? Why do some religious groups believe in specific rules, taboos or sanctions?

Cultural understanding takes time and effort; it takes time to "walk in someone else's moccasins," to study other lifestyles and value systems and social structures. When this tack is undertaken, the road to cultural understanding will allow some measure of effective intercultural communication to occur. Both parties in the process will find it possible to move towards the other in a cognitive sense.

The fundamental plank of schooling is curriculum, namely the subject matter content that is studied by students throughout their sojourn in that institution. Naturally the selection of content is important and should be made on the basis that it represents a fair cross-section of the foundational knowledge of society. Schools have an obligation to introduce students to the data base on which they will later make adult decisions. This is particularly true of public schools, which have an obligation to provide such a foundation for all future citizens. Schools other than public, be they private, parochial or home schools, do not have this obligation as a first premise. Their first priority is to inculcate their students in the rudiments of the creed, which separates them from the rest of society. Thus their primary objective may be credable, philosophical or even spiritual, depending on the modus operandi of the particular school. These schools, because of their lack of obligation to society, cannot be harnessed with the responsibility of socializing the young to fit into mainstream society. In fact, in many instances, the promoters of these schools have no such intention. As will later be seen, this reality may influence students to develop only limited appreciation for diversity.

## (iii) Acceptance

The mode of acceptance implies coming to terms with something such as a belief, behavior or happening. Most social scientists are probably agreed that there are significant cultural differences among cultures, and the members of each cultural configuration have what they consider valid reasons for behaving the way they do. When students of human behavior cognitively understand why people behave the way they do, there is still another step that can be taken toward fuller understanding, namely to accept the proposed rationale. It is one thing to understand a given belief, enactment or process, but it is quite another thing personally to be at peace with the proffered reason for its practice. To make peace with the explanation requires a deeper comprehension and a conscious motivation to incorporate or inculcate that rationale into one's own modus operandi. People can understand that there are different ways of doing things or different ways of explaining the "same" phenomena, but to accept that these alternate explanations are as valid as those which they personally endorse requires extraordinary effort.

## (iv) Appreciation

To appreciate something requires much more effort than just being aware of, or tolerating, that particular belief or behavior. The act of appreciating something means recognizing the value of it, thinking well of it, or esteeming it. This stance is quite far removed from knowing that members of a specific cultural configuration do things a certain way; it is the act of finding value in the way they do it. Any society with specific ways of doing most things can be quite ethnocentric, and most of its members will probably not be too willing to give their blessing to what they perceive to be unorthodox, unusual or even "weird" beliefs or behaviors for no good reason other than to be generous. This may be the foundational requirement of being a global person – to recognize, study, and understand credable or cultural peculiarities, and once they are understood, commend them for the satisfaction they provide to the people who hold them dear. In pushing the concept to its logical conclusion, it should be mentioned that individuals so convinced might even consider adopting some element of the newly-encountered values for themselves. Such an occurrence could indeed be called cultural appreciation, which is a vital plank of any global education program.

With the agenda of providing something for everyone, public schools do not to have to fret about possible value shifts or adoption of new values by students. No matter what the subject matter, be it orthodox, ordinary or controversial, there are always people in some sector of society who will appreciate the various emphases being promoted in school. Controversial topics such as family life and sex education, substance abuse, religion, or values can probably be bypassed or avoided by educators in non-public schools, but unless there is considerable opposition from any sector, the public school experiences no such restrictions. An institution committed to preparing the nation's young for virtually any possible scenario, must constantly dare to launch out onto new ground, regardless of how philosophically precarious it may be. Nonpublic schools can afford to be cautious in this regard; after all, their obligations are restricted by their constituencies.

## (v) Affirmation

It was Plato who said it first and probably said it best; the ideal society with a truly global outlook is one in which everyone performs the tasks they are best qualified to perform and everyone is equally valued for his or her contributions. In such a society one could conceivably endorse, encourage and even celebrate the fruits of true diversity (Siccone, 1995). Educationally speaking, it is a well-researched fact that students who receive positive feedback from their teachers perform better than those who are insecure or unsure about themselves (Bennett, 1990; Grant, 1995). Thus it is very important to endorse or affirm every student for who they are if their learning capacities are to be maximized.

Teachers in public schools by nature of their calling are obligated to avoid the use of stereotypes or language that could hurt students' feelings. Public school teachers should employ language that is free of sexist or racist connotations and profile people as having varied characteristics other than just race, sex, religion or ethnic background. Such a mode can open students' eyes to the greater potential of human ingenuity and individuality. Once this reality is introduced it may be possible to develop a classroom atmosphere in which everyone feels physically, psychologically, and culturally safe.

## References

Baruth, Leroy, and M. Lee Manning. (1992). *Multicultural Education of Children and Adolescents.* Needham Heights, MA: Allyn and Bacon.

Bennett, Christine. (1990). *Comprehensive Multicultural Education: Theory and Practice.* Second edition. Boston, MA: Allyn and Bacon.

Berry, John W. (1981). Native People and the Larger Society. *A Canadian Social Psychology of Ethnic Relations.* Robert C. Gardner and Rudolf Kalin, eds. Toronto, ON: Methuen, 214-230.

Fleras, Augie, and Jean Leonard Elliott. (2004). *Unequal Relations: An Introduction to Race, Ethnic, and Aboriginal Dynamics in Canada.* Toronto, ON: Pearson Canada.

Fleras, Augie, and Jean Leonard Elliott. (2007). *Unequal Relations: An Introduction to Race, Ethnic, and Aboriginal Dynamics in Canada.* Fifth edition. Toronto, ON: Pearson Canada.

Friesen, John W. (1993). *When Cultures Clash: Case Studies in Multiculturalism.* Second edition. Calgary, AB: Detselig Enterprises.

Friesen, John W. (1989). Institutional Response to Multicultural Policy: A Pilot Study of the Business Sector. *Multicultural and Intercultural Education: Building Canada.* Proceedings of the November, 1987. Canadian Council for Multicultural and Intercultural Education. Sonia V. Morris, ed. Calgary, AB: Detselig Enterprises, 13-24.

Garcia, Eugene. (1994). *Understanding and Meeting the Challenge of Student Cultural Diversity.* Boston, MA: Houghton-Mifflin.

Ghosh, Ratna. (1996). *Redefining Multicultural Education.* Toronto, ON: Harcourt & Brace.

Gibson, Margaret. (1976). Approaches to Multicultural Education in the U.S.A.: Some Concepts and Assumptions. *Anthropology and Education Quarterly,* 7:4, 7-18.

Gollnick, Donna M., and Philip C. Chinn. (1986). *Multicultural Education in a Pluralistic Society.* Second edition. Columbus, OH: Charles E. Merrill.

Grant, Carl A., ed. (1995). *Educating for Diversity: An Anthology of Multicultural Education.* Needham Heights, MA: Allyn and Bacon.

Haycock, Ronald G. (1971). *The Image of the Indian.* Waterloo, ON: Waterloo Lutheran University.

Miller-Lauchmann, Lynn, and Lorraine S. Taylor. (1995). *Schools for All: Educating Children in a Diverse Society.* Albany, NY: Delmar Publishers.

Ornstein, Allan. C. (1990). *Strategies for Effective Teaching.* New York: Harper and Row.

Palmer, Howard H. (1981). *Patterns of Prejudice: A History of Nativism in Alberta.* Toronto, ON: McClelland and Stewart.

Siccone, Frank. (1995). *Celebrating Diversity: Building Self-Esteem in Today's Multicultural Classrooms.* Boston, MA: Allyn and Bacon.

Steckley, John I., and Bryan D. Cummins. (2008). *Full Circle: Canada's First Nations. Second Edition.* Toronto, ON: Pearson Education Canada.

Suzuki, David. (1992). A Personal Foreword: The Value of Native Ecologies. *Wisdom of the Elders.* Peter Knudtson and David Suzuki. Toronto, ON: Stoddart.

Tiedt, Pamela L., and Iris M. Tiedt. (1986). *Multicultural Teaching: A Handbook of Activities, Information and Resources.* Second edition. Boston, MA: Allyn and Bacon.

Tiedt, Pamela L., and Iris M. Tiedt. (1990). *Multicultural Teaching: A Handbook of Activities, Information and Resources.* Third edition. Boston, MA: Allyn and Bacon.

Wallace, Ernest, and E. Adamson Hoebel. (1986). *The Comanches: Lords of the Southern Plains.* Norman, OK: University of Oklahoma Press.

Warry, Wayne. (2007). *Unfinished Dreams: Community Healing and the Reality of Aboriginal Self-Government.* Toronto, ON: University of Toronto Press.

# Eight

# *Storytelling as a Means of Language Maintenance: Ten Dynamic Truths*

"I cannot speak a word of the Blackfoot language, but I am as Blackfoot as they come," a young Peigan woman from southern Alberta announced in our university class one day. The young woman's classmates had been discussing the advantages and disadvantages of language change within a specific cultural configuration, and arguments went back and forth about possible cultural loss when an entire language is replaced or eradicated. The woman went on; "I may have learned the beliefs and customs of my people in other than an Indian language, but they are as much mine as they would be if I did speak my traditional language."

Naturally, no nonAboriginal person in the class wanted to voice opposition to the young woman's testimony, but was she right? How much content does a culture lose when its traditional tongue is replaced with another?

## Introduction

Although many Aboriginal elders have long been concerned about gradually diminishing interest in Indigenous language maintenance, they have been generally at a loss about what to do about it. Antone (2003: 10) points out that at least 50 Aboriginal languages indigenous to Canada will disappear within the next century. The startling reality is that there are only three Aboriginal languages – Cree, Ojibway, and Inuktituk – that have more than 5 000 speakers. Many Native languages have less than 100 speakers, and some languages such as Beothuk, Laurentian, Tuscarora, Tsetsaut, and Wyandot, have already been lost.

A decade ago Kirkness (1998: 95) observed that 13 Aboriginal languages had less than forty speakers, and 23 languages were seriously endangered. This trend has continued. For example, the average age of Haida speakers in British Columbia in 2007 is 80, and the youngest speaker is 59 years of age. Young Haida participate in revivalist activities like song, dance, and art, but have not embraced their threatened language in large numbers (Fultz, 2007: 60).

The impact of serious language loss has stirred significant action in schools and universities, along with several government agencies, and these efforts have been going on for several decades. For example, in the 1980s the University of Manitoba initiated an undergraduate degree in Indigenous languages in conjunction with the Manitoba Association for Native Languages (Norton, 1989), while 14 607 students in Manitoba public schools were enrolled in courses offering Aboriginal languages as subject matter. At about the same time the Province of Saskatchewan boasted an enrollment of 6 316 students in Native language courses. The Province of Ontario established the Ontario Literacy Grants Program designed to deliver adult literacy programs to three communities including Aboriginal, Anglophone, and Francophone. Many of these programs are continuing.

# A Complex Challenge

Government and public school programs are severely limited in terms of assuring success in achieving language maintenance. At best such efforts have academic and political value; the greatest assurance for language maintenance is that the language be used daily, preferably in one's home (Cummins and Swain, 1986; Friesen, 1991). Individuals who are serious about keeping their native tongue alive need to be able to speak that language with at least one other individual on a personal basis. Only then will the language truly be theirs. More specifically, effective language learning must meet three specific criteria. *First,* there must be a high rate of acquisition, not the mere memorization of a series of primary monosyllables. *Second,* language learners must have strong support systems to back the undertaking, namely family, peer group, close friends, or significant others who encourage the pursuit. *Third,* language students must be positively motivated, and they must have ample practice time, using the newly acquired language in real life situations. There is little lasting value in mastering a language if its usage is limited to artificial or contrived situations. This fact underscores the contention that the newly acquired language must be spoken in the home (Friesen and Friesen, 2005a: 138).

Paupanekis and Westfall (2001: 101) caution that school programs cannot maintain or rejuvenate Native languages, and when such programs are introduced, it is mandatory that Aboriginal parents be brought on board. Parents need to realize that a functional Aboriginal language program can add to a child's learning process; therefore, parental support is vital to the success of any such program. Paupanekis and Westfall point out that there have been instances where parents have removed their children from language learning opportunities because of underlying fears about possible assimilative objectives.

Language is undoubtedly a most effective carrier of cultural content. For this reason many Aboriginal elders fear that significant cultural loss occurs when language use is depleted and their fears appear justified. Obviously cultures do not usually disappear, but they change, often through language shifts or for other reasons. In the past many tribal cultural changes occurred over generations, for example, when eastern First Nations migrated west following the fur trade. Some of them, like the Plains Cree and Plains Ojibway adopted a lifestyle built around the buffalo and subsequently added a new vocabulary to their cultural repertoire. Similarly, many other First Nations significantly altered their cultural configurations long before European contact, due to such factors as intertribal warfare, geographic shifts, planned migrations, new spiritual insights, or natural climactic changes. Change per se, is not always a negative happening, but it certainly can affect language structure.

A number of cultural groups in Canada, other than Indigenous peoples, have experienced the necessity of changing or altering language structures and meanings in order to cope in dominant society. Dozens of ethnocultural groups who migrated to Canada in the last century have virtually abandoned their heritage languages (at least their children and grandchildren have). These groups have adopted one of Canada's two official languages as their primary means of communication. Members of these communities still treasure the values of their homeland and continue to practice significant cultural practices that celebrate their heritage lifestyle. Canada, as a multicultural country, not only permits this kind of functioning, but encourages it. The reality is that interest in and responsibility for cultural (and linguistic) maintenance is primarily in the hands of each cultural group. Speakers of a particular language (and perhaps a few interested linguists and anthropologists), are generally the only ones who are familiar with it and who value it sufficiently enough to maintain it. Even if Aboriginal groups obtain government support and funding to develop extensive Indigenous language programs, there is no assurance that they will be effective in the long run. The ultimate target in language maintenance is to interest Aboriginal youth in that objective, but they, like all young Canadians, are probably more interested in learning about and participating in the cultural lifestyle promoted by popular culture and Canadian media.

## Benefits of Language Learning

Learning any language, even a second or third language, has significant personal and social benefits. Learning to function effectively in a cultural setting other than one's own through the vehicle of language can greatly enhance one's perspective and outlook. Familiarizing oneself with alternative cultural knowledge builds understanding and sensitivity towards others. A deeper understanding of someone else's lifestyle can foster tolerance and promote acceptance. Many potential social conflict situations can be alleviated through enhanced understanding. In this context, even a cursory understanding of Aboriginal spirituality, culture, and language could help develop the perspective that First Nations religious symbols are as important to them as other religious symbols are to members of other spiritual orientations or religions. Intolerance is often simply the result of a lack of sufficient knowledge and inadequate knowledge is often due to mis-education, insensitivity, or lack of interest.

Social scientists have known for a long time that language conveys cultural knowledge. The language of any cultural configuration incorporates all aspects of its implicit and explicit structures including social, cognitive, linguistic, material, and spiritual elements. Leavitt (1995) notes that the most significant aspect of language is found in its ways of conceptualizing, preserving, and transmitting knowledge. Indigenous languages, for example, tend to exemplify awareness of happenings, eventuating change, flow, and interrelationships. If these unique linguistic characteristics are to be appreciated, Aboriginal languages must be kept alive. When a language ceases to exist, its implicit ways of conceptualizing vanish and society is poorer for it.

Preserving Aboriginal languages is in everyone's interest. Language losses imply important cultural losses, thereby weakening the fabric of a multicultural nation – which Canada purports to be. Fortunately, many First Nations in Canada are rising to the challenge and developing effective language programs at all age levels, involving schools as well as other community agencies. The bottom line is that the preservation of Indigenous languages is primarily an Indigenous concern and responsibility. Sadly, most Canadians are too deeply involved in other enterprises and do not sufficiently appreciate the effect of language loss on the national fabric. Success in Aboriginal language maintenance will depend on two factors, chief of which is the will of First Nations communities to commit themselves to meeting the challenge. Second, their efforts will need to be bolstered by national and provincial legislation that will legally assure the entrenchment of Aboriginal languages rights. Both factors have a somewhat unpredictable and emotional side to them, the former in the hearts of members of the Aboriginal community in the strength of interest that may be ignited in language maintenance, and the second within the hearts of the Canadian people in the interests of national pluralism. When these two factors mesh, Native language maintenance will be assured.

## Ten Dynamic Truths

Ethnocultural communities who are concerned about language maintenance typically explore divergent ways to build interest. Their leaders often undertake serious efforts to attract and excite their younger members about the importance of maintaining strong ties to their cultural or ethnic past, but often with limited success. One avenue that has probably not received sufficient address is the potential of utilizing storytelling as a means of valuing, teaching, and preserving heritage languages. After all, every cultural configuration, from time immemorial, has relied on stories to teach and perpetuate important cultural beliefs and values. Moreover, in recent decades there has been renewed interest in the art of storytelling. Professional storytellers now tour Canada and the United States, and storytelling conferences and festivals abound and attract wide audiences. Folklore stories such as myths, epics, legends, and fables continue to be favorites (website: 42 eXplore). If one searches the internet for the word "storytelling," at least 22 400 000 items will be identified! On this basis, we have become convinced that the two items can successfully be linked – storytelling and language maintenance. This thesis can be projected through ten dynamic truths.

## First Truth

It is a cross-cultural reality that everyone enjoys a good story, and every culture has a stock of myths, legends, or folktales that are told, re-told, and passed on to the next generation. Many of these stories are so well known that they have, in fact, become universally owned. In many cases, no one even remembers stories about their land of origin. Many of Aesop's fables, Grimm's fairy tales, and Biblical parables have been related and published in countless volumes with little or no recognition of the original storyteller. The story of the lion and the mouse, for example, is allegedly one of Aesop's fables. In the story, a lion is awakened by a mouse and threatens to hurt or destroy the mouse. The mouse begs forgiveness and promises to return the favor if ever he is given the opportunity. The mouse also argues that he is not worthy to be put to death by the great beast. Later it happens that the lion is captured by hunters and tied to a tree; the lion roars for help with all his might. The mouse hears the lion's pleas and frees him by gnawing through the ropes.

People in many countries know the story and enjoy listening to it or telling it. Similarly, many people probably know the story explaining why the bear has a short tail, but few can correctly attribute its origin to the Iroquois (Friesen, 2000: 25-26). The story begins with the observation that the bear once had a beautiful long, bushy tail and loved to show it off. The trickster (Coyote) wants to take bear down a peg, so he situates himself near a hole in the ice of a frozen lake, and pretends to be fishing. A number of fish are situated beside the fishing hole that has been carved out of the ice by the trickster. Bear enquires at to Coyote's fishing apparatus, and the latter informs Bear that he uses his tail to catch fish. Bear asks if he can try, and Coyote obliges, promising Bear that he will awaken him if he falls asleep. Bear puts his beautiful tail into the water, and soon falls asleep. Coyote waits until water in the ice hole, in which Bear's beautiful tail is located, is solidly frozen, and then awakens Bear. When Bear sees how Coyote has fooled him, he tears himself loose from the ice and leaves his beautiful tail caught in the ice. Of course, he never captures the trickster, who goes on to another adventure. And that is why to this day, the bear has a short tail.

Another quite familiar story – how strawberries came to be – has its origins in Cherokee country, but one would not know it from the literary sources where it can be found in print. As the story goes, it seems that a husband and wife had an argument and the wife decided to go for a walk, and her husband followed her. Angrily, the woman walked very quickly ahead of her husband and was soon out of sight. The man tried to catch up to his wife, but was unable to do so. Feeling sorry for the husband, the Creator made some bright red berries (strawberries), and placed them in the woman's path. When she saw them, she stopped to pick one and taste it. Pleasantly surprised at the deliciously sweet taste, she wanted to share her discovery with someone, and she thought of her husband. She waited until he reached the place where she had encountered the berries and shared them with him. Both of them smiled as they ate the strawberries and their argument was soon forgotten. From that day to this, Cherokees have believed that it is impossible to eat strawberries and harbor any kind of ill feeling toward others.

Now, if this kind of story could be told in one's native language, imagine how the two objectives of enjoyment and language learning could transpire simultaneously. Some stories simply fare better when they are told in the language in which they originate.

## Second Truth

Storytelling involves a two-way interaction between storyteller and audience. The responses of the listeners influence the telling of the story. In fact, storytelling emerges from the interaction and cooperative, coordinated efforts of both storyteller and listeners. The Iroquois long ago recognized this and initiated a method by which to assure interaction between a storyteller and his or her listeners. While relating a tale the storyteller would stop periodically and utter the word, "Ho." In return, partly to show they were still awake, the audience was expected to response with "Hey." Imagine the benefits of learning language with such a method!

Storytelling is good pedagogy; it is an effective teaching/learning method. The North American Indians living before European contact knew this, and practiced effective teaching/learning approaches. Adherents to the oral tradition, they did not rely on written records in transmitting valued beliefs and practices to succeeding generations. Respected traditions, ceremonies, rituals, and other forms of Indigenous knowledge were passed on via a series of four steps: (i) listening; (ii) observing; (iii) participating; and, (iv) teaching. If an individual was deemed ready, he or she would first be informed about a specific belief of practice, primarily through storytelling. A legend might be told, for example, about the origin of a particular ritual or ceremony, and its purpose would be explained.

Traditionally every valued belief and practice had at least one legend attached to it. After it was decided that the student was sufficiently informed, he or she would be invited to observe the particular enactment and later maybe even be invited to participate in the event. It was believed that an appropriate amount of participation could qualify an individual to teach about a valued belief, ritual, or practice and thus become qualified to teach it to others. Teaching about such an important item was deemed to be the final, clinching step in learning.

Storytelling or legend telling is an active process. Unlike dance, painting, or mime, storytelling uses words – which is what language learning is concerned with. Storytelling also uses actions such as vocalization, physical movement and/or gesture. These actions are the parts of spoken or manual language other than words. Their use distinguishes storytelling from writing and text-based computer interactions. In the case of the ancient Native North Americans, the act of storytelling conveyed a multiplicity of objectives, not the least of which was language learning. This objective can easily be reinstituted today.

There were other pedagogical structures in place in traditional First Nations communities. Legends, while comprising the major vehicle of listening content were told for a variety of reasons, depending on the intended purpose of the telling, time, and place. Four types of legends maybe identified.

*First,* entertainment legends are often about the trickster, who is called by different names among the various tribes. As Grant (1993: 25) observes, the trickster figure is found in many world mythologies and his role may be interpreted in a wide variety of ways. Among First Nations communities the Blackfoot call him Napi, the Crees call him Wisakedjak, the Ojibway call him Nanabush, the Sioux call him îktômni, while other tribes have different names for him like Coyote, Tarantula, or Raven. Stories about the trickster are principally fictional and can be invented and amended even during the process of storytelling. There is never much difficulty in getting listeners to pay attention to trickster stories because trickster stories usually involve playing tricks. Sometimes the trickster plays tricks on others and sometimes they play tricks on him.

The trickster appears to have the advantage on his unsuspecting audience, since he possesses supernatural powers, which he deploys on a whim to startle or to shock. He has power to raise animals to life and he himself may even die and in four days come to life again. Aside from being amusing, trickster stories often incorporate knowledge about aspects of Aboriginal culture, buffalo hunts, natural phenomena, or rituals, or the relationship between people and animals. In this sense, trickster stories may also be instructional.

*Second*, instructional or teaching legends are basically told for the purpose of sharing information about a tribe's culture, history, or origin. These kinds of stories explain things. They often use animal motifs to explain why things are the way they are. For example, a child may enquire about the origin of the seasons or the behavior of a certain animal and a tale revolving around animal life may be told. Another child may ask, "Where did our people come from?" or "Why are crows' feathers black?" or "Why do frogs live on lily pads?" Stories told in response to these questions could include adventures of the trickster.

*Third*, moral legends are intended to teach ideal or "right" forms of behavior, and are employed to suggest to the listener that a change in attitude or action would be desirable. Since traditional Indian tribes rarely corporally punished their children, they sometimes found it useful to point out or emphasize the inappropriateness of certain behavior by telling stories. For example, the story might be about an animal that engages in inappropriate behavior and the child is expected to realize that a possible modification of his or her own behavior is the object of the telling. The onus is always on listeners to apply the lesson of the legend to themselves if deemed appropriate.

*Fourth*, sacred or spiritual legends were traditionally told only by recognized elders or other tribally approved individuals, since their telling was considered a form of worship. Today it is possible to find tribal origin legends, which are sometimes considered sacred, in written form, but in the minds of some elders this is an unfortunate development. In precontact days, spiritually significant stories were never told to just anyone who asked anymore than they were told by just anyone. Among some tribes, sacred legends were considered property and thus their transmission from generation to generation was carefully safeguarded.

Legends comprised only a part of a tribe's spiritual structure, which also included ceremonies, rituals, songs, and dances. Physical objects such as fetishes, pipes, painted tepee designs, medicine bundles, and shrines of sorts, supplemented these. Familiarity with these components comprised sacred knowledge, and everything learned was committed to memory. Viewed together these entries represented spiritual connections between people and the universe which, with appropriate care, resulted in a lifestyle of assured food supply, physical well-being and satisfying the needs and wants of the society.

Teaching about these things in story form following some semblance of traditional Aboriginal pedagogy, comprises a noteworthy undertaking. Doing so in an Indigenous language would accomplish an even more admirable undertaking.

## Third Truth

Storytelling is usually a group activity; it is something that people do together. In traditional times, it would probably be rare that a recognized storyteller would address only one individual at a time. The presence of an audience was certainly the case in formal storytelling occasions. Similarly, language learning is more productive (and enjoyable), when undertaken in the company and in interaction with others. Combining language learning and storytelling, or conducting language classes with an ample dose of storytelling is a recipe that is hard to beat. The importance of doing things together and sharing is well illustrated in the Cowichan story of the day the Red-Tailed Hawk brought fire (Friesen and Friesen, 2005b: 17-18).

In the old days, the Cowichan people lived without fire. They could not cook their food and their homes were sometimes quite cold in the wintertime. They wished for warmth but had no idea how to get it.

One day a group of people was having supper when a beautiful bird with a bright red tail flew over their heads. Everyone noticed the bird's bright red tail. This was the red-tailed hawk.

"Do you see this red flame on my tail?" said the visitor. "It is called fire. It is my gift to you."

"What is fire?" everyone asked. "Why do we want fire?"

"Gather up some small pieces of light wood," said the red-tailed hawk. "Then follow me. I will show you what fire can do. Whoever keeps up with me can learn about fire."

The hawk began to fly away and everyone grabbed a piece of light wood and ran after it. The people were very excited to learn about the mystery of fire.

The hawk flew quickly and the people had great difficulty keeping up with it. They ran through brush, over stumps, and through swamps. Still the bird flew on. Most of the people could not keep up and stopped running after the bird. Finally, there were only four people left pursuing the bird. There were two men and two women still chasing the bird.

Suddenly the hawk stopped flying and settled on a low branch. "Come and touch my tail," said the bird. "Feel how warm it is. It will cook your meat and fish and warm your homes. One of you can have it to take back to your village."

"Give it to me," said the first man. "I have kept up with you running through the brush, and swamp, and forest. I deserve it."

"No," said the hawk. "You are a selfish man and would not share the fire with others. You do not deserve it."

"Let me have it," said the second man. "I can make good use of fire. I will do many things with it."

"No," said the hawk. "You are too eager and excited. You might start a huge fire and burn down the forest. You cannot have it."

Then a third person, a woman, spoke up. "Give me the fire and I will only share it with the other women in my village. Then we will be able to cook food for our children."

"No, " said the hawk. "The fire is for everyone. It is for men and women and children. It should be shared with everyone in all the villages. It should not be kept from anyone."

Then the hawk spoke to a fourth person. This woman had barely kept up with the bird in flight.

"Bring your wood to me," said the hawk. "You can have the fire."

"Oh no," said the woman. "I have done nothing to deserve it. One of the others should have it."

"Take the fire," said the red-tailed hawk. "You are always doing good and I know you will share the fire with everyone."

So the woman put her wood to the hawk's bright red tail and the wood began to burn. It gave of a soft warm glow.

Quickly the woman made her way back to the village and shared the fire with her friends and neighbors. The people began to cook their food with fire and use it to warm their homes. Everyone was very happy to have fire.

That is how, long ago, the Cowichan people got fire. Everyone still listening?

## Fourth Truth

Storytelling was traditionally a community activity involving individuals of varying generations. Formal Native storytellers were usually respected adults, often older adults. Child discipline, which also involved a significant dose of storytelling, was primarily the responsibility of elders and grandparents. Today, most fluent Native language speakers are members of the older generation. Imagine the joy it would bring too them and the increased rate of effectiveness in language learning that would come about, if their role as formal storytellers in their own language was revived. Students of language could be entertained, informed, and instructed while listening to and learning stories about their cultural heritage – and all of it in their heritage language!

## Fifth Truth

Storytelling, like any other traditional First Nations practice, was viewed as a spiritual process. This perspective adds a special dimension to the teaching/learning process, one usually avoided, denied, or neglected in contemporary pedagogical circles. The Sioux, for example, believe that active storytelling (unlike reading), is a living phenomenon. The Sioux have a saying, "Legends are not about life; they are life." This means that whenever someone tells a story about valued beliefs and practices, something special happens. The story itself comes to life in the verbal enactment. This is particularly true in the case of the storyteller who has the spiritual authority to offer the particular details of a story.

Often the manner of telling a story is just as important as the story itself – sometimes more so. If it is perceived that relating a particular account has a spiritual dimension in that the nature of the telling becomes even more important. Imagine the added benefit of doing so in the Indigenous language in which the story originated.

## Sixth Truth

As previously mentioned, virtually every aspect of traditional Aboriginal culture had a legend attached to it – the nature of things, the way the universe works, animal and human habits, social and spiritual practices, etc. The facts connected to these elements were best remembered in story form, so legend telling abounded. Once an individual reached the point that he or she was given permission to tell a certain story, they might also be allowed to embellish aspects of the tale according to their own experience. Imagine the repertoire of cultural knowledge that an individual could mentally store. Imagine how much easier the challenge became when stored in story form. After all, everyone likes a good story, and stories are that much more meaningful if learned in conjunction with the language and culture in which they originate.

## Seventh Truth

The sheer cultural richness of the First Nations repertoire of stories, myths, fables, and legends is a lure for anyone interested in the topic. It goes without saying that the richness is enhanced when one is familiar with the culture that produced and maintained it. Even greater advantage can be gained if one is familiar with respective Aboriginal language. Perhaps the best way to appreciate the richness of this vast store of knowledge is to enroll in Aboriginal language classes – particularly classes that utilize a curriculum based on Indian legends.

## Eighth Truth

It is common knowledge to individuals who speak more than one language that concepts unique to a specific cultural setting cannot easily be interpreted or transferred to another. Many Native legends are formulated around the teaching of conceptual knowledge, particularly moral legends or legends that are intended to teach lessons.

While the concept of conversing with the creatures of the forest, air, or sea, and learning from them is commonplace to traditional First Nations culture, it is not often that nonNatives can comprehend the benefits of such exchange. The Tsimshian of the west coast have a legend about a wolf that visits a community, but does not eat food offered to him. Still, he continues to linger among the villagers. It seems he is unable to speak and eventually someone discovers that the wolf has a fishhook lodged in his throat and removes it. The grateful but hungry wolf can now consume food and offers his grateful thanks to the villagers. He promises that he will someday return the favor, but the villagers are skeptical. After all, what can a wolf do for humans?

Some years go by and one fall as winter approaches the villagers discover that they have been unable to garner a sufficient amount of food for the season ahead. Game has been scarce and even days and nights of fishing have proven unsatisfactory. Suddenly a wolf appears at the door of the village chief's home and suggests that the people follow him to a potential food source. After some deliberation, a number of hunters follow the wolf into the deep woods, sometimes barely able to keep up with him because of the heavy drifts of snow they encounter. Just as they are about to give up, they spy a mysterious herd of caribou in a small clearing ahead of them. The hunters rejoice at the sight and quickly offer their thanks to the wolf, just before he disappears into the woods (Friesen and Friesen, 2004: 63-65).

The moral of the story is quite obvious; it is a version of the ancient Golden Rule. The events and happenings of the story are also clear and real, although nonNatives would tend to perceive them as metaphoric or fictional. To perceive the story otherwise, one would surely have to know and believe in the culture – including the language in which it was related. Imagine the benefits to be gleaned by hearing the story told in the context of Tsimshian culture – and in their language! A combination of the two would be hard to beat.

## Ninth Truth

Many Aboriginal legends seem to have generic origins and may be traced to several different First Nations communities. The story of the blind man and the loon (sometimes called, "How the Loon Got its Necklace") is a case in point. In the Nakoda Sioux version, a blind man and his wife are left behind when their tribe moves. Unable to hunt, the blind man is aided by his wife who helps him aim his bow and arrow at a nearby buffalo. Somewhere in the story, the man seeks out the loon who helps him regain his sight. As a token of his thanks, the man gives the loon a necklace that the bird wears to this day. The plot of the story tends to remain the same in every tribal history in which the story can be identified, even though the characters tend to change. The end result is the same; the man rewards his friend, the loon.

Traditionally the story line of a valued Indian legend would not change, regardless of who told the story. Embellishing details or changing the identity of main characters was allowed, and depending on the whim of the storyteller, could prove to be quite indicative of individual creativity. Imagine the anticipation and excitement of hearing the same story told by several different storytellers. This would not only serve to alert the interest of the listening audience, but also inform them of alternative linguistic concepts.

## Tenth Truth

There can be no question about it; storytelling is back on the stage, and cannot be replaced by technology. The current generation of youth is probably already somewhat bored with the presentation of media manufactured information or attempts to lure their attention by shallow television plots that allegedly substitute for entertainment. These youth are a ripe market for good storytelling. In fact, people of all ages are still enamored by live performances – including good storytelling. Few means of sharing information or stimulation of the imagination can replace the articulate, dramatic telling of a good story. It is an excellent medium for teaching language, particularly Aboriginal languages, because it is in those languages that some of the best stories unique to North America are contained.

It is difficult to place a value on community commodity, be it physical, spiritual, social, or simply cultural. Each family of humans bases their valued items on what might be called a myriad of reasons, some of which are hidden in antiquity. Language is one of those, and its unique form is prized undoubtedly highly prized by those whose heritage sponsored it. In some ways this truth can be illustrated by the Hopi story of the sacred humming bird (Friesen and Friesen, 2004: 53-56). The story shows why that small bird is revered in Hopi cultural lore. The same phenomenon may be identified with regard to other cultural entities in virtually every Indigenous milieu. Here is a relevant example.

As the story goes, the Hopi people were worried. It had not rained for many months and their corn crop was drying up. Last year it had rained too much and the many plants had been washed away. The year before the frost came early and the corn crop was lost again. The Hopi people always stored plenty of corn for lean years, but now the supply was almost gone. What were the people to do?

Finally, the Hopi people decided to leave their traditional home on the mountain plateau and live elsewhere. Perhaps they would find a place where it would rain. Sadly, they packed their belongings and said goodbye to the homes they had built. It was very hard to leave, but they knew that if they stayed, they might starve.

When the tribe left the plateau, three people were left behind, a boy named Red Fox, and his younger brother and sister. They had no mother or father to take them to the new village and the others seemed to forget about them.

Red Fox tried very hard to look after his brother and sister, but there was very little food. Each day Red Fox tried to find some root or berry bush with dried up fruit on it to feed them. He fashioned a toy bird for his sister from a sunflower stalk. She spent many happy hours playing with her new toy.

"Why not pretend your toy bird is real when you play with it?" Red Fox asked his sister. "Perhaps the Creator will see the bird and send food for it and for us."

His sister did as Red Fox suggested and often threw the sunflower bird into the air to make it look as though the bird could fly. One day when Red Fox came home from hunting for food, he saw his sister crying.

"What is the matter, little one," he asked. "Where is the sunflower bird I made for you?"

To his surprise his sister remarked, "I threw the bird into the air and it flew away!" Then she started crying again.

Red Fox did not know what to do, but he told his sister he would look for the bird. He began to search everywhere, hoping the bird would show up.

Then he heard his sister call out. "Red Fox, come quickly, I just saw my sunflower bird fly by."

"Where did he fly to?" Red Fox asked. He was sure his little sister was playing make believe.

"He flew right into that hole in the stone wall," his sister insisted. "Please get him for me," she begged.

Red Fox asked his younger brother to put his hand into the hole in the wall while he went on looking for the sunflower bird. He was very surprised when his brother cried out.

"Red Fox, you must come and see. I have found a bin of corn. The hole in this wall is the opening to a great amount of stored corn. Now we will have plenty to eat."

Red Fox ran to his brother and put his hand into the hole. His brother was right. There was plenty of corn in the hidden bin. Now they would have food to eat for a long time. The three of them were very happy.

"See, I told you my bird came alive and it showed us the corn bin," the little sister exclaimed. Neither Red Fox nor his brother knew what to say. Then to their surprise a little hummingbird flew past them and into the hole that led to the secret bin of corn.

"Perhaps that was your toy sunflower bird," said Red Fox. "We may never be sure, but we will always be grateful."

Just then, the tiny Hummingbird flew out of the hole and stopped in mid-air in front of the three of them. It beat its tiny wings very fast and remained in one spot for several minutes. It did this as if to say, "Yes, I am the sunflower toy bird."

Before long several people from the Hopi tribe came looking for the three children they had left behind. They were surprised to find that the children had plenty of food. In fact there was enough corn to feed the entire tribe for a long time. Soon the Hopi tribe returned to their traditional home and they have remained there to this day.

When Red Fox and his brother and his sister told the people the story of the sunflower bird that turned into a hummingbird they were very grateful. Since then, the hummingbird has been very special to the Hopi people.

Clearly we have a lot to learn from studying Aboriginal legends and languages. We have much to discover. The late John Snow, Chief of the Wesley Band of the Stoney Nation described it this way:

> And so I say to you, the EuroCanadians; you have discovered our land and its resources, but you have not discovered my people nor our teachings, nor the spiritual basis of our teachings. (Friesen, 1998: 60)

The traditional way of Canada's First Nations was a unique way when it came to expressing truth. It was contained in the very essence of their languages. As Chief Cochise of the Apache nation once said, "You must speak straight so your words may go as sunlight into our hearts" (Friesen, 1998: 50).

May these words have that kind of impact.

## References

Antone, Eileen. (2003). Culturally Framing Aboriginal Literacy and Learning. *Canadian Journal of Native Education,* 27:1, 7-15.

Cummins, J., and M. Swain. (1986). *Bilingualism in Education.* London, UK: Longman.

42eXplore. http//:42explore.com/story.htm

Friesen, John W. (2000). *Legends of the Elders.* Calgary, AB: Detselig Enterprises.

Friesen, John W. (1998). *Sayings of the Elders: An Anthology of First Nations Wisdom.* Calgary, AB: Detselig Enterprises.

Friesen, John W. (1991). The Persistence of Cultural Destiny: The Role of Language. *The Cultural Maze: Complex Questions on Native Destiny in Western Canada.* John W. Friesen, ed. Calgary, AB: Detselig Enterprises, 147-162.

Friesen, John W., and Virginia Lyons Friesen. (2005a). *First Nations in the Twenty-First Century: Contemporary Educational Frontiers.* Calgary, AB: Detselig Enterprises.

Friesen, John W., and Virginia Lyons Friesen. (2005b). *Even More Legends of the Elders.* Calgary, AB: Detselig Enterprises.

Friesen, John W., and Virginia Lyons Friesen. (2004). *Still More Legends of the Elders.* Calgary, AB: Detselig Enterprises.

Fultz, Joanna. (March/April, 2007). Keepers of the Forest. *Canadian Geographic,* 127:2, 52-61.

Grant, Agnes. (1993). *Our Bit of Truth: An Anthology of Canadian Native Literature.* Winnipeg, MB: Pemmican Publications.

Kirkness, Verna J. (1998). The Critical State of Aboriginal Languages in Canada. *Canadian Journal of Native Education,* 22:1, 93-107.

Leavitt, Robert. (1995). Language and Cultural Change Content in Native Education. *First Nations Education in Canada: The Circle Unfolds.* Marie Battiste and Jean Barman, eds. Vancouver, BC: University of British Columbia Press, 124-138.

Norton, Ruth W. (1989) Analysis of Policy on Native Languages: A Comparison of Government Policy and Native Preferences for a Native Language Policy. Unpublished paper, University of Calgary, 35pp.

Paupanekis, Kenneth, and David Westfall. (2001). Teaching Native Language Programs: Survival Strategies. *Aboriginal Education in Canada: A Study in Decolonization.* K.P. Binda and Sharilyn Calliou, eds. Mississauga, ON: Canadian Educators' Press, 89-104.

# Nine

## Role of Women in Plains First Nations Societies

The role of women in the health of family systems from one generation to the next is one of immense power. The immensity of the responsibility of bearer of life and nourisher of all generations is just becoming clear in its relationship to societal functioning. In traditional Aboriginal society, it was women who shaped the thinking of all members in a loving, nurturing atmosphere within the base family unit. (Armstrong, 2001, ix)

"They do not deserve to get back their Indian Status," the woman said emphatically. "They have chosen to renounce their cultural heritage, respect for traditional spirituality, and obligations by marrying out, so they should not be allowed to regain their traditional place in our culture. It has always been the role of Native women to maintain the spiritual traditions of our culture, and if they willingly renege on that responsibility they should remain on the outside."

The occasion for this statement was a conference on Native education in northeastern Alberta some years ago, with many Native and nonNative people in attendance. The federal government had just announced the passing of Bill C31, and the women seated at our table were upset by it. The woman who uttered the above statement was supported by three others at our table. Evidently these women thought that Bill C31 was a mistake. Their interpretation was that once an Indian woman "left the fold" by marrying out, she should not be allowed to retrieve her traditional role.

## Introduction

Historical background to the above event was the passing of Bill C31 in 1985, an Act of Parliament that allowed Indian women who had previously married nonStatus males – Aboriginal or nonAboriginal – and subsequently lost their Status, to apply for reinstatement as Status Indians. Loss of Status would have occurred for a number of reasons, principally because women with Status had married men who did not have Status. There were other ways in which Status might have been lost, for example, if a women married out, children born to her would not be considered eligible for Status. Even though Bill C31 was designed to correct this historical injustice, the retrieval process is not without complications. In addition, many Indian women did not see past government action as constituting injustice. After all, no one forced these women to marry nonStatus men.

It is not surprising, therefore, that when the passing of Bill C31 was announced, leaders of four of eight national Indigenous organizations immediately declared their opposition to it with much the same rationale that the women at our conference luncheon table voiced. Today debate about the merits of Bill C31 is still ongoing in Native circles and it is useful at this point to examine the rationale for the more traditional position that poses opposition to the bill.

As the social sciences continue to mature, a higher degree of critical writing and analysis of research has become evident, thereby affording researchers a more penetrating look at the way things are. This positive development is particularly true of anthropological writings, most of which are now culturally comprehensive and remarkably objective. An examination of much of twentieth century anthropology will reveal that though researchers made an earnest attempt to remain objective, they did not always succeed. For example, the role of Aboriginal women was mentioned only in passing and then only as a segment of cultural life. Today the literature pertaining to the role of First Nations women is growing; much of it inspired or undertaken by Aboriginal women who have entered the world of academe.

## Traditional Concepts of Women's Roles

It was anthropologist Ruth Benedict (1934: 50, 238) who observed that religion has little to do with the status of women, and the correlation between the two cultural elements is accidental rather than causal. Benedict cited the example of early American Puritan culture as proof that women could be mistreated without just cause. The Puritan divines in the eighteenth century were the last persons whom contemporary opinion in the colonies regarded as psychopathic. Today that perception has changed and it is now known that it was the duty of religious leaders to put the fear of hell into the heart of even the youngest member of society and to extract from every convert emotional acceptance of his/her damnation before God. To a modern observer it was the religious leaders who were guilty of psychoneurotics, not the confused and tormented women they put to death as witches. If Benedict taught us anything, it would surely be that the treatment of women in any other cultural configuration should be regarded from the same relativist point of view.

It should be noted that traditionally, Plains Indian gender roles were well-defined, and responsibilities of men and women were equally crucial to societal functioning. Both sexes were respected for doing their jobs well, although this reality was not always captured by well-meaning incoming European writers and anthropologists. Descriptions of female roles were bathed in ethnocentrism, a commodity that sometimes still badgers the efforts of well-meaning social scientists.

Another well-known anthropologist, Ruth Underhill (1953: 158) noted that in traditional Plains Indian society girls were "bred to work hard though not at the really tough jobs, which were left to old women." Underhill concluded that there was little importance for women in the lifeway of Plains societies though they worked harder than the men in putting up teepees, drying meat, and dressing skins. Depending on their tribal affiliation, Native women also cleared fields, planted and hoed crops, and harvested them. They dug pits for storing foods, erected and dismantled lodges, collected wild plants and firewood, hauled water – often from great distances, cleaned utensils, and transported household goods whenever the tribe moved. In the meantime they sewed, mended clothing and made pottery, all the while also rearing children. Grandmothers shared stories with their grandchildren, thereby informing them of cultural customs, instructions, morals and spiritual truths. Many of them also became skilled herbalists (Sterling, 1992; Goulet, 2001). According to early European-inspired observations, men had all the power and sat around smoking, gambling, and occasionally mending a tool or weapon or caring for a horse (Wishart, 2004: 334).

In terms of marriage practices, Benedict assumed that women did some of the flirting required to catch a life partner's attention, but they were expected to remain virgins until marriage took place. Plains Indian women had no right to divorce, as Pueblo Indian women did, but a virtuous wife could brag about her faithfulness with as much vigor as a warrior might brag of his exploits. If she did err, however, she stood in danger of having the tips of her nose and ears cut off. Almost always occupied in household chores, there was little time for a Native woman to be tempted to be drawn into sexual deviance. Her "leisure" time was spent doing beautiful quill-work and beadwork to decorate articles of clothing and moccasins (Josephy, 1968: 120).

Writing in 1896, John Maclean offered the following explanation regarding the role of Indian women:

> There have been no more devoted workers among the native tribes than the women of culture, who have consecrated their talents to the work of elevating the red men and their families in the camp. They have labored assiduously amid great privations, enduring hardships without murmur, and though their influence has been abiding and strong, seldom have we heard their names mentioned, or read them on the printed page. We have not seen a biography of one of these saintly heroines of the lodges, though many of them have been worthy of lasting record, and this want is still more striking through the existence of numerous biographies of missionaries to the Indian tribes. (Maclean, 1980: 344)

Maclean went on to describe the "thrilling records" of Jesuit expeditions among Native tribes, outlining the part played by Indian women in caring for missionaries and explorers. He described these women as industrious and very handy with needles at making shirts, moccasins, leggings, and other Native articles, ornamenting them with beads according to their local customs.

Maclean observed that when a young Indian man wanted a wife he made a bargain with her parents by giving them presents. There was no performed marriage ceremony; the couple simply started housekeeping using the few practical articles bestowed upon them by the bride's parents (Maclean, 1980: 141). Driver (1968: 267-268) describes several different ways of acquiring a wife among tradition-al Plains tribes. One way was by purchasing or by offering a bride price, often by offering horses. The purchase of a bride did not give the husband the right to injure or kill his wife, nor dispose of her by selling her or renting out her sexual favors. The bride's family was expected to provide gifts to the groom's parents in equal value to the gifts given in bride price. Bride price and polygamy were con-sidered economic transactions, so influenced by the competition of the fur trade. Men often sought more wives so they could produce more furs to be traded with European traders. Maclean (1980: 62) noted that the Blackfeet did not marry outside their confederacy, but in times of war they sometimes made wives of enemy female captives. Since men were often killed during times of war or hunting accidents, the number of females in camp exceeded that of males, thus encouraging polygamy as a socio-cultural obligational means of looking after widows or single women.

There were some tribes who permitted young men to court their daughters by living with the prospective bride's family and thereby proving themselves by hard work. This custom often resulted in a temporary matrilocal residence for a year or so after the couple was married, or until their first child was born. After the marriage was regarded as fully consummated the groom often took his new wife to live with his own community members.

Although some observers might perceive of the traditional role of women in Indian societies as "beasts of burden," there were definite limits as to how they could be treated. Joe Dion (1979: 16f) describes the Plains Cree attitude toward women as one of simplicity and respect. Love and friendship prevailed in most marital relationships, and often two families who were friendly with one another would arrange for their children to be married. The Crees did not frequently engage in wife buying or wife beating, but if a man found his wife unsuitable, he could put her away without any formalities of divorce. A wife beater was looked down upon, but a wife was expected to yield to her husband's commands in their home. In one instance where a man beat his wife, two family friends visited him and meted out the same medicine to the offender. If a wife decided to leave her husband, her mother would likely make her daughter look presentable and send her back to her husband.

Blackfoot men generally took multiple wives because the sex ratio was imbalanced by matters of war and hunting accidents. It was not unusual for men in their twenties to be single and living in their parents' lodges, and it was also quite common for men in their sixties or seventies to have six or seven wives, including some young enough to be his grandchildren.

A member of the Kainai (Blood) First Nation, Hungry Wolf (1982: 26-27), defends the custom of multiple wives, by drawing an analogy with the animal world and the philosophy of the survival of the fittest. Older individuals who had survived the ravages of war and wilderness living were much more qualified to care for larger families than young, unproven males. Constant warring with other tribes  raised the fatality rate among young men, with the result that there were more women with children who needed looking after. Young men might seek the company of women their age who were married to older men and therefore quite lonely. Older men with multiple wives might sanction these clandestine relationships and on occasion even give up a young wife to a young suitor. There were also times where secret relationships would result in frustration and unhappiness, and suicide was not uncommon for a young, heartbroken woman who had fallen in love with a younger man.

Hungry Wolf observes that many Kainai parents were quite willing to give up their young girls as brides so they might learn how to cope within their new family or clan parameters. It was thought that if a youthful female grew up in her husband's household she would better adjust to their particular ways. This custom was particularly appealing to parents who were poor or sickly. By giving up their daughters in marriage they did not have to provide for them. Most young women of Kainai affiliation were married by the age of sixteen and were expected to remain faithful to their husbands until death. Women who remained committed to their marriage partners grew to be respected in the community and were permitted to participate in special ceremonies. They could also be considered qualified to call (announce) the revered Sundance. Mike Mountain Horse (1989: 64) observes that eight religious societies were once operant in Kainai society, one of which (the Buffaloe Society) was run by women. Any two societies, male or female, could preside at a day's ceremonies, most of which consisted of dances. Women also provided refreshments at these events – boiled meat, broth of varied ingredients, and hundreds of slabs of fried bread.

Lowie (1963: 82) insisted that the position of women in Plains societies was decidedly higher than was usually assumed. A good woman enjoyed the esteem of her husband and of the community at large. The bond between man and women grew stronger as the marriage endured. When a woman grew older and was less able to perform her chores, the husband might take a second younger wife to help her out. Lowie observed that among some Plains tribes women participated equally with their husbands in ceremonial enactments. For example, both men and women took an active part in the Crow Tobacco Ceremony, and it was a respected, holy woman who announced the celebration of the Sundance. Though these arrangements validated the importance of women in precontact Plains cultures, Radin (1937: 274) suggests that privileges of governance were not made available to women. This did not mean that women did not influence the men, for they did. Property was often owned exclusively by women, and this arrangement gave them unmeasured power in important sectors. These statuses and roles were maintained long after European contact despite attempts on the part of the new arrivals to adapt them to coincide with their own perceptions.

There is some argument among historians as to the impact of the fur trade on Plains cultures, particularly with regard to the role of women. Some researchers have argued that as the demand for furs grew, pressure was put on women to produce more furs. As mentioned, a man might even take additional wives in order to meet the demands of the fur trade. There were also instances of Native women marrying traders, possibly to ensure a productive band's loyalty to a particular post. Some Native women acted as unpaid interpreters for fur-trading companies and achieved a good deal of importance. Peers (1994: 35) suggests that this does not mean these women were pawns used by the band for power and profit. In fact, women had a vested interest in promoting cordial relations with traders in order to guarantee the maintenance of supplies of labor-saving trade goods such as steel needles and kettles. In some cases both traders and Indians could establish kinship relationships through extensive interaction that could result in marriage. Some women even preferred the trader lifestyle to their own and willingly married eligible European bachelors. If such a marriage broke up, a woman whose husband had left her would return to her tribe, but as the economic base of Indian life deteriorated, it became difficult for tribes to reabsorb women and their children. Their vulnerability was confirmed with the passage of the *Indian Act* in 1876.

## Shifting Perceptions in Mainstream America

Many observers credit the origin of the American feminist movement to 1848 when the first women's rights convention was held in Seneca Falls, New York. After two days of discussion and debate, 68 women and 32 men signed a Declaration of Sentiments that outlined grievances and set the agenda for the women's rights movement. A set of twelve resolutions was adopted, calling for equal treatment of women and men under the law and voting rights for women. Two years later, the first National Women's Rights Convention took place in Worcester, Massachusetts, and attracted more than 1 000 participants.

The best was yet to come. In 1963 Betty Friedan published her highly influential book, *The Feminine Mystique*, which described the dissatisfaction felt by middle-class American housewives with the narrow role imposed on them by society. The book became a best-seller and galvanized the modern women's rights movement. On June 10th of that year, the American Congress passed the *Equal Pay Act,* making it illegal for employers to pay a woman less than what a man would receive for the same job. The rest, as they say, is history.

Canadian women have been organizing to redefine their place in society since the nineteenth century. They have been successful in both legal and political arenas and have effected profound changes in the social realm as well. In the Canadian postwar era, women were urged to create modern families characterized by internal family democracy and equal partnerships between spouses (Purvey, 2005: 259). The Cold War, and the fragility it constituted to world peace, was a real threat to potential advancement in this regard. Dysfunctionality among families was enhanced, as social roles were altered to meet the times. The unexpected postwar boom further complicated the picture, but proponents of family stability labored on to establish a measure of vitality to the institution. Purvey (2005: 260) argues that postwar Canada created a particular model of marriage and family that placed specific obligations on both sex roles. Women were encouraged to quash their dreams and wants and avoid exhibiting what were perceived as masculine behaviors. Women who did not do this were socially penalized or pathologized. It was the task of women to keep the family together and make it look like things were going well. Women who did manage to obtain work outside the home usually opted to engage in approved "female" professions such as teaching, nursing, and social work.

By the 1980s, most married Canadian women had paying jobs although for the most part they were still expected to maintain their traditional domestic roles at home. Leaders of the movement to liberate women in the early years of the twentieth century were Nellie McClung, Emily Murphy, and Laura Jamieson. Following their lead, in 1963 the federal government of Canada set up the Royal Commission on The Status of Women to examine the employment inequities that existed, and in its 1970 report the commission made 167 recommendations for greater equality of women.

When it comes to the realm of professional functioning, women have generally had to prove that they were at least as good as men in performing their duties. Callahan (2005: 237) suggests that in the development of social work and child welfare in the period between 1920 and 1960, women had to prove that they could operate as full-fledged professionals in the public domain. They had first of all to distance themselves from the moralistic attitudes of their foremothers whose functioning could best be described as patronizing and offensive, and then establish an alternative perspective. This was accomplished by thinking conceptually and applying that knowledge in ways that would advance their clients and the profession as a whole. During that period, many women labored diligently as managers and workers in both public and voluntary child welfare institutions. They also assumed leadership positions in the development of social work theory and in advancing the status of related social work institutions.

## Changes in Aboriginal Communities

The situation for Aboriginal women is quite different. Although not all observers are agreed, Hungry Wolf (1996: 78) insists that in traditional Kainai society male and female roles were equal and interdependent. Ceremonies given to the people by the spirits were shared by both sexes, and could not take place without participation of both men and women. Usually women had the responsibility of taking the sacred bundles outside each morning and making incense for them. Women also had a special role to play in opening the bundles. Hungry Wolf blames the teachings of the missionaries in lowering the status of Indian women, Missionaries tended to follow the biblical example of the first created women, Eve, who deceived her husband, Adam, in the Garden of Eden. After that incident Eve was blamed for the fall of mankind. Eve's punishment for deceiving Adam is described in Genesis 3:16 (NIV): "To the women he said, I will greatly increase your pains in childbearing; with pain you will give birth to children. Your desire will be for your husband, and he will rule over you." This perspective is reiterated in the New Testament. Saint Paul, writing to Timothy, his young protégé states:

> A woman should learn in quietness and full submission. I do not permit a woman to teach or to have authority over a man; she must be silent. For Adam was formed first, then Eve. And Adam was not the one deceived; it was the women who was deceived and became a sinner. But women will be saved through child-

bearing – if they continue in faith, love and holiness with propriety. (I Timothy 3:11-15 NIV)

Milloy's (1990: xvii) study of Plains Cree trade, diplomacy and war (1790-1870) does not elaborate the role of women, and while this tack is deliberate, it appears to be of some concern to Milloy himself. Milloy justifies the lack of inclusion of data about the role of woman by suggesting that this omission stems primarily from the fact that the work in precontact Indigenous communities focuses on trade and war, which were predominantly male activities. Aboriginal women played a vital internal economic role within the subsistence milieu as small game hunters and gatherers. They also provided the workforce that produced furs to satisfy hungry European markets. Milloy mentions how unfortunate it is that male-produced historical sources provide little information about the actual role of Native women so it is difficult to reconstruct an exact description of their experiences and responsibilities.

In precontact days, it was recognized that household goods generally belonged to women, and the attending chores were their primary responsibility. Property owned by a woman was passed on to her relatives, not to her husband. Many tribes also traced their ancestry through the female line. Radin (1937: 275) observed that this practice did not necessarily afford women a role in tribal government, but there were other ways in which they gained respect. The Iroquois were an exception in this regard because the oldest matron was regarded as one of the most important grades of chiefs, and responsible for selecting a successor to a deceased chief of the family.

When the reserve system was established the role of both sexes changed dramatically. A study by Goldfrank (1945: 46) in the middle of the twentieth century suggests that new laws introduced by government officials actually helped Indian women to gain status because reserve laws protected their property rights and favored them in matters of inheritance. As Carter (2001: 51) points out, this view was grounded in the old-fashioned notion that women were virtually slaves in traditional times. Europeans who first came into contact with Aboriginal communities quickly but erroneously gained the impression that Indian women were bought and sold like chattel and suffered many indignities in their marriage relationships. As more sophisticated observations by more astute anthropologists became available, this perception changed to take into account that First Nations women were generally in charge of their homes, and despite the fact that they often relocated, exercised discipline, modesty and cleanliness, all virtues that nonNatives might believe were impossible in nomadic societies.

Reserve life had a devastating impact on many of the old ways. Sex roles were greatly changed, because reserve rations were handed out, not distributed generously, and often suspended for days at a time. Government officials regarded this responsibility as dangerous and demoralizing, and recipients were discouraged from thinking that the process would continue indefinitely (Carter, 2001: 57). The Indian mortality rate was high and reserve residents were frequently ill because of the lack of availability of a proper diet and adequate health facilities. Wuttunee (1971: 112) points out that Indians suffered from malnutrition and disease in the primeval silence and in an attempt to maintain integrity, tried to turn reservations into permanent havens away from the EuroCanadian mainstream. Gradually the exile that was imposed on them turned into a voluntary exile, but with severely amended social structures. One element that did remain, was the stalwart efforts of female elders, the "old ladies" (Dion, 1979: 114), who endeavored to keep up the spirits of the imprisoned reserve occupants by remaining cheerful in depressing, undesirable and uncomfortable circumstances.

Dion (1979: 115) praises the attitudes and behaviors of the older women on reserves. They exhibited a tremendous work ethic and could always be counted on to help individuals in need. They derived a great deal of enjoyment when, in the company of their sisters and friends, raided Mother Nature in her various stores – gathering maple sugar or sap from birch trees. They gathered berries, fished and dried the spoils, and hunted rabbits. A special cultural custom was the pursuit of the red willow. This was usually a well-organized event, each member of the group being equipped with a sharp knife, while several of them also carried axes. Once cut down, the willow was taken back to camp where a brisk fire had been kept going. Here the outer bark was removed and the inner bark was scraped off. Finally, the pale yellow colored inner bark was removed, dampened slightly, and rolled into a ball, then tightly wrapped in a cloth. Later the bark was dried and added to tobacco.

When cultural changes became necessary, influenced by a variety of factors – migrations, outside interventions, or government policy, women's domestic responsibilities were maintained. Very capable of making necessary adjustments to their lifestyle, for the most part they avoided outside political involvements and devoted themselves to caring for their families (Peers, 1994: 189). As it later turned out, political involvements did become necessary if Native women were to be able to function effectively within their communities.

## Contemporary Interpretations

Voyageur (1996: 93) points out that as the twentieth century got underway, Indian women ranked among the most severely disadvantaged groups in Canada. They were worse off than both nonIndians and Indian men. In many Native communities they were removed from their roles as advisors and respected community members. Some tribes even subjugated women in the spiritual domain. Female deities were replaced by male deities and their significance in this area of leadership was undermined. The *Indian Act* denied women direct participation in their band's affairs before 1951, but women who had experienced some degree of formal education managed to influence community decisions making through informal means (Fiske, 2001: 178). Some them formed voluntary associations while others organized effective protests. Still others attended conferences and meetings in order to gain relevant information to organizing petitions that were forwarded to appropriate government departments. The government finally removed its ban against women's participation in local community politics, and many educated women were ready for the challenge. Then as now, Aboriginal women were on the march (Fiske, 2001: 178).

There are other concerns. Elders today complain that children do not listen to them anymore (Friesen and Friesen, 2005: 130; Cooke-Dallin, Rosborough, and Underwood, 2000: 89). The traditional notion that elders must be respected has faded, just as it has in dominant society. The breakdown in the traditional system of learning and connecting worries Native elders. Native teachers are working hard to restore the old ways of recognizing that with age comes experience and experience, when shared with willing learners, constitutes a vital factor in their accumulation of insight. In some schools elders are being awarded a prominent place along with regular teachers. When they begin to share their knowledge it soon becomes evident that they are repositories of traditional cultural knowledge. Couture (1991: 207) suggests that elders are superb embodiments of highly developed human potential, and should be respected as such. The sharing of knowledge between participants in the classroom – elders and students – can become a reciprocal process, and when it does, it offers mutual benefits. With mutual sharing comes respect, a goal currently sought by those who are concerned about cultural losses. Properly involved, elders can assist in the process of restoring appreciation for valued Indigenous knowledge.

Times change, regardless of who is prepared for them, and after the publication of the White Paper by the liberal government of Pierre Trudeau in 1969, Aboriginal women organized lobby groups such as Indian Rights for Indian Women and the Tobique Indian Women's Group that forced women's issues before band councils and government deliberations. While all of this was going on, women continued to carry out their traditional roles – caring for their homes and fulfilling domestic responsibilities, raising and instructing children, and generally stabilizing the community. These roles have continued to this day, but new challenges have arisen. Today many Indigenous women face many of the same problems that nonNative women do – social, familial, and political. Sadly, their spiritual role has also diminished in many communities and these women will have a difficult time of it, trying to retrieve what is rightfully theirs.

Those who opposed what they perceived to be the discriminative stipulations of the *Indian Act* can give thanks to the passing of Bill C31 in 1985. Traditionally, Native women who married non-Native men immediately lost their status and relinquished the right to live on reserves. Such discrimination, since Native men marrying nonNatives were not affected, was the source of great distress and ultimately political protest for Native women. The passing of Bill C31 is essentially a EuroCanadian attempt at rendering justice because not all Aboriginal women agree that the act does produce justice. Some, in fact, argue that since women were the spiritual purveyors of their society, they needed to be extra careful with whom they were sharing that role. By marrying outside their culture they gave up that role and should not expect to retrieve it. The evidence backing this statement is grounded in the fact the fact that some women who have regained Indian Status with the federal government have not been able to retrieve their band membership. As time goes on, however, this position has been softened somewhat, and the injustice caused by the original Indian Act is increasingly viewed as unfortunate by the majority of Native people.

The current emphasis on women's issues is on childcare, community programming, and family violence. Childcare facilities are being built on many reserves, allowing mothers to enter the world of employment or enroll in upgrading programs. Programs such as distance-learning programs that assist women and families are now being developed in many Native communities so that enrollees do not have to leave their homes to attain high school, college, or university credit for their efforts. Educational programs such as Aboriginal Headstart can assist Indigenous children with school readiness, and family violence, once a taboo topic, can now be addressed openly (Ponting and Voyageur, 2004: 431).

One of the most powerful ways in which the challenges facing Aboriginal women have been made public is through the publication of their stories. Examples of this kind of literature include *Women of the First Nations: Power, Wisdom, and Strength,* edited by Christine Miller and Patricia Chuchryk (2001), *Our Story: Aboriginal Voices on Canada's Past* (n.ed) (2004), *Finding my Talk: How Fourteen Native Women Reclaimed Their Lives after Residential School,* edited by Agnes Grant (2004), and *Hidden in Plain Sight: Contributions of Aboriginal Peoples to Canadian Identity and Culture,* edited by David R. Newhouse, Cora J. Voyageur and Dan Beavon (2004).

Miller and Chuchryk offer a series of twelve essays on a variety of different topics, many of them penned by Native women. The series includes such topics as "The Colonization of a Native Woman Scholar," by Emma LaRoque, "Metis Women at Batoche, 1870 to 1920," by Diane Payment, "An Examination of Sport for Aboriginal Females on the Six Nations Reserve, Ontario, from 1968 to 1980," by Vicky Paraschak, and "The Changing Employment of Cree Women in Moosonee and Moose Factory," by Jennifer Blythe and Peggy Martin McGuire. The topics addressed in this volume are wide in scope ranging from a study of "Art or Craft: The Paradox of the Pangnirtung Weave Shop," by Kathy M'Closkey to "Gender and the Paradox of Residential Education in Carrier Society" by Jo-Anne Fiske. The content of this volume very well illustrates the many fronts on which Native women are laboring today.

Although the book does not acknowledge an editor, Rudyard Griffiths wrote the preface and Adrienne Clarkson provided the foreword to *Our Story: Aboriginal Voices on Canada's Past.* Griffiths emphasizes that EuroCanadians tend to view Aboriginal history "through our systems of understanding" (2004: 2). Clarkson admits that, given the baleful history that they have to live, "It is astonishing then, the extent to which Aboriginal peoples still engage in intercultural dialogue with generosity, understanding and goodwill" (2004: 54). We tend to agree.

The authors of the nine essays in *Our Story: Aboriginal Voices on Canada's Past* include Cree actress Tantoo Cardinal, playwright Tomson Highway, Ojibway historian Basil Johnston, journalist Lee Maracle, and Inuit writer, Rachel A. Qitsualik. Highlights of the book include these contributions. As a starting point, Métis writer, Tantoo Cardinal takes readers back to 1928 when a nonStatus Cree teacher applied his education to help organize the movement that would produce the Métis settlements of Alberta by 1935. Tomson Highway pays tribute to the late Canadian Prime Minister John Diefenbaker for pushing through legislation that granted Native people the right to vote. Lee Maracle documents the sale of the False Creek or Snaq (meaning sandbar) Indian reserve between the years 1913 and 1916. As Maracle notes, sadly the two people who once occupied the reserve, the Tsleil Watuith and the Musqueam, were once quite friendly to one another, but this is not the case today. In fact, a court case has ensued. As Maracle states, "The case has convinced me that Canada must face its history through the eyes of those who have been excluded and disadvantaged as a result of it" (n.ed., 2004: 204).

Agnes Grant's volume, *Finding My Talk*, contains the biographies of fourteen Native women who survived residential school and went on to make their contributions to society. Grant suggests that the women survived the experience, not because they adopted the value system of dominant society, but because they did not (Grant, 2004: ix). In fact, the residential school experiences of these women ranged from being teacher's "pet," to being brutally abused. The fundamental reason they were able to get past the negative aspects of the experience was that they were able to sort the good from the evil and find solace in spirituality. Eleanor Brass, for example, did not finish high school, but worked successfully as executive director of the Friendship Centre in Peace River, Alberta. Ida Wasacase obtained two university degrees and became a consultant for the Indian Language Institute, Saskatchewan Indian Nations, and First Nations Holdings. She was also head of the Commission of Indian Education Inquiry established by the Assembly of First Nations (Grant, 2004: 33). Alice French became an Inuit author, Dorothy Moore entered a religious order, and

Shirley Sterling obtained her Ph.D. at the University of British Columbia. Armed with a B.A. degree in linguistics and a master's degree in education (with a teaching certificate), Bernice Touchie took up the academic path leading to a Ph.D. These Aboriginal women, along with many others, serve as examples of success against severe odds, and appropriate models for Native children to emulate.

Newhouse, Voyageur and Beavon (2004) have rendered a valuable service in putting together a very diverse set of essays that pinpoint many of the legal and public challenges faced by Canada's First Peoples. Topics include a discussion of Indian treaties, arts and media, literature, justice, culture and identity, sports, and military. Many of the twenty-five authors selected from a potential group of fifty, are Aboriginal, all of them expert in the topic addressed by them. A series of profiles of influential Native leaders offer an enriching aspect to the book – for example, profiles of political leaders like Harold Cardinal and Albert (Billy) Diamond; poetess Emily Pauline Johnson; artists Norval Morrisseau, Daphne Odjig, Allen Sapp, and Robert Charles Davidson; and, writers Jeannette C. Armstrong, Thomson Highway, and Basil Johnston. Profiles of individuals involved in sports include Alwyn Morris, Wayne "Gino" Odjick, and Thomas Charles Longboat. Profiles of women are in equal number to men, no doubt representing a successful attempt by the editors to right a past wrong. A brief biography of professor Freda Ahenakew (University of Manitoba), for example, ends with this observation: "Freda Ahenakew is a remarkable women who deserves much recognition for her efforts to protect and promote the Cree language. As a result of her hard work, the Cree language will live forever in print" (Newhouse, Voyageur, and Beavon, 2004: 294).

In the preface to the book, David Newhouse of Trent University informs readers that the general perspective of Native peoples in Canada held by Canadians can be summarized with adjectives offered by his students when asked to describe the contemporary Aboriginal social and political situation – poverty, dispossession, anger, marginalization, and hostility. Newhouse also asked his students to list the contributions made by Indigenous peoples to Canada and they had a great deal of difficulty doing so. His co-editor, Dan Beavon experienced the same situation when he consulted with his colleagues at Indian and Northern Affairs Canada. He discovered that few Canadians know very much about Native people because most of them are fed a steady diet of media clips and sound bites that describe a people in conflict with society. This type of coverage does little to encourage interaction between Aboriginal people and mainstream society" (Newhouse, Voyageur, and Beavon, 2004: xii).

As the twenty-first century progresses Native women continue to make headway. In most Plains communities women are more likely to have completed high school and college than men. They are also more likely to hold jobs outside the home. Wishart (2004: 334) notes that today Aboriginal women are often the chief providers for their households, while men are charged with child-care, cooking, and cleaning. This change of roles has provided Indian women with increased authority and closer father-child relationships for men. However, they also bring the stresses of new responsibilities and altered self-images.

And so the saga continues. In July 9-11, 2007, the Fifth Continental Meeting of Indigenous Women of the Americas convened with the theme, "Restoring Our Balance." Stated objectives of the meeting included the development of capacity-building strategies for Indigenous women, analyzing and exchanging information on best practices to affect the lives and wellbeing of Indigenous women across the Americas, and consolidate long-lasting partnerships that might lead to the development of new projects among women of north, central, and south America. Recognizing that women in the Americas have been shortchanged in terms of political influence, the continental meeting hopes through its efforts to contribute to the reinforcement of leadership and organizational capacity of Indigenous women.

# Projections

Aboriginal women in Canada still have a long agenda. Their roles still somewhat shattered by the cultural clash of European influence, there are a number of fronts, which they must address. Commenting on the Fifth Continental Meeting of Indigenous Women of the Americas, the *Calgary Herald* (July 16, 2007) had this to say:

> Aboriginal women are Canada's forgotten demographic. The rates of family violence are higher among them than for non-aboriginal women, and when they live in abusive situations on isolated reserves, the lack of counseling and shelter resources

traps them in ways non-aboriginal urban women do not have to contend with. Only recently have governments and band councils begun to deal with the inequities . . .

Aboriginal women have reached a point in their political and individual growth that they will not sit by helplessly while others decide their future. They will undoubtedly develop new roles that combine elements of their traditional heritage along with a successful appropriation of aspects of the contemporary Canadian lifestyle that will enhance their effectiveness in their own communities. History has shown that they have always managed to do this, and they will again achieve this kind of synthesis.

## References

Armstrong, Jeanette. (2001). Invocation: The Real Power of Aboriginal Women. *Women of the First Nations: Power, Wisdom, and Strength.* Christine Miller and Patricia Chuchryk, eds. Winnipeg, MB: University of Manitoba Press, x-xii.

Benedict, Ruth. (1934). *Patterns of Culture.* New York: The New American Library.

Callahan, Marilyn. (2005). Beyond Stereotypes of Old Maids and Grand Dames: Women as Insurgents in Child Welfare in British Columbia. *Child and Family Welfare in British Columbia.* Diane Purvey and Christopher Walmsley, eds. Calgary, AB: Detselig Enterprises, 235-258.

Carter, Sarah. (2001). First Nations Women of Prairie Canada in the Early Reserve Years, the 1870s to the 1920s: A Preliminary Inquiry. *Women of the First Nations: Power, Wisdom, and Strength.* Christine Miller and Patricia Chuchryk, eds. Winnipeg, MB: The University of Manitoba Press, 51-76.

Cooke-Dallin, Bruce, Trish Rosborough, and Louise Underwood. (2000). The Role of Elders in Child and Youth Care Education. *Canadian Journal of Native Education,* 24:2, 82-91.

Couture, Joseph E. (1991). The Role of Native Elders: Emergent Issues. *The Cultural Maze: Complex Questions on Native Destiny in Western Canada.* John W. Friesen, ed. Calgary, AB: Detselig Enterprises, 201-218.

Dion, Joseph F. (1979). *My Tribe The Crees.* Calgary, AB: Glenbow Museum.

Driver, Harold E. (1968). *Indians of North America.* Chicago, IL: University of Chicago Press.

Fiske, JoAnne. (2001). Gender and the Paradox of Residential Education in Carrier Society. *Women of the First Nations: Power, Wisdom, and Strength*. Christine Miller and Patricia Chuchryk, eds. Winnipeg, MB: The University of Manitoba Press, 167-182.

Friesen, John W., and Virginia Lyons Friesen. (2005). *First Nations in the Twenty-First Century: Contemporary Educational Frontiers*. Calgary, AB: Detselig Enterprises.

Goldfrank, Esther S. (1945). Changing Configurations in the Social Organization of a Blackfoot Tribe during the Reserve Period (The Blood Indians of Alberta, Canada). *Monographs of the American Ethnological Society*. No. 8, A. Irving Hollowell, ed. Seattle, WA: University of Washington Press.

Goulet, Linda. (2001). Two Teachers of Aboriginal Students: Effective Practice in Sociocultural Realities. *Canadian Journal of Native Education*, 25:1, 68-82.

Grant, Agnes, ed. (2004). *Finding My Talk: How Fourteen Native Women Reclaimed Their Lives after Residential School*. Calgary, AB: Fitzhenry and Whiteside.

Hungry Wolf, Beverly. (1996). Living in Harmony with Nature. *Women of the First Nations: Power, Wisdom, and Strength*. Christine Miller and Patricia Chuchryk, eds. Winnipeg, MB: The University of Manitoba Press, 77-82.

Hungry Wolf, Beverly. (1982). *The Ways of My Grandmothers*. New York: Quill.

Josephy, Jr., Alvin. (1968). *The Indian Heritage of America*. New York: Alfred A. Knopf.

Lowie, Robert H. (1963). *Indians of the Plains*. New York: The American Museum of Natural History.

Maclean, John. (1980). *Native Tribes of Canada*. Toronto, ON: William Briggs. Reprinted by Coles Publishing Company.

Miller, Christine, and Patricia Chuchryk, eds. (2001). *Women of the First Nations: Power, Wisdom, and Strength*. Winnipeg, MB: University of Manitoba Press.

Milloy, John S. (1990). *The Plains Cree: Trade, Diplomacy and War, 1790 to 1870*. Winnipeg, MB: The University of Manitoba Press.

Mountain Horse, Mike. (1989). *My People, The Bloods*. Calgary, AB: Glenbow Museum.

NA. (2004). *Our Story: Aboriginal Voices on Canada's Past*. Toronto, ON: Doubleday Canada.

Newhouse, David R., Cora J. Voyageur, and Dan Beavon. eds. (2004). *Hidden in Plain Sight: Contributions of Aboriginal Peoples to Canadian Identity and Culture*. Toronto, ON: University of Toronto Press.

Peers, Laura. (1994). *The Objiway of Western Canada, 1780 to 1870.* St. Paul, MN: Minnesota Historical Society Press.

Ponting, J. Rick, and Cora J. Voyageur. (2004). Multiple Points of Light: Grounds for Optimism among First Nations in Canada. *Hidden in Plain Sight: Contributions of Aboriginal Peoples to Canadian Identity and Culture.* David R. Newhouse, Cora J. Voyageur, and Dan Beavon, eds. Toronto, ON: University of Toronto Press, 425-454.

Purvey, Diane. (2005). "Must a Wife do all the Adjusting?" Attitudes and Practices of Social Workers Toward Wife Abuse in Vancouver, 1945-1960. *Child and Family Welfare in British Columbia: A History.* Diane Purvey and Christopher Walmsley, eds. Calgary, AB: Detselig Enterprises, 259-282.

Radin, Paul. (1937). *The Story of the American Indian.* Garden City, NY: Garden City Publishing Company.

Sterling, Shirley. (2002). Yetko and Sophie: Nlakapamux Cultural Professors. *Canadian Journal of Native Education,* 26:1, 4-10.

Sterling, Shirley. (1992). Quaslametko and Yetko: Two Grandmother Models for Contemporary Native Pedagogy. *Canadian Journal of Native Education,* 19:2, 165-174.

Underhill, Ruth M. (1953). *Red Man's America: A History of Indians in the United States.* Chicago, IL: University of Chicago Press.

Voyageur, Cora. (1996). Contemporary Indian Women. *Visions of the Heart: Canadian Aboriginal Issues.* David Alan Long and Olive Patricia Dickason, eds. Toronto, ON: Harcourt Brace & Company, 93-116.

Wishart, David J. (2004). Native American Gender Roles. *Encyclopedia of The Great Plains.* David J. Wishart, ed. Lincoln, NB: Centre for Great Plains Studies, University of Nebraska – Lincoln, 333-334.

Wuttunee, William I. C. (1971). *Ruffled Feathers: Indians in Canadian Society.* Calgary, AB: Bell Books.

# Ten
# Perceptions of Aboriginal Art: The Struggle for Recognition

To the American Indian, everything he made had a function. . . . We might even say that Indians tended to decorate almost everything they used, as time and materials allowed. (Norman Feder, 1971: 8, 21)

They extended symbolic thinking to many everyday acts; for example, when a woman did some beadwork or painted a skin bag to beautify it, the designs she used were given names suggesting hidden meanings and sometimes ideas of deep religious import. (Clark Wissler, 1966: 110)

. . . many Native people have taken political action aimed at changing the way Native arts and cultures are represented in museums and university curricula. (Ruth B. Phillips, 1989: 162)

"I was so spiritually moved by the work of artist Susan Point that I immediately set about gathering all the information I could find about her. Her work definitely inspired me." This was the testimony of a student enrolled in our course on "Aboriginal Art and Spirituality," and she is only one of many to experience this kind of reaction.

There is definitely something unique about Indigenous art but it seems to have taken western civilization a series of many generations to discover this. Like any other cultural genre of art, Aboriginal art comprises a unique format and dimension, and it deserves to be equally regarded with all other schools of art. Fortunately, the tables are turning and First Nations art is slowly being awarded the status it deserves on the world front. By making it the subject of academic study, students can now immerse themselves in an entirely unique genre not previously made available to them.

# Introduction

The first nonresident visitors to North America were not particularly taken with Aboriginal art, primarily because it was different than that which they had seen back home, and so they did not understand it. Their evaluations of it therefore, were quite biased. In a book, published in 1932, New Zealand anthropologist, Diamond Jenness (1977: 209) observed:

> On the plains there was no sculpture worthy of mention, and the realistic paintings on robes and tents were pictorial records rather than expressions of artistic impulse. . . . Their repetition of straight lines, zig-zags, triangles, and rectangles, had the taint of monotony.

Jenness' assessment of Native art was clearly a reflection of his personal cultural upbringing and the inability to apply any form of cultural relativity. Another anthropologist Paul Radin (1937: 332, 336), a contemporary of Jenness, had this to say about West Coast Native North American art:

> He painted representations of them [ancestors] on the walls of his house and on various receptacles; he carved them in wood and he set these statues in front of his house. . . . No one can study the customs, read the legends and the songs, stand bewildered by the art of this much discussed region, without feeling its unutterable rawness, its lack of subtlety, its messiness and its blatant unrelieved egocentricity.

Art historians intrigued by Aboriginal art have tended, until recently, to freeze its productions in time – usually to the time of European contact. Thus much of twentieth century Native art, for example, has been classified in terms of the old regime, namely that it was more craft-like than artistic. Phillips (1989: 172) observes that the nineteenth perception was that Aboriginal art was basically representational. This view essentially rendered Native artists virtually invisible through much of the twentieth century. Most critics preferred to cast Aboriginal art in its classic traditional period and only reluctantly gave in to admitting that it too could be transformed by Indigenous artists themselves.

Freeland (2001: 73) describes a telling illustration of this perception in relation to a traditional dance performance by Australian Aboriginal dancers in a European theatre. Wearing traditional clothing, the dancers enacted a story to eerie-sounding didjeridu music, miming the ancient murder and rebirth of the hero. Then, according to Freeland, the lead dancer, still clad in a loin-cloth and body

paint, stepped out of character, grinned, shouted "G' day," and invited the audience to purchase CDs of the group's performance. The
quick transformation in scenario may have been startling to the
audience, but observers were clearly given to understand that many
cultural groups have adjusted quite well to technological change
while maintaining some semblance of their traditional lore.

A parallel shift that acknowledges the reality of cultural change
is occurring in the academic world. Now, thanks to the efforts of
new art historians working from an interdisciplinary perspective, has
Native art become recognized as comprising a unique genre, one
that has its own distinct identity but manages successfully to mix
the old with the new. Even then, much of its content is shrouded in
historical mystery and should be perceived as such. Phillips (1989:
175) states quite bluntly; "As art historians we must ask ourselves
whether we still believe that there are things which can be
expressed visually but cannot be perfectly translated into words."

One of the difficulties in writing about Native North American art
is that Native languages have no exact equivalent for the post-
Renaissance term, "art" (Berlo and Phillips, 1998: 9). This implies
that Native artists traditionally were unreflexive in creating art and
functioned without the aid of specific criteria by which to determine
value or aesthetic quality. This left European-inspired critics to classify Indigenous art as fundamentally representational. This view
was erroneously arrived at because of two factors. First, European
explorers arrived with a healthy dose of ethnocentrism on their
hands, believing that their way of life back home was immeasurably
superior to any other. This perspective hindered them from making
objective appraisals of Indian art. Second, these explorers were
either unequipped or unable to make sense of an entirely different
genre of art and therefore virtually dismissed it. It was well into the
early part of the twentieth century when ethnographic descriptions
of Aboriginal art portrayed Indigenous art as an expression of ethnic culture. Generations later, when the turbulent 1960s arrived and
the various elements of social societal life were under scrutiny, that
perception was also questioned. The 1960s in North American history gave rise to an abundance of serious questions about both
American and Canadian lifestyles motivated by Vietnam war pro-
testers, hippies, Black power and Red power advocates, and the
American Indian renaissance movement (Lincoln, 1985).

When the decade of the 1960s was finally over and a time of
peace (some would call it lethargy) set in, the social climate was

such that new explorations of Aboriginal culture and spirituality could take place. Many former hippies and new age worshippers quickly endorsed First Nations cultures and spirituality, and with that thrust came a new perspective on Native art. Museums and institutions of higher learning responded by re-examining time honored approaches to Indian art and gradually a new history of Native American art emerged. Phillips (1989: 168) suggests that the new art history replaces the notion of a universal "history of art" with a number of discrete but overlapping "histories of art," for example, the art of women, art of social strata, and ethnic art. As a consequence, new art history seeks to establish a series of new non-hierarchical redefinitions of the term, "art," to include many forms of visual representation formerly excluded from the canon and depicted as craft or curios, folk art, or popular art.

A change in attitude was evident during the 1970s when museums began to display Indigenous art as art. Exhibitions at the Whitney Museum in New York City, the Walker Center in Minneapolis, and the Nelson-Atkins Museum in Kansas City seemed to have changed the longstanding perception of Indian art as craft or merely representational (Bernstein, 1999: 60). These exhibitions portrayed Indigenous art in terms of its spiritual or ceremonial implications instead of as ethnographic productions. Gradually, the public began to catch on, paralleled by the efforts of many First Nations promoters who agitated for the construction of Native operated galleries and museums, paralleled by movements on the part of nonNative collectors to seek out Aboriginal artists. These factors encouraged the foundation of Native-run galleries and museums.

## Theories of Art

Cynthia Freeland, Professor of Philosophy of Art at the University of Houston, has published widely on topics in philosophy of art and film. Freeland (2001: xvii) suggests that there are many different theories of art including ritual theory, formalist theory, imitation theory, expression theory, cognitive theory, and postmodern theory. Theories are intended to help things make sense rather than create obscurity through the development of in-house jargon and use of weighty words. A difficulty arises, however, when specific art forms cannot immediately be interpreted through the channels of a single theory. This is particularly true of the genre of contemporary Indigenous North American art because its forms have been affected by a variety of influences from colonialism to postmodern developments. Traditional Indigenous art, however, while it may seem to be easier to categorize, no longer exists in what might be called classic or pure forms.

Gebhard (1974: 9) projects four possible embellishments or bases of art including: (i) technical; (ii) simple aesthetics; (iii) ideographic; and, (iv) sacred. The first two categories, technical and aesthetic, pertain to form; that is, they may be described as comprising art for art's sake. Ideographic art is viewed as a pictographic link emphasizing cultural beliefs and values. Hidden meanings behind artistic expressions vary in the sense that they may be representative of different cultural aspects. Pictographic art, a third form, is intended to tell a tale or relate an episode of history. This art form is therefore instrumental as an avenue of expression; it serves as an additional guidepost to cultural maintenance. Analyzing such an art form should assist viewers in gaining clarity or enhanced appreciation for specific cultural aspects. The fourth category, sacred art, which perhaps best describes traditional Native art, poses some difficulty unless it is understood that the original inhabitants of North America believed that every behavioral enactment, including art, had spiritual or theological implications. In fact, their works of art were often expressions of spiritual relation and obligation.

There is little or no evidence to indicate that First Nations artists traditionally categorized cultural obligations as different than spiritual obligations. Individual obligations were just that – they were spiritual obligations, and therefore also cultural. The concept of interconnectedness, so deeply imbedded in Indigenous thought, mandated that individuals were spiritually accountable for their every thought and action. Creating art for art's sake or engaging in purely technical acts would clearly violate this belief. In this sense, although traditional Native art would generally to be considered representational, it was much more than that. All drawings and designs, and other forms of artistic expression, whether implanted on rocks, teepees, shirts, or war axes, were indicative of something, but also had spiritual implications. Artistic designs were traditionally placed on everyday items such as moccasins and positioned facing  the wearer, rather than toward others. The symbolism of the design was for the wearer's benefit and appreciation (Ewing, 1982: 20). This was true of decorated birch-bark dishes, wooden bowls, effigy pipes and pipe bags, drums, woven bags, flutes, and other items. Among the Iroquois, self-directed effigies were often carved on pipes. Directed toward the smoker, these effigies represented the individual's guardian spirit. Smoke was believed to be a kind of incense or intermediary avenue by which to connect with the spirit world. Therefore it was the responsibility of the smoker to maintain as close a connection as he could with the effigy. A contemporary interpretation might be that placing decorative symbols in any direction would be to display their beauty, but in fact artistic designs were not intended for the aesthetic enjoyment of others. Their symbolism was strictly intended as a reminder of deeper truths to the user. When the Europeans arrived, they influenced the transfer of decorative designs on certain items to the viewer's direction so they could be admired for their aesthetics by them.

This arrangement fit in better with their worldview. Although sacred in focus, traditional Indigenous art was not without technical awareness or embellishment. The cosmological principle of balancing antithetical elements was hinted at subtly in the asymmetrical use of color in decorative designs on formal clothing. Contrasting colors could be used on either side of otherwise symmetrical designs, or pairs of designs might alternate colors (Penney, 2004: 67). Art traditionally implied a multiplicity of meanings among the First Peoples of Canada. Among Plains Indians, for example, artistically decorated garments symbolized community identity, but could be used to express individual personal wealth and accomplishment. Many designs were rooted in their cosmological beliefs using the principle of balancing antithetical forms. Interestingly, Blackfoot male artists, for example, usually painted life forms related to war or hunting exploits, while women created geometric designs such as borders, boxes, hourglasses, or feathered circles.

In traditional First Nations societies the universe was viewed as an interrelated entity with all parts and processes closely intertwined. Its workings were to be honored in all human activities. To interfere with one component would affect others. Obligations to one aspect could not be severed from obligations to the others. The earth was perceived as a unity in which humans played only a small part. The role of humans was to be good stewards of the resources available to them and they were mandated to show respect and appreciation for them in every human enactment.

The Aboriginal concept of the God of the universe, the Creator or Great Spirit, did not provide for any notion of the Supreme Being as a personal friend, protector, or comforter; the Creator was traditionally regarded from a distance with awe. It is important to recognize that the Indigenous people saw the origins of all of their works of art and craft as the result of what they had been shown in dreams and visions and these were connected to the Supreme Being. Something about the form and decoration of each item always moved the owner to a point beyond its earthly purpose (Mails, 1997: 5). To understand Indigenous art then, requires delving into their spiritual belief system.

Young Man (1992: 81) suggests that it is virtually impossible to comprehend the meaning of Aboriginal art unless one understands the arguments that rage around it. He insists that when judging Aboriginal art, a Native perspective should be applied, rigidly and boldly, and made an integral part of the various critical, analytical, and historical instruments that make up the lexicon of art. This is particularly necessary whenever the edges of the Native American art world rub against that of dominant society. Some observers, for example, are reluctant to buy into the notion that First Nations cultures like any other, are apt to change with the times. Native artists, however, now face hard decisions about their role and opportunities as artists. Many of them, trained in modern art institutions, are familiar with recent global art movements. However, they feel an obligation to stick to the forms of their traditional culture, but are also attracted by postmodern developments (Freeland, 2001: 81). The perspective seems to be, "Dominant society is expected to change, but Aboriginal cultures are best left as they are." The reality is that Native cultures should be allowed to enjoy the right to change just as any other society does. Aboriginal people may add elements and meanings to their cultural repertoire or amend them at will, and their art will reflect these changes. Pen and ink drawings, for example, are now being used by Aboriginal artists to represent an art form that was traditionally accomplished with porcupine quills and birchbark. This evolution of change is a basic right, but western society does not always practice what it preaches. Too often the view is that classic forms of Indian culture should be maintained not only as a token of the past, but in order to provide perpetual subject matter for historians of the First Nations past. In this sense there is no such a phenomenon as "authentic" Indigenous art because each example is only authentic in so far as it reflects a particular historical moment (Berlo, 1992:4).

# Outside Influences

The European invasion of North America influenced a major transformation of Indigenous art. The introduction of new materials into any cultural configuration usually affects traditional styles, and the First Nations were no exception. The fur trade introduced brightly colored glass beads, silk ribbons, rolled copper, tinned cones, and aniline dyes to replace more pastel colors of native pigments. Aboriginal women adopted European methods of weaving and needlework and adapted them to suit the needs of their people. The introduction of beadwork enabled a greater variety of art work because beads were easier to work with than native materials such as porcupine quills. Many changes occurred after 1800 due to the intensified contact experienced by First Nations with Europeans.

The arrival of various European groups such as explorers, fur traders, and settlers motivated many Native artisans to adapt their craft to meet the demands of trade and later tourism. Many introduced materials had no prototype in classic Indian culture. New products translated into art forms required new and often manufactured visions and interpretations to accompany them. Some new art forms were invented entirely devoid of tradition or spiritual overtones because they were simply copies or downgraded versions of traditional forms. The widespread use of whole animal skins as containers also disappeared from everyday Aboriginal use after the First Nations acquired steel pots and were exposed to a variety of European pouches and bags. Envelope-shaped pouches with triangular flaps became very popular among the Delaware, Shawnee, and Cherokee tribes. Beautifully decorated, these pouches (parfleches) were desirable items of exchange among Indian bands and were frequently found far from their place of origin. It was typical of casual visitors not to be able to differentiate between valid traditional forms and those that were invented and produced strictly for the emerging market. This trend comprised another indication of the creative genius of Aboriginal cultures although informed observers might interpret the move as a weakening rather than a shift of traditional belief systems.

The introduction of the reserve (reservation) system also affected Native art because a sedentary lifestyle eliminated the need for many traditional forms of interaction. Warfare was virtually abolished, thereby affecting the decoration of weapons like shields and war clubs; hunting became a minor activity, and thereby reduced pride in hunting tools. The vision quest also became less important.

Military societies were disbanded, and what remained of First Nations ceremonial life was transported underground.

The current need in the field of art is to encourage artists of Indigenous descent to infuse the contemporary scene with the fruit of their own visions, not too much bothered by the philosophies, language, dance, drama, and worldview of dominant society (Young Man, 1992: 86). Too often there is real conflict between the values of a conquering, consuming society and one that descended from a more naturalistic view. As Young Man (1992: 86) states, ". . . there is a deep-seated need in Western and Native American thinking to resolve these conflicts to our mutual satisfaction."

## The Spiritual Dimension

Unlike the sociopolitical tumultuous decade of the 1960s, when many protesting groups defied all forms of social structure including organized religion, more recently it has become quite appropriate to engage in discussions of religious or spiritual matters. This change in social practice and perception has probably come about because religious beliefs are so often affiliated with current developments on the world scene. Many international sites of political unrest are connected to religious fanaticism of one kind or another, and television viewers are becoming more familiar with references to related underlying belief systems. Unfortunately, a deeper understanding of basic fundamentals of the represented belief system is not often pursued.

A similar situation prevails with regard to Indigenous faith perspectives, which, in the past, have often been construed by EuroCanadians as just another form of religious belief, even heathen or comprised of superstitions. Historically, it was a nonNative habit to describe alternative belief systems as "heathen" simply because these systems were nonChristian. There was no middle ground; belief systems were either categorized as Christian or heathen and the latter simply had to be converted. This ingrained perspective obviously made it very difficult for the European newcomers to appreciate the intricacies of Aboriginal metaphysics. This narrow point of view also made it difficult for European newcomers to understand other aspects of Indian culture.

Although some scholars still use the word "religion" when discussing traditional Aboriginal spirituality, it is fundamentally inaccurate to describe their belief systems as religious in the modern sense. Analysis of traditional Indigenous belief systems reveals that the word spiritual is much more appropriate since theirs was a perspective that pervaded all aspects of life. It was not a part-time occupation or simply a Sunday obligation. This statement cannot easily be exaggerated because the ancients daily spent much time in spiritual activities. As Santee Sioux elder Charles Alexander Eastman (Ohiyesa) once stated, "In the life of the Indian there was only one inevitable duty – the duty of prayer, the daily recognition of the Unseen and the Eternal. His daily devotions were more necessary to him than daily food" (Friesen, 1998: 21).

For Aboriginal people, spirituality has always been understood as an effort to participate in the mystic; the search represents a need to deal with grand existential and metaphysical questions that each individual must all face for himself or herself (Rushing, 1999: 170). As Tatanga Mani (Walking Buffalo) of the Stoney tribe (Nakoda First Nation) once noted; "We saw the Great Spirit's work in almost everything: sun, moon, trees, wind, and mountains. Sometimes we would approach the Great Spirit through these things" (Kaltreider, 1998: 138).

Among traditional Indigenous societies, the earth was regarded as a foundation for spiritual activities and even for being itself. Mother Earth was regarded as the Provider and Caregiver, the Sustainer of life itself. Paula Gunn Allen (Houle, 1991: 61) describes it in these words;

> The earth is the source and the being of the people, and we are equally the being of the earth. The land is not really a place, separate from ourselves, where we act out the drama of our total destinies; the witchery makes us believe that false idea. The earth is not a mere source of survival, distant from the creatures it nurtures and from the spirit that breathes in us, nor is it to be considered an inert resource on which we draw in order to keep our ideological self functioning, whether we perceive that self in sociological or personal terms.

Walters (1989: 18) adds;

> To the Indians, all life is sacred, part of the infinitely renewable cycle that permeates and defines their cosmology. A critical element in this cycle is their relationship with the land – their reverence for Mother Earth. . . . they viewed themselves as caretakers of a realm that defied individual ownership and, more important, was beyond value.

Although scholars have reliably documented significant cultural differences among the various North American Aboriginal peoples at the time of European contact, their metaphysical systems feature a degree of unanimity. Fundamentally, the daily spiritual activities of the First Nations of North America centuries ago overshadowed and completely absorbed their lifestyle. Arts and crafts were no exception because spirituality was perceived as an all-pervading phenomenon. By contrast, contemporary EuroCanadian forms of religion may be defined as fulfilling a separate, innate category of the human consciousness that issues certain insights and indisputable certainties, about a Superhuman Presence (Runes, 1967). There are other differences; formalized religion can generally be dichotomized, broken down, analyzed, and separated into parts, and it may be differentiated from other life concerns. Being religious means to be sincere about something; it could be an activity, a cause or campaign, or an enterprise, and it will absorb a great deal of devotion and energy. By contrast, Aboriginal spirituality does not target an activity or cause, it is not a separate component of life; in a very real sense, it constitutes life itself.

Typically, in North America, people think of a religious individual as one who believes in the existence of a Superior Being (traditionally called  God), and the way to connect with Him is through recipes or formulae originated by an organized religious form. To be religious is to be committed to and act in accordance with a code of ethics derived from sources outside and considered "greater" than oneself. The code may not necessarily incorporate a personalized theism, that is, belief in Almighty God per se. Melford Spiro (Banton, 1966) defined religion as consisting of some form of organized or patterned social behavior, wherein religious adherents respond, both in daily activities and specific rituals, to the perceived will of some entity that is seen as having greater power than themselves. Durkheim suggested that the gods of religion may be nothing more than collective forces, incarnated, and hypostatized under a material form. Thus religion becomes a series of beliefs by means of which individuals represent the society in which they are members and the relationships, obscure but intimate, which they have with it (O'Toole, 1984).

A schematic of three components is sometimes employed to analyze religious systems including: (i) beliefs, which inspire fear, awe or reverence; (ii) a prescribed or implied list of expected behaviors; and, (iii) a long-term promise of eventual respite perpetuated by hope (Hewitt, 1993; Friesen, 1995). If individuals have been raised in a particular environment with an explicit religious bent, they may contend that the attending code posits implicit mandatory expectations for the individual, and even for society as a whole. It will make little difference if the cultural milieu in question fosters alternative beliefs. An orientation without theistic implications would hold that the cosmos is a given and its origins, cycles, and mandates are not questioned because they are perceived as perpetual. They are because they are. However, there is an implied obligation on the part of the human race to care for the earth, keep its air and water pure, and reprimand anyone who violates this code.

The original peoples of North America had fairly definitive beliefs about the universe and their role within it, but these beliefs were rarely formally articulated nor mandated as individual obligations. Their creed could hardly be perceived as that. The universe, the earth, and all natural resources were perceived as gifts from the Creator, the Great Spirit. It was assumed that appreciative behavior for these gifts would be a logical response on the part of recipients and expressed in various forms of ceremonial life. Expectations of appreciation were not explicitly spelled out; neither was any form of institutional membership required as one might expect in a Bahai, Christian, Jewish, Muslim, or Sikh organization.

The First Nations of North America traditionally built their cultures on a foundation of reverence for the universe and for all living things. They did not necessarily differentiate between material and nonmaterial phenomena or necessarily between humans and animals. The threads of ordinary life and spirituality were so tightly interwoven that the sacred and the secular were indistinguishable (Zimmerman and Molyneaux, 1996: 767). Theirs was an holistic perspective which meant that all living things, indeed every living entity should be perceived as having a connection to every other living entity including humans, animals, birds, fish, and plants. The universe was viewed as a complex unity, made up of variety and diversity, but still comprising a synthesized whole. The implied obligation of humankind, therefore, was to live in harmony with the rhythms of nature and respect its balance. For Indigenous people, this implied affording equal respect to all living entities.

There are other traditional Indigenous beliefs worth noting, particularly the Indigenous concern about remaining spiritually in tune with the universe. In the First Peoples' spiritual quest little emphasis was placed on activity per se because activity was always viewed as a means to an end, indeed a spiritual end. Being, not doing, was

perceived as a higher virtue. Another highly valued axiom was looking after family members. Any band member in need or, for that
matter, anyone who was even remotely related to an individual with
resources, could expect to have their needs attended to by that
individual. These expectations were even more firmly cemented in
tribes that featured clan systems. The biblical injunction, "It is more
blessed to give than to receive" (Acts 20:35b KJV), was core to the
essence of Indigenous faith. Anyone who had resources to share
was expected to do so; it was never appropriate or necessary for
anyone to beg for help. Community meant just that.

Eschatology is the division of metaphysics that deals in final
events, and its principal concerns have to do with the destiny of
individuals and the final state of the universe. Related questions
include, "What happens when people die? Is there life after death?
What should individuals do to prepare for life in the hereafter (if
there is one)? and, "What will be the future state of the universe?"
There are no scientifically supportable answers to these questions,
of course, but that reality has never stopped theologians and
philosophers from speculating. Some have even dared to elaborate
their suppositions in volumes of print. As time passes and their fore-
casts prove wrong, the originators sometimes had to scramble to
recalculate and reinterpret their faulty prognostications.

Traditionally the Aboriginal peoples of North America were hardly practicing eschatologists. The First Nations of North America valued the challenge of the "perennial now" (Couture, 1991) too much
for that. Adherence to the oral tradition also precluded that possibility because life was viewed as a phenomenon of the here and
now; it was to be lived with a perpetual appreciation of the present.
That appreciation would be demonstrated in any and all forms of
individual action. As Eastman (1980: 149) stated,

> The attitude of the Indian toward death, the test and background
> of life, is entirely consistent with his character and philosophy.
> Death has no terror for him; he meets it with simplicity and per-
> fect calm, seeking only an honorable end as his last gift to his
> family and descendants.

Traditionally Aboriginal Shamans did not delineate a difference
in kind between the spirit world of their existence and any possible
future state. They perceived the human world as permeated by
spirit beings who enter and leave the human domain. Traditional
Aboriginal philosophy does not differentiate between human and
animal spirits, but assumes that every living thing, soul or spirit pos-

sesses spirit as an animating and personifying principle (Berlo and Phillips, 1998: 24). Much of Indigenous art portrays these beliefs, albeit in a manner not readily appreciated by the uninformed or casual observer.

If the spirit world perceived by Indigenous people could be separated from Immanuel Kant's perceived phenomenological realm, there have always been nonAboriginal individuals willing to try to make contact with it through various means. Traditionally, Indigenous people believed in an afterlife domain of the spirits, but procedures for making contact with that world were not specifically spelled out except perhaps for such rituals as the vision quest celebrated by Plains Indians. That there was a future state was never in dispute, but its precise specifications were not speculated nor elaborated. What mattered was how individuals lived out their daily lives in response to the design that the Creator had designated for them. They were expected to live life purposefully and try to understand life and its learning opportunities in terms of the process of becoming complete (Cajete, 1994: 148). This expectation included the world of art.

## Spirituality and Art

Most religiously-inclined individuals are misinformed about the meaning of spirituality, because they have been influenced into thinking that its expressions are less valid than their own religious affiliation. Partly this happens because religiously-influenced individuals are not usually trained to investigate alternative ways of thinking or believing. They have probably been taught that spirituality implies belief in spirits (pantheism) rather than belief in monotheism. The notion of spiritualism has not fared well in organized religious circles because of the emphasis on the role of the "medium" which allegedly serves as the contact between the seen and unseen worlds. Aboriginal spirituality was for several centuries classified as form of spiritualism because of the inherent belief that individuals could receive messages or learn lessons from any living entity including humans, animals, birds, fish, and even plants. The primary difference between contemporary forms of spirituality and traditional Aboriginal spirituality is that the latter does not mandate the necessity of mediation, but it can happen as a supplementary source of inspiration.

Having been so long bypassed as a "legitimate" way of believing, Aboriginal spirituality offers a great deal of intrigue. Harrod (1995: 30) emphasizes that religious beliefs have always been central to the Indian way of life. Harrod unfortunately uses the term religion when the word "spirituality" would be more accurate in this context. Harrod (1995: 30) states;

> Religion [spirituality] was an essential ingredient in the creation and maintenance of the social identities of all these peoples, and religious energies were foundational in the construction of new social relations as they responded to either improved or chosen alterations in their environment.

Today's more open attitude to appreciating the wider parameters of both spirituality and art is encouraging. Some students of Aboriginal culture and spirituality are beginning to realize that the propensity of First Nations past and present, to link spirituality to every human activity could have implications for modern life. Some scientists and philosophers have come to the conclusion that metaphysical notions such as nihilism and postmodernism tend to ignore the important sector of ontological meaning. The increased interest in spirituality is most fortuitous because it would be very limiting to ignore the study of promising alternative belief systems. If the Indigenous worldview had been explored and appreciated a bit more a few centuries ago, the realms of philosophy and art would have been richer for it. It may not be too late to make up for this deficiency.

## The Challenge

Some philosophers, academics, and even art critics might not be in agreement with the proposal that contemporary society could benefit from incorporating elements of a traditional Indigenous worldview. Nor would these individuals necessarily be convinced of the merits of its hidden meanings or degree of sophistication. It would be easier to dismiss it as belonging to an earlier, more primitive stage in the evolution of civilization. Dissanayake (1990: 92, 95), for example, raises doubts about the claims of individuals who intimate that their personal visions may be influenced by a Divine connection (shamans, for example). No doubt Dissanayake would have the company of academics who refuse to accept the premise that otherworldly experiences can mandate sacred obligations.

Assuming a more positive stance, however, one that holds promise in terms of furthering pedagogical excellence through better, fuller understanding could provide intriguing benefits. To begin with, serious study of Aboriginal philosophy (or any alternative worldview) can open up new vistas of learning and offer expansive ideas for consideration. Second, Aboriginal thought is uniquely focused on spirituality, a quality that heretofore has not played a significant role in the scientific community. Perhaps this "objective" attitude needs to be changed and, like true scientists, we ought to consider every possible resource in learning about, analyzing, and perhaps resolving global issues.

In the traditional world of the Aboriginal, prayer was a vital component of spirituality. Today, spirituality, particularly the appreciation of prayer may be making a comeback. A contemporary proponent of the need to explore the spiritual domain, Larry Dossey is a medical doctor who gave up practicing medicine to study prayer (Dossey, 1997b). Overwhelmed by the mounting evidence of hundreds of studies that proved the efficacy of prayer in hospital settings, Dossey quickly discovered that the medical community was reluctant to buy into the phenomenon of prayer for at least a dozen reasons including the following: (i) the notion that spiritual healing is often equated with mysticism; (ii) healing power is believed to be possessed only by individuals who are strange or different; (iii) lack of replicability; and, (iv) the fact that healing has laws that appear to be different than those of other sciences (Dossey, 1997b: 278).

## Projections

It may now be the time to reevaluate the rather slipshod way in which spirituality has been dismissed as a legitimate avenue of research. In traditional Aboriginal societies the perception of spiritual power was not limited to human beings. It was believed that spirits infused all animate and inanimate phenomena. Animal, birds, fish, and plants were all considered to possess spirits with which humans could communicate. Individuals did not regard lightly the divergency of creation because the interrelationships of these various entities were considered complex. The First Nations of Canada believed that art may be utilized to make visible the spiritual elements of a way of life. They viewed the arts as an avenue by which to express one's respect for and understanding of the spiritual mysteries of the universe. The hope of this pursuit being undertaken is now more encouraging than ever, and no doubt great rewards of understanding can come of its engagement by both seekers and scholars.

Perhaps American Indian Commissioner John Collier was correct when he urged a reconsideration of the traditional Indigenous worldview, particularly their respect for the earth, indeed the universe and its spiritual workings. As Collier observed: "They [the First Nations] had what the world has lost. They have it now. What the world has lost the world must have again, lest it die" (Bordewich, 1996: 71). For the Aboriginal people of the past, art was one avenue by which to express earth respect. That belief in modified form still exists today. To ignore this unique worldview is to neglect a significant component in the search for academic, scientific, and pedagogical excellence.

## References

Banton, Michael, ed. (1966). *Anthropological Approaches to the Study of Religion.* London, UK: Tavistock.

Berlo, Janet Catherine. (1992). Introduction: The Formative Years of Native American Art History. *The Early Years of Native American Art History: The Politics and Scholarship and Collecting.* Janet Catherine Berlo, ed. Seattle, WA: University of Washington Press, 1-21.

Berlo, Janet Catherine, and Ruth B. Phillips. (1998). *Native North American Art.* New York: Oxford University Press.

Bernstein, Bruce. (1999). Contexts for the Growth and Development of the Indian Art World in the 1960s and 1970s. *Native American Art in the Twentieth Century: Makers, Meanings, Histories.* W. Jackson III, ed. London, UK: Routledge, 57-74.

Bordewich, Fergus. (1996). *Killing the White Man's Burden: Reinventing Native Americans at the End of the Twentieth Century.* New York: Anchor Books.

Cajete, Gregory. (1994). *Look to the Mountain: An Ecology of Indigenous Education.* Durango, CO: Kiva Press.

Couture, Joseph E. (1991). Explorations in Native Knowing. *The Cultural Maze: Complex Questions on Native Destiny in Western Canada.* John W. Friesen, ed. Calgary, AB: Detselig Enterprises, 53-76.

Dissanayake, Ellen. (1990). *What is Art For?* Seattle, WA: University of Washington Press.

Dossey, Larry. (1997a). *Prayer is Good Medicine.* New York: HarperCollins.

Dossey, Larry. (1997b). *Healing Words: The Power of Prayer and the Practice of Medicine.* New York: HarperCollins.

Eastman, Charles A. (Ohiyesa). (1980). *The Soul of the Indian: An Interpretation.* Lincoln, NE: University of Nebraska Press.

Ewing, Douglas C. (1982). *Pleasing the Spirits: A Catalog of a Collection of American Indian Art.* New York: Ghylen Press.

Feder, Norman. (1971). *Two Hundred Years of North American Art.* New York: Praeger.

Freeland, Cynthia. (2001). *But Is It Art?* London: Oxford University Press.

Friesen, John W., ed. (1998). *Sayings of the Elders: An Anthology of First Nations Wisdom.* Calgary, AB: Detselig Enterprises.

Friesen, John W. (1995). *Pick One: A User-Friendly Guide to Religion.* Calgary, AB: Detselig Enterprises.

Gebhard, David. (1974). *Indian Art of the Northern Plains.* Santa Barbara, CA: University of Santa Barbara.

Harrod, Howard L. (1995). *Becoming and Remaining a People: Native American Religions on the Northern Plains.* Tucson, AZ: University of Arizona Press.

Hewitt, W. E., ed. (1993). *The Sociology of Religion: A Canadian Focus.* Toronto, ON: Butterworths.

Houle, Robert. (1991). The Spiritual Legacy of the Ancient Ones. *Land Spirit Power: First Nations at the National Gallery of Canada.* Diana Nemiroff, Robert Houle, and Charlotte Townsend-Gault, eds. Ottawa, ON: National Gallery of Canada, 43-73.

Jenness, Diamond. (1977). *The Indians of Canada.* Seventh edition. Toronto, ON: University of Toronto Press.

Kaltreider, Kurt. (1998). *American Indian Prophecies: Conversations with Chasing Deer.* Carlsbad, CA: Hay House.

Lincoln, Kenneth. (1985). *Native American Renaissance.* Berkeley, CA: University of California.

Mails, Thomas E. (1997). *Creators of the Plains.* Tulsa, OK: Council Oak Books.

O'Toole, Roger. (1984). *Religion: Classic Sociological Approaches.* Toronto, ON: McGraw-Hill Ryerson.

Penney, David W. (2004). *North American Indian Art.* London, UK: Thames & Hudson.

Phillips, Ruth B. (1989). What is 'Huron Art'?: Native American Art and the New Art History. *The Canadian Journal of Native Studies,* IX:2, 161-186.

Radin, Paul. (1937). *The Story of the American Indian.* Garden City, New York: Garden City Publishing Co., Inc.

Runes, Dagobert D. (1967). *Dictionary of Philosophy.* Totowa, NJ: Littlefield, Adams & Co.

Rushing III, W. Jackson. (1999). Editor's Introduction to Part III. *Native American Art in the Twentieth Century: Makers, Meanings, Histories.* W. Jackson Rushing III, ed. London, UK: Routledge, 169-173.

Walters, Anna Lee. (1989). *The Spirit of Native American Beauty and Mysticism in American Indian Art.* San Francisco, CA: Chronicle Books.

Wissler, Clark. (1966). *Indians of the United States.* Revised edition. Garden City, NY: Doubleday & Company.

Young Man, Alfred. (1992). *îndîgena: Contemporary Native Perspectives.* Gerald McMaster and Lee-Ann Martin, eds. Vancouver, BC: Douglas & McIntyre and Hull, PQ: Canadian Museum of Civilization, 81-99.

Zimmerman, Larry J., and Brian Leigh Molyneaux. (1996). *Native North America.* Norman, OK: University of Oklahoma Press.

# Eleven
## The Changing Role of
## Aboriginal Leadership

Decision-making was conducted not by fiat or by majority vote; rather the aim in band council, as in the extended family, was reaching consensus. . . . A band chief . . . best understood not as a position of authority but of stewardship, of caring for the people who looked to it for leadership and guidance but not control. (Chief John Snow, 2005: xxii)

When the Europeans arrived in North America they encountered a series of social systems that functioned radically different than those they left behind. Local residents, the First Nations of North America over the centuries had developed finely tuned social and political institutions that worked well for them. Suddenly resident First Nations were confronted by ethnocentric representatives of foreign nations who sought to change their way of operating and at the same time demean the underlying assumptions of their way of life.

Much of European thought at this time was influenced by ideas posited by such writers as British philosopher John Locke. Locke did recognize that the First Nations of North America had developed workable institutional forms of governance, but he considered them inadequate in terms of what he deemed to be the universal criteria for developing a political society. Locke observed that Aboriginal "kings" did not have exclusive rights to declare war or peace, and their governing bodies lacked three essential distinctives – an institutional judiciary, a legislature, and a functioning executive. Locke did allow that the indigenous peoples probably did not have a need for these forms, but he also made note of the lack of desire on the part of the Indigenous people to develop them (Baptiste, 2000: 24-25). Apparently, they should have wanted to develop them, despite the fact that their arrangements were working quite well for them. Backed by this kind of thinking, the first European arrivals in North America were hardly in a position to make objective evaluations about the institutional life of their new neighbors. Their idea of leadership was based on the notion of kings and princes who had absolute authority over their subjects. This, in fact, was almost completely opposite to the First Nations system that was based on consensus and individual freedom (Dempsey, 1997: 13).

# The Traditional Way

After centuries of experience and experimentation, most Indian societies in North America had developed efficient systems of governance. Most tribes operated with a system of chiefs who usually arrived at their position of authority through the hereditary process. These individuals were usually trained early for the role he or she would serve in later life.

It would be erroneous to assume that the various First Nations across Canada designed very similar socio-political systems for they did vary from one cultural region to another. Each tribe or nation over time developed an arrangement that worked for them, whether they were Eastern Maritime First Nations, Woodland, Plains, Plateau, West Coast, or Northern First Nations. The various First Nations were broken down into some 50-53 tribal systems based on language distinctions.

Traditionally there were certain common features among the various systems, to be sure; for example, all tribes posited respect for the individual (regardless of age), respect for spiritual elders, and governance by consensus. Chiefs, who usually obtained that position by hereditary means, were not politicians in those days, nor were they necessarily warriors, hunters, or individuals with great wisdom. They were, however, expected to care for their people, try to provide for their needs, consult with elders, and serve as representatives for their people when in contact with outside groups.

When a chief passed on and it came time to choose a successor there was sometimes confusion about whom to choose if a chief had several sons or daughters. Sometimes a would-be successor would attempt to claim the office by expressing his or her abilities in ways to attract attention and gain approval of the band. After all, successor selection was by consensus, not by open vote. Dempsey (1997: 14) notes that when Red Crow of the Kainai First Nation sought the office of chief he competed with his older brother by openly seeking the favor and backing of tribal members. When Red Crow attained the office of chief, his brother and followers loyal to him then left the camp and joined another band. Denig (2000: 38-

39) notes that a similar practice was in place among the Assiniboines. When a chief passed on, by either death or assassination, his successor absolutely had to possess the requisite governing powers, known and acknowledged bravery and wisdom, moderation, and justice. If a near relative did not have these characteristics, someone else with strong family connections would likely be chosen for the office. Mandelbaum (1979: 290) confirms this practice among Plains and Woodland Cree among whom merit alone gave title to the position. Red Tailfeathers (Dempsey 1997: 15) of the Kainai First Nation stated it this way:

> To be chief or leader among the Indians in those days, one had to be chivalrous and to fight his way to it. One had to prove himself during encounters with the enemy. One step in this ladder to fame was to be able to capture many horses and come home safely with them. . . . You have to make yourself one by your deeds.

The governance system of traditional Plains people revealed a measure of flexibility when a new chief came to office (McFarlane, 2000: 50). As mentioned, it was not the case that the eldest son or daughter necessarily became chief when the respective parent who had served in that office expired. Sometimes an individual who seemed logically destined for that office might be passed over because he or she did not exhibit the necessary characteristics to carry out effectively the duties of the office. A number of tribes also practiced having more than one chief, each charged with specific duties. A permanent war chief, for example, could call a raid whenever he felt it necessary to do so and he did not require approval of band council (Driver, 1968: 371). Temporary chiefs were also in vogue in some societies; these individuals might be appointed by band council to serve during a hunt or the formation of a war party.

Traditionally there were checks in place for chiefs who might not have the best interests of the people at heart, one of them being the formation of a new band headed by a new chief. Bands were often subdivided for a number of reasons, only one of them being disillusionment with the current chief's behavior. Sometimes new bands broke off or members simply drifted away because band population grew too large; for example, for nomadic tribes it was easier to break camp with smaller numbers. Sometimes emerging charismatic individuals were able to lure tribal members to a new vision and a new band would result. In addition, quarrels and squabbles among tribal members often rose to such levels that leaders came involved and a new band was formed. An older band might dissolve after the death of a prominent chief in the hearts of the followers, if there was no one to take his or her place. Some bands might have changed their name after this happened, perhaps in the memory of the individual who passed on (Ewers 1989: 96-97). Despite practices which outsiders might perceive as somewhat dysfunctional, the system worked and there was still an element of unity in it. For example, despite their differences all bands related by culture in the plains usually met together during the summer months for fellowship and the celebration of the Sundance. This meant that the various Cree, Ojibway, Tsuu T'ina, and Stoney bands met together, as did member tribes of the Blackfoot Confederacy.

Generally speaking, Aboriginal chiefs were respected leaders, but they did not warrant respect merely because they held office. They were expected to provide what was expected of a chief in the sense that they brought people together and commanded consensus. Band council meetings would often continue well into the night until consensus was reached. A chief's abilities were often judged on the basis of his or her capacity to bring about unity. Many chiefs had other recognized talents related to hunting, wisdom, or possessing spiritual knowledge. In the latter case, they worked closely with elders who basically constituted and provided the spiritual foundation for the tribe.

Most Plains tribes recognized a head chief who usually presided at band council meetings. The head chief's role would be more prominent during the tribal encampment in the summer when important decisions regarding the next year were made. Generally speaking, the role of chief included such responsibilities as presiding at meetings of band council, making decisions that affected the general welfare, and managing trade or negotiating peace treaties with other tribes (Dunsmore, 1979: 132). Internally, chiefs were often called upon to settle disputes among the membership, arrange food and other provisions for needy families, and participate in all tribal ceremonies. In instances of food or other shortages, chiefs would often offer up their own resources or go without rather than see their people suffer. This was expected behavior. Chiefs did not usually mete out punishment to wrongdoers. That was taken care of by selected men's societies who policed the camp. Their role was quite limited during the rest of the year when the various bands went their own ways.

# Contemporary Trends

When the Native hereditary system of leadership selection was replaced by the election process, the very foundation of what had been an effective system of governance was shaken. Traditional Aboriginal leadership grew out of social systems that were organized around kinship groups whose relationships and responsibilities were defined by tradition and custom. Individuals were essentially responsible to anyone even remotely related to them by bloodlines. The system worked, and if there were resources of any kind anywhere in camp, no one was left in need.

In later generations and to this day, due to outside influences, instead of serving as stewards and caregivers, Indian chiefs have become politicians – individuals who run for office and, predominantly have to do whatever it takes to become elected. Now responsibility has shifted from people to process; it has become less human, less personal, and, in plain words, purely political. Changes in leadership patterns among the Ojibway, for example, used to be the result of human as well as natural forces. Changes in fur trade company structures and policies and the decline of fur and game bearing animal populations affected their lifestyle and very social structure. Missionary pressure, exerted through European forms of schooling, coupled with governmental regulations virtually transformed their way of doing things (Peers, 1994: 138-139).

The business of electing officers to manage band affairs is still in many ways alien to Canada's First Nations, and for more than a century, the Canadian government has purposefully aimed its policies and practices toward replacing traditional Native leadership systems with colonial structures, philosophies and norms (Boldt, 1993: 120). The Indian Affairs Branch has been able to justify its actions by acting under the authority of the *Indian Act* which has served as the primary vehicle for undermining traditional leadership systems.

# The Elder Phenomenon

Tribal cultures of the past featured a spiritual leadership stratum and a well-defined role for individuals who were believed to possess vital knowledge of the faith. These individuals were also authorized to perform related rituals and ceremonies. In certain contexts these leaders were also considered experts on life. Generally known as elders (or priests or shamans) these individuals were responsible for carrying forth to the next generation the valued beliefs, traditions, and practices of their respective tribes.

During the centuries before European contact, Indian elders were considered very important members of their communities, and they exerted a profound, political, social, and spiritual influence in their neighborhoods. Elders and grandparents were essentially responsible for raising children and transmitting tribal customs and traditions to younger members of the community. In some tribes they also played an important role in identifying tribal members for leadership positions. Among the Iroquois Confederacy nations, for example, clan mothers had power to appoint chiefs and depose them if they did not live up to expectations.

In precontact days, Aboriginal elders were not typically older people with experience; they were recognized because they exhibited a variety of gifts and talents. True, some of them were recognized for their knowledge and wisdom and were frequently sought out for guidance on tribal or individual matters. Others possessed the gifts of counselling and healing – spiritual, psychological, and physical. They often performed ceremonies that provided recipients with the relief they needed. There were also elders who had the right to perform revered rituals and ceremonies, often having derived the privilege of doing so via a period of apprenticeship.

Although the role of respected elders has made a recent comeback, in modern times a kind of "circus elder" has emerged in the form of individuals who "look elderly" and who are willing to perform minor rituals publicly for a price. These individuals are not usually recognized nor respected in their local communities and they do not function in that capacity at home. Medicine (1987: 143) cautions that elders who have "lost their way" are not true representatives of authentic Native ways of knowing. Unfortunately, although members of the older generation may have lost their Aboriginal cultural focus, they may still attempt to serve in the role of elder. The status of elder may appeal to such individuals as a means of trying to get back some of the authenticity they have lost, or never were party too. By acting as elders they may hope to redeem themselves. Organizational leaders  interested in having Indian representation on their boards often engage circus or seeking elders because they appear to be interested in serving in that capacity. Too often their role is merely that of figurehead or tokenism (Stiegelbauer, 1996: 40). NonAboriginals need to be aware that not every short sentence uttered by an elderly Indigenous individual in broken English is worthy of being categorized as an elder saying.

For the most part the elderly are still treated with respect in First Nations communities, but not all are regarded as spiritual elders. Native cultures fully realize that all elderly people have valuable knowledge to share about their life experiences, but only a few have specialized knowledge about the workings of the cosmos that uniquely equips them to provide counsel to their communities (Knudtson and Suzuki, 1992: 179-180). These individuals usually have a deep abiding humility and a reverence for life and the natural world. They also carry out a teaching role as facilitators and guides. Today, as historically, these individuals see their mandate as one of guiding their people toward a better knowledge of their rituals and growth processes that might help them become more aware of themselves as well as the natural world and their place within it.

Today Indigenous rituals of spirituality are once again presided over by elders, that is, men and women who over time have demonstrated to their communities their appropriateness for that office over time. They have also received a kind of formalized community approval. Consistent with the "vagueness" or elusiveness of the oral tradition, even today spiritual elders are not elected nor appointed, nor do they have special training for their task. They simply "emerge over time" and their wisdom and knowledge is informally recognized by their community.

In some tribes there is still observable a definite process by which certain individuals become elders. The individual's motivation to take up that role could have been sparked by a personal, spiritual, or political event or events that turned them towards the traditional way. As Stiegelbauer (1996: 47) points out, such experiences may motivate individuals to take up the challenge of learning tribal teachings and ceremonies in an active and involved way by practicing them. They in turn may be called upon by the community to "give those teachings back" and through that process become "recognized" as teachers and elders. However, their corollary experiences outside of learning those teachings may also contribute to their ability to help others find their culture and regain a healthy self-esteem.

The verification of eldership is the local Aboriginal community. Elders develop their stature through interaction with their neighbors. Their statuses and gifts are reinforced by the people who respect them and come to them for guidance. The current resurgence of interest in seeking direction from these spiritual advisors is evident among many North American tribes today and comprises a strong indication of the increasing importance of their role and the vitality of the Aboriginal ways (Couture, 1991b; Lincoln, 1985). In recent years elders have been invited to participate in Aboriginal organizational structures while continuing to consult with troubled youth on an individual basis (Medicine, 1987: 148). It might be too much to hope, but it would be encouraging to discover a genuine intrigue on the part of both Native and nonNative observers to share in this revival.

When incoming Europeans first encountered the various cultural configurations of the North American First Nations, they did not appreciate the nuances of the office of shaman (or spiritual elder), particularly the belief that some shamans were perceived as having strong supernatural powers. Commonly dubbed "medicine men" or "medicine women" by the newcomers, they questioned the belief that the powers of some elders went far beyond the arena of healing. They were seen as being able to establish direct contact with the spirit world or themselves be possessed by the spirit. They were approached by individuals in the tribe about such matters as success on a hunt, the time for planting crops, or seeking good fortune in war.

## Formal Societies

Plains Indian tribes have always featured formal religious societies known as sodalities or secret societies. These operated much like the religious orders committed to specific purposes within certain Christian denominations. Members of sacred societies, like the Horn Society in the Blood (Kainai) tribe, were believed to have special spiritual powers and they were feared and respected by their compatriots. Even today, for example, people are not to walk in front of a Horn member, even other elders, lest the power of the Horn members affect them (Taylor, 1989).

At one point in the mid nineteenth century the Blackfoot had seven age-graded men's societies in their religious structure, the youngest being called the "Mosquitos," and the oldest, the "Buffalo Bulls" (Ewers, 1989: 105). When older members of the latter group passed away their secrets died with them and a new society, the "Pigeons" (or Doves) was organized. As a new society, however, it held the lowest rank among the seven. To make things more complicated, the members of these societies also belonged to different hunting bands which were only active during the summer months. At times the head chief of the summer camp would call on one or two of the societies to police the camp and the summer hunt. Each society performed its unique ceremony during the celebration of the Sundance, which was practiced during this time.

Formal societies of the First Nations played an important role in preserving and passing on spiritual knowledge. During the years when governments banned certain religious practices, societies took their practices underground until it was safe to reveal them again. The passing of the *Indian Act* in 1876 greatly affected the role of elders and therefore they were not longer perceived as having important political influence (Boldt, 1993: 119). Instead, chiefs who now had to adhere to the mandate of official government forces were viewed as those to be reckoned with in terms of tribal decision-making. They in turn became responsible to officials of the Indian Affairs Branch of the Department of Indian Affairs and Northern Development.

Today a revival of many First Nations sacred practices has spread throughout out many North American Native communities (Lincoln, 1985). Couture (1991b) contends that elders today hold the key to the survival of humankind because they alone have access to the knowledge that may save Mother Earth from being extinguished. Today elders are also being sought out for healing and inspiration, and interpretation of past and present events. Battiste (2000: 201) emphasizes that elders are a critical link to Aboriginal epistemology through their knowledge of Indigenous language. The last vestiges of the traditional forms of Aboriginal languages exist in the hearts and minds of Indigenous elders.

# Identifying Elders

Someone once asked, "What is an elder?" Neither age nor gender plays a role in the definition of an elder. Elders are teachers of wisdom and traditions because they know the secrets of life; they have walked the path. They know the way to inner peace, which is one of life's ultimate goals. They know not anger, nor spite. They are the ones who would tell you that among the great values of life the most precious are spirituality, compassion, and honesty. (Wilton Goodstriker, 1996: 25-26)

In the days before European contact, an individual's status as elder had to be welcomed, recognized, and affirmed by the community. Their various gifts were affirmed by the manner in which members of the community approached them. They might be consulted for advice, for healing, to conduct a specific ceremony or ritual, or for the assignment of an Indian name. Eva McKay (1999: 298), a Dakota Sioux elder explains the functioning of elders this way:

> For approaching an elder it depends on what kind of help they are asking for. Is it spiritual help, or is it healing, or do they want us to visit? You have come here to visit, you wanted to ask me something. For spiritual help, like asking for a name, they would bring Tobacco. It is so important for everyone who is an Aboriginal person to have a name, an Indian name. One of our stories is how we can be recognized by the Creator if you do not have a name?

The duties and expectations of Native elders were traditionally quite complex. Among other things, some already mentioned, elders sometimes gave formal recognition to tribal members. Male members, for example, were often recognized for their talents as hunters, warriors, or guides, but before they could be formally executed these enterprises required a form of spiritual confirmation. This enactment was the responsibility of the shaman or elder who had been affirmed by the community to perform such a task. As Lakota elder Beatrice Medicine (1987: 141) has explained; elders are ". . . those people who have earned the respect of their own community and who are looked upon as elders in their own society." This recognition was more than the assignment of status; it was also a form of affirmation for specific expectations and responsibilities.

Since the office of elder has been revived and strengthened in recent decades, the functions of the office have been magnified and expanded. Today elders are being called upon to help communities with decisions regarding everything from education and health issues to community development and self-government. Others are involved in developing "culture-based" programs, language instruction, and curriculum-making. Still others have become active planners and decision-makers in education (Castellano, Davis, and Lahache, 2000: 98). It has been concluded that elders can offer input that takes the minds of their apprentices beyond the walls of the classroom. "Such strategy provides the community with contact with tradition, traditional beliefs, ceremonies and experiences, and a philosophy unique to First Nations cultures" (Stiegelbauer, 1996: 40).

Meili (1992: x), who spent many months researching the elder phenomenon in Alberta, came to this conclusion:

> The elders I met were happy to chat. . . . They had much in common, but the most significant was a deep concern for young people. They urged young people to get an education and take their rightful place in the patronizing, dominant society, taking the best from Native and non-Native worlds. The elders live prayerful lives in the arms of the sacred, some blending Indian and Christian beliefs learned from their mission schools days. All have strong work ethics and are active in their communities, health permitting.

## Projections

Over the years that we have been privileged to study First Nations ways, we can honestly say that elders in all of the communities we have worked in have been very kind to us. Many of them, now deceased, went well beyond the call of mere hospitality by informing us of valuable information and proper protocol in a variety of situations. We have met, conversed with, and learned from these rare individuals in church and school settings, private conferences, and public gatherings. We owe them a great debt and can only hope that some of it can repaid by our carefully handling and sharing the truths they gave us and which are contained in this book as well as in our other research publications.

Today there are significant economic and social forces at work that are greatly affecting the role of elders as large populations of Indigenous people leave their reserves and move to urban areas. Some elders have also migrated to nearby cities and towns along with their families. There they have carved out a unique niche for themselves as ritualists, consultants, and counsellors. Some elders even make house calls in response to individual or family requests for counselling or prayers. Once again, as is so typical of their history, they have demonstrated an ingenious ability to change with the times. These changes, however, have only affected their geographic location, not their spirituality. Perhaps the time will come when the nonNative world will also seek out the kind of advice that Aboriginal elders can offer to a needy world.

Soon it may be possible to observe with evidence and conviction – Aboriginal elders – their time has come!

## References

Battiste, Marie, ed. (2000). Maintaining Aboriginal Identity, Language, and Culture in Modern Society. *Reclaiming Indigenous Voice and Vision.* Marie Battiste, ed. Vancouver, BC: UBC Press, 192-208.

Boldt, Menno. (1993). *Surviving as Indians: The Challenge of Self-Government.* Toronto, ON: University of Toronto Press.

Castellano, Marlene Brant, Lynne Davis, and Louise Lahache. (2000). Innovations in Education Practice. *Aboriginal Education: Fulfilling the Promise.* Marlene Brant Castellano, Lynne Davis, and Louise Lahache, eds. Vancouver, BC: University of British Columbia Press, 97-100.

Couture, Joseph E. (1991a). The Role of Native Elders: Emergent Issues. *The Cultural Maze: Complex Questions on Native Destiny in Western Canada.* John W. Friesen, ed. Calgary, AB: Detselig Enterprises, 201-218.

Couture, Joseph E. (1991b). Explorations in Native Knowing. *The Cultural Maze: Complex Questions on Native Destiny in Western Canada.* John W. Friesen, ed. Calgary, AB: Detselig Enterprises, 53-73.

Dempsey, Hugh A. (1997). *Tribal Honors: A History of the Kainai Chieftainship.* Calgary, AB: Kainai Chieftainship.

Denig, Edwin Thompson. (2000). *The Assiniboine.* Edited by J.N.B. Hewitt. Regina, SK: Canadian Plains Research Center.

Driver, Harold. (1968). *Indians of North America.* Chicago, IL: University of Chicago Press.

Dunsmore, Frances. (1979). *Chippewa Customs.* St. Paul, MN: Minnesota Historical Society Press.

Ewers, John C. (1989). *The Blackfeet: Raiders of the Northwestern Plains.* Norman, OK: University of Oklahoma Press.

Goodstriker, Wilton. (1996). Introduction. *The True Spirit and Original Intent of Treaty 7.* Treaty 7 Elders and Tribal Council, with Walter Hildebrandt, Sarah Carter, and Dorothy First Rider. Montreal, PQ: McGill-Queen's University Press.

Knudtson, Peter, and David Suzuki. (1992). *Wisdom of the Elders.* Toronto, ON: Stoddart.

Lincoln, Kenneth. (1985). *Native American Renaissance.* Berkeley, CA: University of California Press.

Mandelbaum, David G. (1979). *The Plains Cree: An Ethnographic, Historical and Comparative Study.* Regina, SK: Canadian Plains Research Center.

McFarlane, Peter. (2000). Aboriginal Leadership. *Visions of the Heart: Canadian Aboriginal Issues.* David A. Long and Olive P. Dickason, eds. Toronto, ON: Harcourt Canada, 50-80.

McKay, Eva. (1999). If they read what you are writing, this is the teachings, this is some of the teachings that we want them to read about. *In the Words of Elders.* Peter Kulchyski, Don McCaskill, and David Newhouse, eds. Toronto, ON: University of Toronto Press, 289-310.

Medicine, Beatrice. (1987). My Elders Tell Me. *Indian Education in Canada: Volume Two, The Challenge.* Jane Barman, Yvonne Hébert, and Don McCaskill, eds. Vancouver, BC: University of British Columbia Press, 142- 152.

Meili, Dianne. (1992). *Those Who Know: Profiles of Alberta's Elders.* Edmonton, AB: NeWest.

Peers, Laura. (1994). *The Ojibway of Western Canada: 1780-1870.* St. Paul, MN: Minnesota Historical Society Press.

Snow, Chief John. (2005). *These Mountains are Our Sacred Places: The Story of the Stoney People.* Calgary, AB: Fitzhenry and Whiteside.

Steigelbauer, S. M. (1996) What is an Elder? What do Elders Do? First Nations Elders as Teachers in Culture-based Urban Organizations. *The Canadian Journal of Native Studies,* XVI: 37-66.

Taylor, Fraser. (1989). *Standing Alone: A Contemporary Blackfoot Indian.* Halfmoon Bay, BC: Arbutus Bay Publications.

# Twelve
# Land Claims:
# A Perpetual Challenge

The political process that has become known as "land claims and in which many of our First Nations are involved with the federal and other governments, is devastating to our cultural values. In order to participate in the process, our statements and language are forced to become sterile and technical. Our documents must be written in language suggested by lawyers and understood by judges. The legal jargon we must use contains concepts of ownership that directly contradict our spiritual understanding of life. As a marginalized people, forced to live on tiny plots of land, we encounter the worldview of the wealthy and powerful in the land claims process and are forced to compromise or die. (Chief Dan George in Bird, Land, and Macadam, 2002: 29)

Anyone even vaguely familiar with or participated in even a brief conversation about Indian land claims will have encountered at least once an individual with this viewpoint; "I do not understand why our government is continually engaged in discussions about land claims with the Indians. We beat them in battle and took over their lands. What's to bargain about? It's as simple as that!"

Needless to say, the forgoing perspective is not only without logistic merit but historically incorrect. Land treaties negotiated with Canada's First Nations were undertaken on a nation to nation basis, each side apparently recognizing the other as an equal partner in the process. As history reveals, at least one partner (government) was not negotiating in good faith.

## Introduction

The subject of Aboriginal land claims was allotted a great deal of press during the last half of the twentieth century and will likely be discussed well into the twenty-first century. It all started in 1763 when the British took over French holdings in the New World (North America), and issued an edict about ownership of Indian lands.

Formally known as the Royal Proclamation of 1763, the edict stated that land could not be taken from Aboriginal communities and used for settlement unless the Crown first made a treaty with local First Nations. The Proclamation confirmed that Aboriginal inhabitants had land rights that were to be respected by subsequent governments and immigrants.

In the years that followed, many treaties were signed between governments and First Nations, but as Chief Dan George pointed out (quote on previous page), negotiations required that Indians first learn to bargain in language they did not understand, and in a language that was founded on entirely different ideas about land ownership than what they were used to. The end result was that most treaties compensated Indian people with limited land space, small amounts of money, and other commitments – many of which were not adequately met by government. Another difficulty was that a number of signed treaties were friendship treaties or peace treaties, and were not to be construed as having anything to do with land. Finally, when the dust of formal treaty-signing (during the 1870s and the 1880s) had settled there were areas that remained legally unaffected. These areas included much of the land on the west coast of Canada, two-thirds of the Province of Quebec, and various other assorted areas across the nation.

When the treaties were signed, the process of land settlement began, and the two cultures – European and Aboriginal had opportunity to mesh and/or clash. The federal government's role in all of this was basically to fulfill the dream of nation-building – to form a nation from coast to coast. What hindered that dream, at least partially, was the existence of many Indian bands who occupied lands that were viewed by incoming settlers as ideal farming and ranching lands. Political and business leaders of the new Canada were geared to negotiate for some of those lands with First Nations so that western Canadian expansion could begin. As several historians have suggested, one of the primary goals of the plan was to provide an outlet for the overflow of population created by dwindling farmlands of the Canadian West. In order for western migration to flow peacefully, the west had to be made safe for settlement. This implied the removal of Indians from desired lands and settling them on smaller tracts to be called reserves (Treaty 7 Elders and Tribal Council, with Walter Hildebrandt, Dorothy First Rider, and Sarah Carter, 1996: 207).

As treaty-making got underway, it was the intention of the federal government to make treaties across the whole prairie region to the mountains. In the summer of 1873, however, the federal cabinet changed policy and decided to proceed on the basis of settler need. When settlers migrated to specified areas, representatives of government began negotiations with local Aboriginals, but basically forged ahead with a clear idea in mind of what they wanted final settlements to look like. They tended to ignore their protests when the latter insisted on remaining on occupied lands (Taylor, 1999a: 15-16). A compensating feature appears to be the fact that First Nations in the Treaty No. 8 area were required to give up proportionately less land than their counterparts in Treaties Nos. 6 and 7 areas (Daniel, 1999: 70). No doubt incoming settlers preferred areas further south.

## Treaty Intent

The fact that many land claims are currently being pursued in Canada is founded in the history of treaty-making. Chief John Snow (2005: 39) suggests that the process of treaty-making was bathed in uncertainty and confusion. The result is that the first major ten treaties in Canada (made between 1871-1899) have a great deal of variation among them. There was also conflicting content between the published reports of the federal government and the personal correspondence of treaty negotiators. Apparently treaty negotiators performed their duties without being familiar with Aboriginal laws and procedures, and certainly without knowledge of Indian languages. Many land claims today are based on this misunderstanding.

Traditionally, Canadian Indians regarded oral language as living, binding, and permanent. Under North American Aboriginal unwritten law, whatever words were spoken and oral promises given during formal negotiations, were committed to memory and considered legally binding. By contrast, government negotiators considered only written promises binding. Thus the cultural clash that occurred resulted from failure to communicate to one another the manner in which knowledge, truth, and commitment were viewed. Adding to the confusion was the problem that everything said by either party had to be translated and interpreted, usually by someone who was inadequately equipped to do so. Some have suggested that the government cared so little about treaty negotiations that their representatives only haphazardly recorded the wishes and demands of

Aboriginal leaders. Government negotiators were cynical about the whole process and were basically eager to get Aboriginal people out of the way so they could get on with nation building. Once the First Nations were outnumbered by incoming settlers, they could be ignored or put off without much consequence. This is exactly what happened (Treaty 7 Elders and Tribal Council, with Walter Hildebrandt, Dorothy First Rider, and Sarah Carter, 1996: 209-210).

Specifically, the treaties were designed to meet five federal objectives. The *first* was to provide the government with legal title to lands occupied by First Nations. *Second*, the government hoped to lure Canadians living in Eastern Canada to migrate to the west. *Third*, the government hoped to relocate Métis and Status Aboriginals to new locations with as little cost as possible. *Fourth*, government officials were worried about possible American expansion into western Canada so they wanted to populate the area as a means of assuring claim to the land. They were not at all oriented to recognizing Aboriginal settlement in the West. *Fifth* and finally, it appeared that many First Nation leaders, fearing encroachment on their lands, actually favored treaty-negotiation with the hope that benefits might be obtained (Treaty 7 Elders and Tribal Council, with Walter Hildebrandt, Dorothy First Rider, and Sarah Carter, 1996: 212). One thing is certain, not everyone had the same idea about treaty-making.

Taylor (1999b: 44) points out that a variety of opinions existed about treaty-making. With regard to Treaty No. 6 and Treaty No. 7, for example, the former Indian negotiators bargained hard for better benefits because they were aware of what they were losing. Their leaders agreed to give up surface rights for the benefit of incoming farmers. In their view, treaty benefits were, in part at least, compensation for what they were giving up or sharing. Unlike the Indian signers of Treaty No. 7, they had less of an idea in mind about the Queen looking after her subjects through treaty signing. Treaty No. 7 people, on the other hand, believed very strongly that this was the case. They believed negotiators who insisted that the Queen Mother would not let them down.

## Treaty Aftermath

The ink was barely dry on the treaty papers when Aboriginal people began to realize that the government had little intention of carrying out their promises. In fact, government officials were not being entirely honest when they conceived the idea of setting aside certain lands for Indian reserves. Moreover, they acted without obtaining the necessary information before proceeding with the reserve concept.

There were other complications. Most First Nations in British Columbia, for example, did not and do not have treaties with the federal government. Theoretically, this means that they have never ceded title to lands they occupy, and they should be considered rightful owners of said lands. Provincial and federal governments brushed the issue aside and tried to ignore it. In 1916, an organization known as the Allied Tribes of British Columbia was created to undertake legal proceedings towards government recognition of their ownership. Ignored by Canadian governments, in 1926 this organization sent a delegation to London but was rebuffed; they were told to settle the matter with the dominion government. The Canadian government did not want to deal with the matter because if they did, any decision made could also affect other areas where First Nations lived who also did not have signed treaties – Quebec, northern Ontario, Yukon, and Northwest Territories. The British Columbia government did begin to pay treaty money to Status Aboriginals, but beyond that, little happened. In fact, the federal government passed legislation making it illegal for anyone to raise money from Indian band members for the purpose of pursuing land claims (McFarlane, 2000: 66). The government justified this action on the basis that the legislation would stop unscrupulous parties from acting on the Indians' behalf, with only self-interest in mind. Indian leaders regarded the legislation as racially motivated and devastating to their inherent rights.

When Canadian government officials conceived the idea of creating Indian reserves, their maneuvers were founded in the British imperial tradition. That tradition smacked of blatant colonialism, and to a certain extent (and to their credit), Canadian officials were able to break away from that tradition. For example, the Canadian government did avoid the tradition of treating First Nations as "conquered" peoples and thus exercising wardship or guardianship over them. Paternalism, however, has not been avoided, and a number of parties including church officials and school administrators have certainly demonstrated that characteristic.

The British tradition inherited by the Canadian government of 1867 was to respect the land base of Indigenous people; this was assured by the British in the Royal Proclamation of 1763. In 1860, even before Britain transferred its responsibilities for "Indians and Indian lands" to Canada, officials had been under pressure from nonNative settlers to modify its policies. In its defense, the Canadian government held firm and did not yield to the pressures exerted by a protest group of nonNatives representing a population of two and a half million compared to less than two hundred thousand Indians (Melling, 1967: 34-35). Despite this resistance on the part of government, the establishment of reserves was not by any means done in the interests of the Indigenous people. Several factors were in play.

*First,* it helps to keep in mind that Indian reserves were created primarily to set aside specific areas for settlement by nonNative people. No reserves were created in areas where nonAboriginals had ample opportunity for any settlement in which they might be interested (Melling, 1967: 37). In fact, the best land was always kept for EuroCanadian settlement. Later it was discovered that pursuing an agricultural lifestyle was particularly difficult for First Nations because the land most suitable for farming had been taken away from them.

*Second,* it should be noted that to a certain extent reserves were invented for the administrative convenience of government. If rations were to be given to Indians during the time in which they made the transition from buffalo hunters to farmers, the government wanted to undertake the task with a minimum of expense. By assigning First Nations to specific plots of ground and having them governed by powerful Indian agents, the government essentially created a simplified administrative pattern for itself. As Henlin (2006: 93-94) notes, the *Indian Act* of 1876 set a framework in place that configured Indian communities as rural municipalities with a simple governmental administrative pattern. The arrangement effectively isolated First Nations on lands outside mainstream society and thus made it easier to control their communities. The intent was to replace traditional Indian governments with band councils and assign them comparatively little power. This gave government the opportunity to seize control of valuable resources located on reserves, take charge of band council finances, and impose an unfamiliar system of land tenure. This form of colonialism continued until quite recently. Today, armed with better education and a higher degree of familiarity with standard governmental procedures Native leaders are hard at work trying to undo the past and negotiate more equitable arrangements.

A *third* factor to consider in the formation of Indian reserves is that because the poor land on which Natives were placed, was simply not suitable for farming (Snow, 2005: 62-63). As a result, with limited economic prospects, many reserves became centres of disillusionment and despair. A welfare mentality set in, and coupled with the near dictatorial powers of the Indian agent, the atmosphere deteriorated into hopelessness and dependency (Melling, 1967: 38). This trend continued well into the 1960s when a movement of cultural revitalization began among the various Indian tribes of North America (Lincoln, 1985).

By 1921 the reserve system had been formalized to include most areas of the country. Essentially the system functioned to dichotomize Indian people and the rest of Canadians. Efforts to "civilize the Indian" and turn him to farming were underway with accompanying slogans such as, "Don't hunt for $100 a season if you can make $1 000 by farming. Learn farming" (Robertson, 1970: 130). Government efforts were to little avail, however, because the cultural adjustment from following the buffalo to scratching the surface of the ground and planting seeds was often too much. Several Plains Cree tribes did take up successful farming, but other tribes had greater difficulty in doing so. Some men refused to work with "digging sticks" because they considered it demeaning; if anything, they deemed it women's work. The Stoney Indians at Morley, Alberta, were assigned land near the Rocky Mountains, generally unfit for farming. After a few years several families took up cattle ranching with better results. This situation prevailed until the Stoney Nation discovered gas reserves on their land and began to mine them.

*Finally*, the subject of commissions and expropriations of Indian lands must be addressed (Dickason, 2006: 219). There are areas of land in many regions of Canada developed by EuroCanadians that legally belong to First Nations, but unfair and secret negotiations have deprived them of the land. In Treaty No. 6 area, for example, the southeast portion of the City of Edmonton was taken from the Pahpahstayto (Passpasschase) Indian band by squatters. The band was forced to abandon the area, withdraw from the treaty, and accept scrip. As Dickason (2006: 221) points out;

> By 1886, the reserve counted only 13 families remaining, who later agreed to join the Enoch band to the west of Edmonton, completing the surrender. Today descendants of the disbanded group are seeking reinstatement as a band and a settlement for their lost lands.

Another Treaty No. 6 fiasco occurred in central Saskatchewan, twenty years after this treaty was signed with Cree First Nations. A tract of land situated about an hour's drive north of Saskatoon was homesteaded by Lutheran and Mennonite farmers in the late 1800s with federal approval, since there were no Aboriginal people living there. Without consulting the Cree First Nation, the government gave the settlers permission to settle the land. Many years later these settlers discovered that they were indeed occupying Indian land. In 1977 a group of young Native activists came to the region to raise the issue of their loss of land. Their expressions of concern made local farmers feel quite uneasy and tensions between the two groups lingered. In 2006 the situation was resolved with original Aboriginal land occupants acknowledging ownership of said lands by local farmers. The farmers, in turn, resolved to support the First Nations in government dealings for justice (*Mennonite Reporter*, October 30, 2006).

The history of Manitoba is rife with similar examples of government and Aboriginal land dealings. Shortly after treaty-signing, the Indians were preyed upon by land speculators and dishonest settlers who tricked them into selling off parcels of land, which the Indians were led to believe were privately owned. The land predators then mined timber from the land without providing any form of compensation. Despite making promises to work towards restitution, the federal government adopted a spectator stance and did nothing to intervene. It has been estimated that during the prime ministership of Wilfred Laurier, some 600 000 to 700 000 acres of Indian land in Canada were sold for an average of ten to fifteen cents per acre. Reasons for government inaction were premised on the idea that incoming settlers had to be accommodated (Treaty Days, 1971: 56; Friesen, 1977: 127).

## Turn of Events

Now dial forward to the 1950s and 1960s. The prairies are changing; young people are flocking to the cities and small towns are being abandoned. In larger perspective, Indian reserves were victims of the same economic forces that were driving nonNative farmers out and luring their children to urban centres. The difference was that Aboriginals really had no place to go; they were not welcome in the cities, and they did not have sufficient education even to take casual labor jobs. If they did relocate to the city, many of them soon ended up in most undesirable social situations.

In fact, there were three categories of Indian youth who sought a better life in the city. The first group consisted of students and job-seekers; they were people with purpose. Bored with the futility of trying to get ahead on the reserve, these bold individuals risked becoming the targets of racism, discrimination, and prejudice, and forged ahead (Buckley, 1993: 93). The second and largest group of urban migrants, sometimes rudely labelled "welfare Indians," were philosophical traditionalists. Caught in a severe time warp, few of them managed to obtain employment and after a few months of trying, ended up back on their reserves. The third group was people caught in the middle. Although they had strong work habits and plenty of purpose, they ended up working at menial jobs and for low wages. They lived in slum-like homes and because they were far away from family and friends, were often lonely. Some managed to obtain advice and assistance from local manpower offices, but the best they could expect was short term or part time work for inadequate pay (Buckley, 1993: 95).

As the 1960s got underway, new developments became evident. Small numbers of Indian young people began to attend postsecondary institutions and became quite successful in adapting to city life. Some of them returned to reserve life where they assumed positions of leadership. Now educated in government ways, these new leaders were often quite helpful in negotiating with industry, oil companies, and government agencies. According to Adams (1995: 177f), some them took the opportunity to endorse the colonizing policies of federal and provincial governments and thus dominate their own people. Adams insisted that that these Native colonizers did not have community support nor credibility, and for the most part local residents let them get away with it.

## Projections

Most students of the treaty signing phenomenon are familiar with these phrases; "As long as the rivers run, as long as the sun shines," and, "as long as the grass grows," as indicators of the alleged long term intention of keeping promises made in the treaties. Aboriginal people are well aware that the promises have not been kept, but, a number of attempts have been made to rectify the situation. A first serious effort was made in 1969 with the publication of the White Paper by the Liberal government of Prime Minister Pierre Elliott Trudeau. In effect, the government recommended the abolition of Indian treaties and the *Indian Act,* and suggested that Indian people be regarded as all other Canadian citizens and begin to receive health, education, and welfare services from provincial sources. The Red Paper, authorized by forty-four chiefs of Alberta in 1970 posted the first resistance to the idea. The chiefs suggested that the government honor the intent of the treaties and the *Indian Act* and not merely try to abolish them.

The challenge now before Native communities is whether or not to reopen and perhaps revise the treaties so tribes can gain access to resources that will allow them to develop sustainable economies and end their reliance on government welfare and other subsidies (Warry, 2007: 132; Cockerill and Gibbins, 1997: 385). One way to accomplish this, although somewhat undesirable from an Aboriginal point of view, would be to extinguish the treaties in exchange for settlement of land claims. At the very least is the option of trying to reinterpret the intent of the treaties. Henlin (2006: 259) emphasizes that government policy and legislation has remained unchanged for over a century, and left intact a government structure that is unfair and often oppressive to Indigenous peoples. Essentially the system disempowers a substantial portion of the Aboriginal population and concentrates power in the hands of a small elite group. The end result produces a culture of dependency sporting the adjoining factors of corruption, mismanagement, resource waste, lateral violence, and other forms of abuse.

Today it is mandatory that a new political philosophy be initiated that more fairly distributes power, goods and services implies political and legislative change. Henlin suggests that the first step towards new system building will require that Indian bands clean up their own back yards. Members of First Nations communities must see to it that their politicians become responsible to them, not merely to the safety of distance to the governmental Indian Affairs office in Ottawa. Henlin's view is that the current lack of private ownership under the *Indian Act* should be examined to determine how best to allow individual members to raise monies using reserve based property as collateral. Given this arrangement, Indigenous people will better be able to join and compete in Canada's successful economy. Today Canada is in the best position ever to create constructive change for moving First Nations forward. Obviously one cannot simply rely on government action to fulfill this need. A strong supportive public will is needed.

# References

Adams, Howard. (1995). *A Tortured People: The Politics of Colonization.* Penticton, BC: Theytus Books.

Bird, John, Lorraine Land, and Murray Macadam. (2002). *Nation to Nation: Aboriginal Sovereignty and the Future of Canada.* Toronto, ON: Public Justice Resource Centre.

Buckley, Helen. (1993). *From Wooden Ploughs to Welfare: Why Indian Policy Failed in the Prairie Provinces.* Montreal, PQ: McGill-Queen's University Press.

Cockerill, Jodi, and Roger Gibbins. (1997). Reluctant Citizens? First Nations in the Canadian Federal State. *First Nations in Canada: Perspectives on Opportunity, Empowerment, and Self-Determination.* Toronto, ON: McGraw-Hill Ryerson, 383-403.

Daniel, Richard. (1999). The Spirit and Terms of Treaty Eight. *The Spirit of the Alberta Treaties.* Third edition. Richard T. Price, ed. Edmonton, AB: The University of Alberta Press, 47-100.

Dickason, Olive Patricia. (2006). *A Concise History of Canada's First Nations.* Toronto, ON: Oxford University Press.

Friesen, John W. (1977). *People, Culture & Learning.* Calgary, AB: Detselig Enterprises.

Henlin, Calvin. (2006). *Dances with Dependency: Indigenous Success Through Self-Reliance.* Vancouver, BC: Orca Spirit Publishing & Communications, Inc.

Lincoln, Kenneth. (1985). *Native American Rennaisance.* Berkeley, CA: University of California Press.

McFarlane, Peter. (2000). Aboriginal Leadership. *Visions of the Heart: Canadian Aboriginal Issues.* Second edition. David Long and Olive Patricia Dickason, eds. Toronto, ON: Harcourt Canada, 49-80.

Melling, John. (1967). *Right to a Future: The Native Peoples of Canada.* Don Mills, ON: T.H. Best Printing Company.

Robertson, Heather. (1970). Reservations are for Indians. Toronto, ON: James, Lewis & Samuel.

Snow, Chief John. (2005). *These Mountains are Our Sacred Places: The Story of the Stoney People.* Calgary, AB: Fitzhenry and Whiteside.

Taylor, John Leonard. (1999a). Canada's Northwest Indian Policy in the 1870s: Traditional Premises and Necessary Innovations. *The Spirit of the Alberta Treaties.* Third edition. Richard T. Price, ed. Edmonton, AB: The University of Alberta Press, 3-8.

Taylor, John Leonard. (1999b). Two Views on the Meanings of Treaties Six and Seven. *The Spirit of the Alberta Treaties.* Third edition. Richard T. Price, ed. Edmonton, AB: The University of Alberta Press, 9-46.

Treaty Days. (1971). *Manitoba Indian Brotherhood.* Winnipeg, MB: Centennial Commemoration Historial Pageant.

Treaty 7 Elders and Tribal Council, with Walter Hildebrandt, Dorothy First Rider, and Sarah Carter. (1996). *The True Spirit and Original Intent of Treaty 7.* Montreal, PQ: McGill-Queen's University Press.

Warry, Wayne. (2007). *Ending Denial: Understanding Aboriginal Issues.* Peterborough, ON: Broadview Press.

# Thirteen
## The Challenge of Economic Development

The band does not owe its membership dependency. It owes them opportunity and a chance to be come independent. (Chief Clarence Louie) (Henlin, 2006: 233)

We have the best-educated generation of First Nations people ever. They are well trained and equipped to make their way in the global, knowledge-based economy. The rest of the country, especially the business sector, is starting to wake up to this reality – Robert Nault, Minister of Indian Affairs and Northern Development, April 4, 2004. (Indian Affairs and Northern Development website)

A significant happening that drew the attention of the nonNative business world in 2006 was the publication of Calvin Henlin's book, *Dances with Dependency: Indigenous Success Through Self-Reliance*. Originally from a small coastal community in British Columbia, Henlin is the son of an hereditary chief of the Gitlan Tribe of the Tsimshian First Nation. Trained in law, Henlin is a descendant of long line of hereditary chiefs and quite familiar with the phenomenon of Aboriginal leadership. His main thesis is to challenge Indigenous leaders to direct their people towards self-reliance through full economic integration. He believes that such a move could permanently throw off the yoke of EuroCanadian colonialism.

Henlin posits that Canadian government policy and legislation, which is essentially colonial in nature, has remained unchanged for the past two centuries. Unless Canada's Native people take steps to climb out from under the somewhat despotic system, which holds them in its clutches, the format will remain in place. Well aware of internal forms of colonialism, Henlin insists that elected chiefs and band councils must be also be made accountable to their people. In the first place, the electoral process, by which they come into office must be streamlined to make it more democratic. The appointment of an ombudsman could help in this process, provided the ombudsman maintains an arms-length position. Henlin draws attention to the urgent need for transparency and accountability in Indian affairs, both in local communities as well as in governmental quarters. Local band ledgers should be open to any and all band members who desire to examine them (Henlin, 2006: 260).

A very positive recent development is that business entrepreneurs have gradually become aware of the potential labor force available in the Aboriginal community and are starting to tap into it. In the meantime, some 27 000 self-employed individuals of Indian, Métis and Inuit background have created economic opportunities for their fellow citizens in their own communities. The rate of expansion for this kind of venture has increased by more than thirty percent since 1996. The Aboriginal economy is booming in northern regions as well. Several diamond mines are in production, and oil and gas activity in the Northwest Territories has increased markedly. The latter industry will be enhanced significantly when the Mackenzie Valley Pipeline Project is completed. This will happen when treaty negotiations with locals have been completed. Henlin (2006: 177-181) believes that with the appropriate environment, Aboriginal businesses are poised to be a major contributor to the Canadian economy.

## Going Back a Bit

Historically First Nations communities were fairly steadily involved in trade, usually with other tribes, because they desired or lacked resources that were not locally available. Many times they negotiated alliances on the basis of trade and these were often considered more important than the goods themselves. Member tribes of the Blackfoot Confederacy traded among themselves, and eastern Algonquians traded with their close relatives, the Ottawa. The Three Affiliated Tribes of North Dakota – Arikara, Hidatsa, and Mandan – were successful agriculturalists, but they needed horses for which they traded with the Lakoda Sioux further south – only to see their horses often stolen by the Assiniboines. The more northerly Crees wanted corn, and they were able to trade for it with furs they managed to obtain from the Three Affiliated Tribes. When the fur trade began on the west coast, the Native people of the British Columbia plateau acted as middlemen between Plains Indians and those who had direct contact with incoming European traders.

Before European contact, neighboring tribes shared more than trade goods. Trade negotiations involved social contact, and so ideas and stories and customs were often passed on from one people to another. Sometimes members of their tribes even intermarried. Dickason (1984: 97) points out that because of intertribal relations, Indian nations also shared legends about animals and culture heroes. This is why many similar stories can be identified in the historical lore of contemporary tribes even though the story line of a legend may vary from one community to another. The content of these legends, which are still alive, has a repertoire ranging from entertaining to providing cultural knowledge to comprising spiritual truths. Many of these stories included a central character known as the trickster, and even though he had different names among the various tribes across Canada, his whimsical and sometimes notorious actions were much the same in every setting.

Traditionally, the Indigenous peoples of Canada were very serious about trade, and many of the goods they exchanged travelled great distances. Dickason (1993: 78) makes note that obsidian, for example, probably originated in mines in British Columbia, but samples of it have been found in archaeological sites far from its place of origin. Similarly, copper goods have been identified across the country, many of them probably originating in copper mines in what is now Ontario. Many goods that were traded were not merely for their commercial value, but for ceremonial purposes. The Iroquois, for example, believed that wampum had spiritual powers and traded for it to enhance their spiritual ceremonies. Once obtained, the Iroquois made wampum into collars and belts that were worn to provide or assure good fortune.

Despite language differences tribes were able to negotiate trade, many of them relying on a universal sign language that probably reached its most sophisticated level on the Plains. Eventually some tribes developed a trade jargon that speeded up the process when trade negotiations were underway. No doubt the fact that intertribal trade involved social negotiations affected existing worldviews, including spiritual outlooks. Perhaps because of such extensive forms of interaction it is possible today to identify epistemological commonalities among the various First Nations across Canada, many of them probably having their roots in precontact days. Even traditionally, however, most Indigenous communities manifested many similar characteristics such as hospitality, cultural pride, and a unique sense of humor. The First Nations of Canada generally had in common a deep respect for the Creator and Mother Earth, the workings of nature, love for animals, and aptitude for sharing.

However, these commonalities do not necessarily provide convincing support to the notion that a kind of panIndian overview can be assumed. After all, such was the perspective of early explorers, who must have been surprised when they eventually discovered significant cultural differences among the various culture areas of the continent.

# Fur Trade Influence

There is little doubt that the most pervasive force influencing the economic and political development of Western Canada between 1660 and 1870 was the fur trade. In many ways it was a movement that provided mutual benefit for traders and locals and served as an integrating force between Aboriginals and Europeans. In the broadest sense, it was a partnership for the exploitation of natural resources. It was not an equal partnership, to be sure, but before 1870 a climate of peace and respect did exist between Indians and traders (Ray, 1974: xi). Writers who have a penchant for describing the fur trade as an economic take-over by outsiders may want to take another look. After all, the Indigenous people were willing participants in the process and when the traders arrived and local residents discovered their wares, they were eager to acquire some of the incoming goods – colored fabric, beads, steel hatchets, guns and ammunition, pots, and various related items.

The introduction of the horse and gun caused significant changes in traditional Aboriginal lifestyle. The North American horse culture began in the early 18th century in southwestern United States via the Spanish colonies of Mexico. The horse fit in well with the nomadic moves of the Plains people since the animal allowed longer lengths of travel in shorter periods of time and carried heavier loads than was possible with dog travois. Soon the horse became a status symbol and contributed to the development of the skilled horse-mounted warrior stereotype that emerged. Horses were also used to barter for brides and were regarded with a reverence not unlike spiritual adoration. By the 19th century, the demand for horses skyrocketed to almost unbelievable proportions. It became popular to steal horses as a means of proving one's qualities as a warrior. Partially the deed was magnified in importance by the amount of danger involved in stealing. To steal a tethered horse of an enemy was a very brave thing to do, to say nothing of the value which a good horse could bring in trade or as a sign of individual wealth (Driver, 1968: 233). Ownership of horses also provided tremendous military might. When the Shoshone acquired the horse, for example, they became militarily superior almost overnight. When their enemies, the Crees, obtained the rifle, however, everything changed and the Shoshone were reduced to the status of handmaiden. Horses, it seems, were no match for a good rifle.

The arrival of the horse also affected changes in social structure. Class distinctions were often made according to the number of horses a man possessed. Often horseless families would attach themselves to a family with horses, and a new band or tribal subdivision was formed. Social mobility of a sort also became a reality when a young man with lower status acquired horses. This was often accomplished through raiding parties in which sons of wealthy families also participated, sometimes being motivated to do so by teasing (Patterson, 1972: 93). Undoubtedly, the high level of interest shown in rodeos today by young Aboriginals is a carryover from the status and significance which the horse wove into the fabric of First Nations culture.

As an indication of the popularity of the fur trade, Indian tribes competed with one another for guns and ammunition. At first Western tribes who preferred to hunt buffalo actually preferred more traditional means of doing so – using spears or bows and arrows. Muzzle loading rifles were slow and enabled only a single shot before reloading. It was also quite difficult to get repairs for guns because trading posts were often located a long distance from hunting sites. Loud rifle shots startled herds and caused stampedes, whereas the silence of the bow and arrow did not have this disadvantage. As the quality of the gun eventually improved, its users found that they could not live without it. American historian, Walter Webb (1931) of the University of Texas, postulated that elements as simplistic in nature as the six-gun, barbed wire, and the windmill made the west inhabitable for emigrating settlers. Imagine the surprise on the enemy's face when he discovered that his gun-toting foe was able to shoot more than one bullet without having to reload. This was the superiority of the new gun – both the six-gun and the repeating rifle. Not only could the hunter stalk his prey, if he missed his shot the first time, he could quickly fire another round – and that from a greater distance. To complete the account of the three elements introduced by Webb, he also noted that the windmill made it possible to access water on the plains from deep wells, and barbed-wire made cattle ranching a possibility. Now a rancher could physically lay claim to specific areas of land and protect his claim by surrounding his lands with secure fences that held cattle in.

Trade items other than guns offered their own unique legendary history. Fabric or cloth was almost immediately popular. More than 200 yards of cloth were acquired by Indians as early as 1690; thereafter the volume increased dramatically. Ice chisels, used to open frozen beaver lodges, were at first eagerly obtained by inland groups, but started a downward trend by the early 1730s. Kettles, which were large, heavy and bulky, saw a steady demand although only limited numbers could be shipped from Europe because of their heavy makeup. Ray (1974: 85) has documented that the annual peak amount of rum and brandy (864 gallons) was reached between the years 1720 and 1753. Thereafter it remained relatively constant until a peak of 761 gallons was bartered to the Indians in one trading season. These peaks of trade items were reached at times of maximum trade rivalry. Ray concludes that data support the conclusion that the consumption of alcohol generally increased through time, and its damage to Aboriginal social structure has been well documented.

As the fur trade reached the Great Plains the Crees and Ojibway followed it, some of them even taking up the buffalo way of life. Member nations of the Blackfoot Confederacy did not directly take up with the fur trade because the demands of the fur trade conflicted with those of buffalo hunting. The Blackfoot managed to obtained trade goods through the Assiniboine and Cree networks. The preferred role of Blackfoot in the fur trade was to serve as guides and interpreters and providers of buffalo meat. Dickason (2006: 112) notes that the Blackfoot complained that they were not being treated fairly in trade as well as their enemies who were fully engaged in it, particularly when it came to the provision of firearms. The situation eventually deteriorated into an atmosphere of distrust, particularly so because the Blackfoot were involved in both Canadian and United States localities. Occasionally the standoff between traders and First Nations erupted into violence; in 1781, for example, the Natives burned the prairie around trading posts, allegedly to chase game away. Contrarily, there were times when the cross-border situation worked to the advantage of the Blackfoot. They became adept at raiding posts built in what they deemed to be their territory, but claimed by the government of the

United States. After the raid the Blackfoot sold their bounty in more northerly regions.

The early years of the fur trade were extremely rewarding for European traders. Fisher (1977: 2f) reported that great profits were reaped by those who brought European goods, often to the debilitation of fair trade. On July 2, 1787, for example, Captain George Dixon negotiated a trade with the West Coast Haida, and received large numbers of furs and cloaks in trade for relatively few items. Apparently some of the locals quarrelled with one another about who could engage in trade first. Some of them threw their furs on board ship even if there was no one to receive them. In one half hour, Dixon obtained 300 furs. A month later he left the west coast with 1 821 furs on board. Another trader, John Kendrick, made one of the best deals when he traded 200 pelts at the rate of one pelt for one chisel. Another trader collected $20 600 when he arrived home, all from his first trip to the area.

As the west coast trade continued to flourish, local First Nations traders became more adept at negotiating for goods. By now they were used to seeing virtually dozens of ships in their harbors and were less impressed with what their crews had to offer. One of the most desired commodities were items made of iron and brass, but local Natives had gradually grown to realize the true value of them. They were no longer willing to offer one fur for a single item. Market saturation was one factor in this development, but there were other reasons for the change. John Boit, who made a return trip to the west coast in 1795, found that the price of pelts had gone up nearly 100 percent. Other traders reported that prices had quadrupled (Fisher, 1977: 5). Not only did local Aboriginals quickly learn to demand a better quantity in the goods they were purchasing, but they became quite discriminate about the quality of goods offered to them. Experience, it seems, was their best teacher.

One of the practices related to the fur trade was gift-giving, at first as an indication of good will, and later as a bribe to encourage increase in production. Gifts were also given as a means of enhancing the status of those receiving them. Often the same leaders were given annual gifts because traders liked to deal with the same individual every year. Naturally, this practice changed the role of chiefs who formerly served primarily as caregivers; now their office took on an economic dimension as well as enhanced political authority. Not only did this change the status and role of chiefs, it also affected the way they dealt with their people and hence with fur traders.

Other changes were also in the offing. In addition to shifting relations between European traders and Indians, there was competition between the Hudson's Bay Company and the North West Company resulting in economic rivalries. Sometimes both companies recognized different individuals as chiefs in the same band and confusion resulted. At other times both companies were dealing with the same individuals in the same band. More lavish gifts accompanied continuing negotiations, each company trying to win favor with local producers.

Gradually the fur trade wore down. Then, in 1821 the Hudson's Bay Company and the North West Company merged, and a unique way of life came to an end. As time passed it became increasingly difficult for the Plains Indians to make a living as hunters, trappers, canoe men, boatmen or cart drivers, and they were forced, many times unwillingly, to become farmers or work as hired hands on the farms of settlers. Still, as late as the 1860s the Plains Indians, particularly the Crees, were still in the habit of sending representatives to fur trading posts to pick up goods in advance of the arrival of trading parties. They received their usual presents of tobacco, sugar, and tea (Ray, 1974: 196). By the time of Confederation, however, large numbers of First Nations bands were making their living in the more conventional way of working in the labor force or farming. Their more sedentary lifestyle was welcomed by religious orders that were eager to enroll their children in day schools and try to assimilate them to European ways.

## The Métis Factor

After the merger of the Hudson's Bay Company and the North West Company, a number of company employees lost their jobs because of redundancy. Most these employees were Métis, individuals with Indian-European ancestry who had begun to congregate in the Red River Valley of what later became Manitoba. As time went on they developed a strong sense of cultural identity, having borrowed from both parental cultures in forming their unique way of life. At the time of the company merger, about 500 Métis had settled in the vicinity of the Pembina River post, and were somewhat feared by colonial authorities. Rapid population growth, strengthened military might, and a strong sense of peoplehood lent credence to colonial suspicions whose leaders tried to encourage the Métis to move further north. The times were changing; new arrivals from Europe were laying claim to Métis lands and this invasion was not pleasing to local Métis.

The rise in population of European immigrants from Scotland was encouraged by Thomas Douglas, Earl of Selkirk, and local governor, Miles Macdonell. The arrival of these settlers put pressure on the Métis. They resisted the infiltration of outsiders and decided to quash the growth of the Selkirk settlement, as it became known. Under the leadership of Alexander Macdonell (no relation to Miles Macdonell), a plan was devised by which to impede the growth of the Scottish settlement. The campaign to discourage expansion included threats of invasion and attack, terrorism – such as burning crops, stealing cattle, horses, and machinery, and destroying fences and buildings (Purich, 1988: 36). A quick turn of events was motivated by the appointment of a new governor, Robert Semple, who adopted a more militarist stance. When he heard that the Métis had raided Hudson's Bay Company boats and confiscated pemmican, he took twenty men with him and accosted a group of fifteen Métis face-to-face. It was a temporary standoff, and it soon became obvious that any form of peaceful accommodation seemed impossible because of increasing cultural differences and growing economic strains.

A strong factor in aiding the emerging Métis identity was the formation of distinct communities including Fort William (now Thunder Bay), Ontario, and Manitoba communities – Red River (now Winnipeg), and Pembina, Hair Hills, and Deer Lake. In many ways the lifestyle of Métis communities resembled those of nonNative communities; many of the men dressed like nonNatives, but distinguished themselves with their blue capotes (cloaks), red belts or sashes, and corduroy trousers. The primary means of employment included farming and home construction, and fur trade-related jobs, acting as interpreters, intermediaries, and distributors. The Métis thirst for recognition and self-consciousness was clearly a Manitoba phenomenon, but it was enough to spirit the patriotism of their membership well towards the end of the 20th century.

Relations between Europeans and Native people generally – Métis and Status Indians – deteriorated after the merger of the two trading companies, partially because of a decrease in fur trade related activity. In 1835 the Hudson's Bay Company enacted legislation pertaining to mixed marriages for employees. This anti-Métis move strengthened existing Métis identity, who by now comprised a major factor in the area partly because of the restrictions on intermarriage. In 1949 a Métis trader named Guillaume Sayer broke the trade monopoly of the Hudson's Bay Company by selling furs to the United States without permission from company officials. He was charged and reprimanded, but no harsh punishment was meted out because the Hudson's Bay Company feared Métis reprisals. In 1867 Canada became a new nation and had to deal with the various factions that made up the new nation. Eager to join confederation, the Province of Manitoba was formed in 1870, largely influenced by the leadership of Métis leader, Louis Riel. Prime Minister, Sir John A. Macdonald, however, had little respect for Riel and did not acknowledge his efforts on behalf of Manitoba. In fact, Riel was thrice elected to parliament, and three times expelled.

The Métis were a cultural-political force to be bargained with. They were great buffalo hunters and had sufficient military might to be able to drive the Sioux south, so they could operate their annual buffalo hunt undisturbed (Friesen and Friesen, 2004: 61-62). It has been estimated that the Métis annually killed 100 000 buffalo and sold the meat and hides – all of this in addition to hunting for their own needs. The annual buffalo hunt involved nearly one thousand individuals and covered about 400 kilometres in a month. Métis-designed Red River carts, pulled by oxen, hauled the spoils home where the meat was dressed and pounded into pemmican. A well-built cart could carry over 400 kilograms of buffalo meat while making its way, virtually floating across a river, behind a yoke of oxen. The adaptability of the cart greatly assisted the Métis in developing a semi-nomadic lifestyle and abandoning their traditional nomadic ways (Sealey and Lussier, 1975: 22).

After a series of military skirmishes, Riel and his troops were defeated in 1885 and the Métis essentially became an invisible people. Many of them left their established homes and migrated north in search of a hunting/trapping lifestyle. Others, who had connections in Indian communities, joined their relatives on reserve locations. Still others situated themselves near small towns, often on road allowances (Adams, 1975), and worked at odd jobs, often part-time. Essentially an unwanted people, these were times of economic depression for the Métis.

## Changing Times

Although First Nations were regarded as allies during the days of the fur trade where negotiations were undertaken with each party viewing the other as equals, the end of the fur trade brought dramatic changes to their communities. The period from 1821 to 1870 was one of decreasing opportunities for First Nations. Declining resources and growing economic dependency placed the Native people in a vulnerable position with company representatives who had administrative responsibilities for the industry. By the 1870s the independence of the Plains Indians was threatened by the incursion of other groups who competed with them in the buffalo market. Soon thereafter, the bison were wiped out and a permanent state of economic dependency became a reality.

The assignment of reserve lands to First Nations began with the signing of Treaty No. 1 with the Peguis (Ojibway) Band in 1871 and continued over the next two decades. The last of the ten major treaties was signed in 1899. Shortly thereafter, the battle over reserve lands began, many observers believing that the Indians had been allotted too much land or assigned land in the wrong areas. A royal commission, published in 1916, recommended the "cutting off" of specified reserve lands, and their substitution of areas of lesser value (Dickason, 1993: 324). As a result, hundreds of hectares of Indian land were sold to settlers without any consideration of Aboriginal needs. For example, among reserve lands sold by government action included almost half of the Blackfoot (Siksika) reserve near Calgary in 1910-11. Treaty-making in British Columbia halted, much for the same reason; the demand for land by incoming settlers influenced government officials to put a stop to treaty-making.

As the 20th century approached, public attitudes toward First Nations shifted from regarding them as unfortunates to "poor doomed savages" (Haycock, 1971: 1). Those who had compassion on them and wished to assist them in coping with changing times basically had a welfare mentality; it never occurred to them that the First Nations could successfully adapt to economic challenges. These well-wishers preferred to muster handouts instead of encouraging economic change. It took several decades for this attitude to shift to one of humanitarianism to concerns about human rights. Only when the Canadian government passed the *Multicultural Act* in 1971 did it occur to observers and analysts that the First Nations were in a unique political position. Legally they could appeal to the *Indian Act* and the signed treaties for special regard, and thus perceive of themselves as "Citizens-plus" as they did in the Red Paper of 1970.

Two decades earlier, a happening that drew attention to the need for urgent Native participation in economic development occurred in 1957 when Prime Minister John G. Diefenbaker came to power and soon thereafter "discovered the north." Northern Aboriginals soon found out that resources in their home domain would be harvested without much local consultation and they quickly determined to do something about it (Harrison and Friesen, 2004: 209). Diefenbaker did support consultation with local Natives and his government even awarded First Nations voting rights. So intrigued by the north, Diefenbaker was even referred to as "Lincoln of the North" by other politicians (McMillan, 1995: 314).

Eventually the potential of the Aboriginal labor force was realized. During the 1960s when the Quebec government began development of a dam at James Bay, a requirement was the hiring of Aboriginal labor. By 1981, service industries employed 35 percent of the local Aboriginal population. On the negative side, when the Churchill Nelson River Hydroelectric Project at Pike Lake, Manitoba was launched, and Natives were told that tremendous benefits would accrue to them, the end results were quite disappointing. There was little consultation with local leaders and local job training was limited, so outside help was brought in instead (Bone, 1992: 167). By the 1970s Indian leaders had accumulated sufficient experience with companies who invaded their territories with promises of benefits from economic development. In response to their concerns, when the Mackenzie Valley Pipeline was in the planning stage, the federal government established a commission to investigate the role of and effect on northern Native communities. The report of the commission has been described as the first significant public study of the environment and social effects of economic development ever conducted in Canada (Harrison and Friesen, 2004: 211). The First Nations of northern Canada were major instigators of environmental concern and the report reflected this.

Economic development in First Nations communities is closely related to the realization of Aboriginal self-government. Unless local control is initiated, particularly over natural resources, outside organizations have only to deal with governments that often have many other interests and concerns and their headquarters are often a long distance away – at least so it seems. The good news is that a number of positive changes toward the goal of self-government are being made. In 2006, for example, the Desmarais-based Bigstone Cree Nation in Alberta reports that their partnership with

Petrocare Services Ltd., is very successful. Active in oil and gas exploration, Petrocare Services have hired many locals to the point that nearly 90 percent of their employees have Bigstone connections. The company is also involved in a variety of community activities such as trades apprenticeship programs as well as helping community development in other areas such as sponsoring high school sports teams and social clubs (Copley, 2006: 11).

The move to engage in joint projects between industry and local Native communities is a recent, but already successful way to proceed. Agreements usually provide preferential hiring and contracting to local residents and businesses as well as ongoing consultation with Aboriginal leaders and their representatives. The Déline Land Corporation, working in the Great Bear Lake region of North West Territories, has demonstrated a successful partnership with the Sahtu Dene in mining ventures (Copley, 2006: 21). In March 2006 Syncrude Canada received two accolades from the Alberta Business Awards of Distinction for excellence in Aboriginal relations and in providing workplace learning. Syncrude had been successful in implementing a training program for Aboriginals that resulted in providing employment opportunities for them. The program focused on employment, business development, individual capacity development and community relations. Its operation gave mutual benefit to both Aboriginals and the company.

The story is not complete. The latest move in the saga of Native economic development has been for Indian tribes to invest and manage resource development on their own terms. Their past experience has taught them well, and although they still cooperate with outside agencies and organizations, essentially they run newly-formed companies that manage a wide variety of business ventures. Today the media are reporting stories of successful and rapidly growing Aboriginal owned and operated business enterprises.

## Success Stories

The Department of Indian Affairs and Northern Development website reports that the number of Aboriginal business start-ups has exceeded the rest of the Canadian population by more than one hundred percent. There are now 20 000 registered First Nations businesses across Canada, 4 700 of them in British Columbia. Over the next decade it is expected that the Aboriginal labor force will grow at twice the rate of the total Canadian labor force. At least fifty percent of Canada's Aboriginal population is under the age of 25, and if properly trained, will assure a continuing labor force.

Henlin (2006: 184) notes that resource and business development is burgeoning and corporations out of necessity will have to seek an alternative labor force. That force exists in the Aboriginal community so cooperation with and training of Aboriginals is of utmost importance. Henlin describes a number of enterprises that have managed to make use of the First Nations labor force, many of them operated by Natives themselves.

A number of years ago the Peguis Ojibway First Nation of Manitoba documented more than 50 business ventures, begun and managed by the band, all of them profit-making. Included in the list is a cabinet-making business, a hotel located in Winnipeg, local retail outlets of different kinds, and a publishing house. When these programs began Chief Louis Stevenson insisted that if domestic or commercial building ventures were to be started, local help should be hired first. As projects got underway, the band trained the local labor force in the various required trades – carpentry, electricity, plumbing, sheet metal work, and so on. In August 2007, the tribe launched out on an historical venture by restoring the St. Peter, Dynevor Church in cooperation with the Canada/Manitoba Economic Development Partnership Agreement. The church now stands as a tribute to the late Chief Peguis and his people and serves as a symbol of cooperation between Aboriginal people and European settlers.

Another success story originates with the Osoyoos Indian Band of south central British Columbia. Strongly encouraged by their chief, Clarence Louie, who has been elected eleven times since 1985, the band manages its own health, education and welfare services as well as nearly a dozen successful business enterprises. Over the last decade the band has engaged in a variety of successful business ventures and now yields seven times the revenue it receives from the federal government. Its annual business revenue totals more than fifteen million dollars. Band-run businesses include a golf-hotel-residential complex, a vineyard, a campground, a recreational vehicle park, a construction company, a ready-mix concrete company, and a gas bar and convenience store. In 2006 the band opened an eight million dollar interpretive centre that deserves a visit by any Canadian interested in learning about Western Canada's First Nations Plateau desert culture. On our own visit we were privileged to examine a series of intriguing indoor displays as well as ride on an escorted golf cart trip to explore the grounds. The motto of the Osoyoos Indian Band Development Corporation is, "Working with Business to Preserve our Past by Strengthening our Future" (Henlin, 2006: 235).

First Nations bands in every province are garnering their human and natural resources in an effort to establish a new Canadian identity based on a self-defined form of integration. By all counts many nonNative Canadians will need to formulate a much more admirable perception of the nation's original peoples.

## References

Adams, Howard. (1975). *Prison of Grass: Canada From the Native Point of View.* Toronto, ON: New Press.

Bone, Robert M. (1992). *The Geography of the Canadian North: Issues and Challenges.* Toronto, ON: Oxford University Press.

Copley, John. (February, 2006). Bigstone Ventures puts Community Members at Work. *Alberta Native News,* 23:2, 11, 16.

Copley, John. (March, 2006). Companies and Communities Benefit from Access Agreements. *Alberta Native News,* 23:3, 21.

Dickason, Olive Patricia. (2006). *A Concise History of Canada's First Nations.* Toronto, ON: Oxford University Press.

Dickason, Olive Patricia. (1993). *Canada's First Nations: A History of Founding Peoples From Earliest Times.* Toronto, ON: McClelland and Stewart.

Dickason, Olive Patricia. (1984). *The Myth of the Savage and the Beginnings of French Colonialism in the Americas.* Edmonton, AB: University of Alberta Press.

Driver, Harold E. (1968). *Indians of North America.* Chicago, IL: University of Chicago Press.

Fisher, Robin. (1977). *Contact & Conflict: Indian-European Relations in British Columbia, 1774-1890.* Vancouver, BC: University of British Columbia Press.

Friesen, John W., and Virginia Lyons Friesen. (2004). *We Are Included: The Métis People of Canada Realize Riel's Vision.* Calgary, AB: Detselig Enterprises.

Harrison, Trevor W., and John W. Friesen. (2004). *Canadian Society in the Twenty-First Century.* Toronto, ON: Pearson Canada.

Haycock, Ronald G. (1971). *The Image of the Indian.* Waterloo, ON: Waterloo Lutheran University.

Henlin, Calvin. (2006). *Dances With Dependency: Indigenous Success Through Self-Reliance.* Vancouver, BC: Orca Spirit Publications and Comunications.

Indian Affairs and Northern Development website. http//www.ainc-inac.gc.ca

McMillan, Alan D. (1995). *Native Peoples and Cultures of Canada.* Second edition. Vancouver, BC: Douglas and McIntyre.

Patterson, E. Palmer. (1972). *The Canadian Indian.* Toronto, ON: Macmillan.

Purich, Donald. (1988). *The Métis.* Toronto, ON: James Lorimer.

Ray, Arthur J. (1974). *Indians in the Fur Trade: Their Role as Hunters, Trappers and Middlemen in the Lands Southwest of the Hudson Bay.* Toronto, ON: University of Toronto Press.

Sealey, D. Bruce, and Antoine S. Lussier. (1975). *The Métis: Canada's Forgotten People.* Winnipeg, MB: Manitoba Métis Federation Press.

Webb, Walter Prescott. (1931). *The Great Plains.* New York: Gosset and Dunlop.

# Fourteen
# The Challenge of Aboriginal
# Self-Government

The issue of Aboriginal rights is the oldest question of human rights in Canada. At the same time it is also the most recent, for it is only in the last decade that it has entered our consciousness and our political bloodstream. (Thomas R. Berger 1982: 219)

As a participant in the failed constitutional conferences on Aboriginal issues ending just weeks before the Meech Lake Accord was signed in June of 1987, I witnessed first hand how little significance was given to legitimate demands. It was not surprising to me, or to many other Aboriginal leaders, that we were left entirely out of the Meech Lake Accord. Aboriginal Peoples were not even considered one of the founding partners of the constitutional package. (Elijah Harper, Hylton, 2001:7)

Someone once asked the late John Snow, Chief of the Wesley Band of the Stoney First Nation, if he thought the Aboriginal peoples were ready for Self-Government, should it be granted to them by the federal government. He smiled mischievously, then responded; "Well, we do have some experience in self-government; we did manage to govern ourselves for many centuries before the Europeans came to this land."

In his book, *These Mountains are Our Sacred Places,* Chief Snow stated that "a migratory people are not necessarily a people who lack civilization, not if 'civilization' is taken in the sense of a law-abiding and caring society" (Snow, 2005: 8). In other words, the First Nations of North America, like any other people the world over, have always developed a means of governance since their intention has been to function and persist as a people. The First Nations of North America are no exception in this regard.

Chief Snow's point is well taken. Before European contact the many varied North American Indian tribes did have in place rather elaborate forms of governance. In fact, when formulating the Constitution of the United States, one of America's founding fathers, Benjamin Franklin, apparently acknowledged the functionality of the

241

Iroquois Confederacy and suggested that the American system of representative democracy be patterned after it.

# The Iroquois Confederacy

At the peak of its existence the Iroquois League was the largest and best-organized political unit in North America. The league comprised five First Nations: Cayuga (The Great Pipe People), Oneida (People of the Stone), Onondaga (People of the Mountain), Mohawk (People of the Flint), and Seneca (The Great Hill People). The League added a sixth nation, the Tuscaroras, in 1722; hence the more recognizable name by which they are known in Canada is Six Nations.

At the time of European contact the Iroquois Confederacy was the only confederacy north of Mexico and was probably founded around 1570. Matrilineal descent was the prevailing format among the Iroquois and leadership in all its forms tended to be inherited matrilineally. Each of the five confederate nations was made up of sibs and clans which were further subdivided into two "phatries," which were exogamous (Goldenweiser, 1968: 565). So divided, the presence of the two phatries was evident in all activities including the practice of ceremonies, games, and feasts. Although they varied somewhat in function among the five tribes, the sib and clan organizations were the units that made up the towns and tribal locations, and normally both spiritual and political offices were confined to particular lineages and sibs, which were matrilineal (Driver, 1968: 344-345). The Cayuga, Onondaga, and Seneca, for example, had more than eight clans each, while the Mohawk and Oneida had three clans each. Essentially the operational terms of Iroquois clans were these: (i) the clans were exogamous; (ii) each clan had its own set of names; (iii) most clans had a representative chief in the overall organizational body; (iv) each clan had its own burial ground; (v) in ancient times, clans were associated with specific longhouses and villages; (vi) clans could adopt outsiders if they preferred; and, (vii) clans elected their own ceremonial officials (Goldenweiser, 1968: 569). Essentially the entire social-political structure of the Iroquois was permeated by a maze of channels through which respected women guided the affairs of the people.

The judicial and executive power of the Iroquois confederacy was invested in a body of fifty chiefs, each of whom was associated with a specific clan. When a chief died, the clan mothers held a meeting and decided who would fill the vacant place. A woman (or clan mother) carried the name of the chosen candidate to the council of chiefs, and usually the woman's choice was accepted by the chiefs. Clan mothers had further powers; it was they who kept a close watch over the actions and behavior of a new chief, and if he deviated from the preferred pattern, he would be reprimanded. If he did not fall into line after a series of such visits, there would be one more visit. The clan mother made the visit, accompanied by a warrior chief. If the visit was unsuccessful, the new chief would be denounced in public and later impeached.

Despite its careful complexity, the Iroquois model was a most appropriate one for Benjamin Franklin and his colleagues to emulate. It represented exactly what Franklin and his colleagues were looking for. When Franklin and his peers had formulated their charter and the Canadian-American border was established, member nations and clans of the Iroquois Confederacy had to choose on which side of the international border to live. It was not an easy decision to make, and today many descendants of the Six Nations live on both sides of the border.

A second example of a carefully crafted form of traditional government was the Mikmaq plan. This governing plan consisted of seven governing districts, each of which was presided over by a chief. A grand chief, who called and chaired meetings of the seven councils, lived on Cape Breton Island. These meetings basically dealt with matters that affected all seven districts which otherwise operated on their own. The names of the seven districts reflected their locations, for example, ground nut place, foggy land, lying in the water, and where explosions are made (Miller, 1995: 354-355).

The duties of a Mi'kmaq chief were not unlike those of a provincial premier or prime minister today. Duties included calling council meetings as required, touring the district and consulting with lower chiefs, feasting with visiting chiefs, and participating in Grand Council meetings. Chiefs were also responsible for apportioning hunting territories to family heads or reassigning them as needed. Chiefs were expected to be generous individuals, with responsibilities of supplying needs and sharing with members of the extended family. Respected chiefs were often quite poor because they gave away much of what they had. Lower chiefs, those who functioned just beneath district chiefs in terms of rank, were assigned on the basis of their geographic domicile. Each of them headed a group composed of their bilocally extended family, with added responsibilities to individuals who might be unrelated but who may have chosen to ally with the chief. The majority of Mi'kmaq were ordinary citizens who organized their lives along the lines of a gender division of labor. The men hunted, fished, and participated in war, and the women transported household goods when the tribes moved, dressed, cooked, and distributed meat, collected plants and dug ground nuts for food and medicine. In short, they took care of all household-related duties. It was at once a well-organized and smoothly functioning society, and like that of the Iroquois Confederacy, a classic example of precontact Aboriginal self-government.

The First Nations of the Plains were generally governed by hereditary chiefs and band councils, and decisions were made by talking things through to consensus. A band chief had no authority to hold people to his own perspective against their will. If a considerable number of individuals disagreed with the chief on an important matter, they were always free to leave and form a new band. Indeed the traditional office of chief is best understood, not as a position of authority, but of stewardship, of caring for the people who looked to that office of leadership and guidance, not control (Snow, 2005: xxii).

In addition to chiefs, each tribe had among them respected men and women who were regarded as elders – usually older individuals who over the years had revealed themselves to have the wisdom of their years. They had special gifts among them, some of medicinal knowledge, some of ceremonial knowledge and authority to call or conduct them, and others to offer advice, consolation, or encouragement. It was a system that worked effectively for thousands of years.

## After European Contact

European motivation for entering North America was strictly business, based on an imperial model. The newcomers did not come as tourists or to learn about North American ways. They came to conquer, plunder, and integrate existing systems into their way of thinking. Many explorers wanted to expand the empires they represented, while others wanted to win the souls of their new acquaintances to Christianity. Spain was particularly interested in accessing the dazzling riches they believed to exist in southwest United States. France wanted to add new territories to her holdings, and

Britain was probably more interested in defeating France than any-thing else. These objectives were not even remotely related to the concept of visiting the newly-identified continent to discover new ideas.

Most early European perceptions of Indian life in North America were uninformed, insulting, and negative. The European forebears did not seem to have in their vocabulary or in their mindset a con-cept of compromise or withholding judgment. They tended to regard all cultural differences as inferior. Dickason (1984: 129) quotes from diaries of early explorers to note that they saw First Nations as living like animals, functioning freely in their natural state, and following their natural desires. Those who did examine the Native way of life a bit more closely were often surprised at the skill and complexity the First Nations had built into their social struc-tures. Still, an overall negativity prevailed. Francisco de Vitoria (1480-1552), a professor of moral theology at the University of Salamanca took considerable interest in Aboriginal ways, and while he concluded that European nations had no right to confiscate Indian lands, he also believed that the First Nations of North America had no proper laws, and no literature or arts of any kind, so they were not competent to administer their own affairs.

The approach to dealing with North American Indians differed somewhat among the three major invading nations – Britain, France, and Spain, with the latter two being more attuned to the idea of integrating the cultures of Aboriginal locals, even through intermarriage. Apparently the French saw no contradiction between their own assertion of sovereignty and the recognition of Aboriginal occupancy rights. Natives often spoke of the kinship relationship they had with the French and many of their warriors fought side by side with French soldiers when their claims were threatened (Conrad, Finkel, and Jaenen, 1993: 219).

Despite a somewhat amiable relationship, both French and Spanish invaders built settlements in Indian country and eventually tried to impose their cultures on the locals. Incoming missionaries, however, opted for a slightly different route, choosing instead to live among the First Nations, learning their languages and studying their society in order to more effectively convert them. They combined their evangelical efforts with schooling, the Recollects establishing schools among the Huron as early as 1615. Many tribes resisted efforts at colonizing them; for example, between 1609-1915 the Iroquois engaged in open warfare to protect their lands. When a form of peace was finally negotiated the French embarked on a vig-orous recruiting program to people New France. Before long the First Nations were either geographically displaced or lost vast num-bers of population by being affected with imported diseases.

In 1867, when Canada became a nation within her own right, significant changes regarding Aboriginal self-government were enacted – specifically through the *Indian Act* of 1876. Essentially the *Indian Act* consolidated earlier legislation and assured that vir-tually all activities of Canada's First Nations were regulated by gov-ernment. Hereditary chiefs were replaced by the election process, and Indian agents with far-reaching powers were placed on reserves. The Indian agent made all decisions related to reserve life and wrote full reports to the federal government on all reserve activities (Buckley, 1993: 43). The Six Nations of Ontario strongly opposed the new law and managed to continue elements of their traditional practice of respecting the rule of clan mothers. The power of band councils, however, was essentially reduced to gov-erning peripheral matters. This arrangement persevered until the 1960s when the office of Indian agent was dissolved.

# Reclaiming Authority

The 1960s were interesting times in North America with the rise of the hippies (flower children), anti-Vietnam demonstrations, the Black Power movement, and an Indian cultural renaissance. Having coped successfully with the debilitating experience of poor housing and near poverty levels of living, inadequate health care, substan-dard education, and continuing colonization, the First Nations of Canada were finally able to fight back. Although they had always believed in their inherent right to self-government, they were never in a strong enough position politically to assert those rights. The publication of the Indian White Paper by the Trudeau government in 1969 brought things to a head. Aboriginal leaders protested against government proposals to cancel the *Indian Act* and ignore Indian treaties, and demanded to have their voices heard.

The years between 1969 and 1983 when the Penner Report (Penner, 1983) dealing with Aboriginal self-government was pub-lished were marked by public protests and confrontation. With the repatriation of the nation's constitution, the time seemed ripe to deal with the controversial subject of First Nations governance. Russell (2000), a practicing Aboriginal lawyer in Toronto, suggests that the concept of Aboriginal self-government is a fairly recent notion, but he makes it clear that he does not mean to imply that the idea is new – only the language has been changed to modern nomenclature. Native peoples have always governed themselves, but the structure of their forms of governance did have to accommodate other arrangements foisted on their communities by incoming political powers.

The Penner Report of 1983 recommended that First Nations be allowed to establish their own level of government, distinct from that of municipalities and that contained in the Indian Act. The report included a number of positive recommendations regarding Aboriginal self-government including expanded jurisdictions, the exclusion of provincial jurisdictions from Aboriginal lands, and a process of Aboriginal government accountability to its people. However, detail regarding the scope of jurisdictions that First Nations governments would control were lacking in the report. Instead the report suggested that these be arrived at through negotiation (Russell, 2000: 7).

Soon after the Penner Report was published, in agreement with the conditions related to the repatriation of Canada's constitution from Britain, a series of constitutional conferences to determine the nature of Aboriginal rights were held, the first chaired by then Prime Minister Pierre Elliott Trudeau. The remaining three conferences were hosted by the Conservative government of Prime Minister Brian Mulroney. Aboriginal leaders representing virtually every area of Canada were present including Métis leaders. Although there were many discussions on the matter, essentially the conferences accomplished nothing pertaining to this important agenda item. Shortly after the last conference the Mulroney government and the provincial premiers signed the Meech Lake Accord that recognized Quebec as a distinct society. Naturally the Native people of Canada were severely disappointed with this action, and launched a public awareness program. Why was Quebec acknowledged and the First Nations of Canada ignored? Now it was up to provincial legislatures to ratify the Meech Lake Accord, but Elijah Harper, a Cree Member of the Manitoba Legislature, voted against ratification, and the Meech Lake Accord died on the order paper (Dickason, 2006: 285). Since then the legislative status of Aboriginal rights in Canada have been in a quandary, some local bands having negotiated elements of the concept, but unilateral agreement is lacking.

# Foundations of Aboriginal Rights

One of the basic principles on which Aboriginal self-government is based is the right of first occupancy; in other words, the Indians were here first. Some would go so far as to suggest that the First Nations were always here; North America was their original home. Critics of this view like to argue that everyone on this continent has immigrant ancestors, and cite the Bering Strait myth as evidence. True, they may contend, the Aboriginal people arrived first, but they too are immigrants. These critics may also inject the "conqueror takes all" position, implying that the French and British invasions of Canada justified the subsequent domination of the First Peoples. After all, the invaders won the war. This position ignores the reality that the treaties negotiated with First Nations were bargained on a nation-to-nation basis; both parties recognized the equal and legitimate status of the other. Such is hardly a situation of winner takes all. In addition, it must be remembered that the Aboriginal peoples of Canada have not relinquished their treaty rights and the *Indian Act*, with all its flaws, is still a law of the land.

Still another argument to justify ignoring Indian rights is the contention that First Nations cultures are no longer distinct and therefore do not qualify for special status (Warry, 2007: 35). Some Indian communities have lost their language and many of their traditional practices, rituals, and ceremonies have all but disappeared. Their children attend public schools, and their parents regularly avail themselves of services of the various institutions of dominant society – stores, hospitals, and government institutions. Of course this argument is based on the fallacious notion that Aboriginal cultures, unlike others, are not allowed to change. For some reason, in order to remain authentic, they alone must remain stagnant.

One of the most significant happenings to affect Indian status in Canada was the publication of the Royal Commission on Aboriginal Peoples (RCAP) in 1996. The commission recognized the right of First Nations to possess self-determination, but did not spell out the details of self-government. Basic principles of self-determination recognized by the RCAP include the right to a land base, the right to hunt and trap on Crown land, and the right to receive quality health care, education, and welfare through federal auspices. In the meantime, the inherent right of Aboriginals to practice self-determination has not been entrenched in the Canadian constitution.

# Determining Format

In examining concerns about Aboriginal self-government in the north, Kulchyski (2005: 15-17) has identified four significant theses about the concept. *First,* in Native communities, the politics of form is of considerable importance. Achieving a measure of self-government, for many Aboriginal leaders, is not simply a matter of transfer of powers from government to local bands. The matter of form – what kind of governance will be initiated – is of immense importance. *Second,* it must be acknowledged that First Nations communities in Canada are ready for self-government. They have quite wearied of being regarded as wards of the government. *Third,* they are well aware that the underlying objective of federal negotiation is to try to fit Aboriginal self-government into the existing operations of the state. Government bureaucrats do not seem to comprehend that existing structures are not necessarily appropriate nor functional in Native communities. *Fourth,* and finally, Aboriginal self-government must take into account that its application must be specific to some extent – specific to each and every community. Unless this is accomplished, it will be another case of applying universal or national structures without determining local needs.

The foundation on which the claim for Aboriginal self-government is made, rests on three planks (Schouls, 2003: 115-116). The *first* is the claim that the First Peoples of Canada should be recognized as having rights of first occupancy. They were here first, if not always, which implies that as originally sovereign nations, they have an inherent right to create and maintain their own identities and cultures, languages, values and practices, and the right to choose their own form of governance. Traditionally, the First Nations always chose the kind of relationships they wanted with foreign governments and this should still be the case today.

A *second* foundational plank put forth by Schouls is that even though Canada's Indigenous peoples live under the Crown's protection, this does not in any way reduce or diminish their historic right to govern their own affairs. The original agreements between government and First Peoples (treaties) were signed on the basis of recognizing the other parties as equals. Self-government, therefore, must be more than merely self-administration. It must encompass Native originated laws and policies based on their culture and way of life.

*Third,* it has been argued that the form and quality of relationship between government and First Nations, established during treaty-making, should be maintained. It is not necessary to invent a new kind of relationship until that traditional format has been properly tested. The treaty-making process was formalized on the principle of reciprocity and consent. There has never been a real reason to ignore or seek to improve this relationship – certainly not by First Nations negotiators. Up till now, treaty rights and the process put in place during treaty negotiations have generally been ignored by governments, but this does not mean that they cannot be fruitful and beneficial – certainly to Canada's First Peoples.

Asch (2000: 67) suggests that the concept of Aboriginal self-government has generally been interpreted in three major ways. *First,* the federal Government of Canada currently has in place a program whereby Indian bands take on financial responsibility for administering government grants in their own communities. In a sense this is not the same as comprehensive self-government because band administrators are essentially deciding how monies received from government sources should be spent. Critics have pointed out that a more comprehensive form of self-government would suggest that self-governing units originate their own funds and then decide how to manage and distribute them.

A *second* existing federal government program is known as the "Inherent Right" policy which purports to recognize that Canada's First Nations have an inherent right to self-government. The difficulty has been for the two parties – the Canadian government and Aboriginal bands – to negotiate the exact form that their relationship will take. The current program sets strict preconditions and guidelines that specify which aspects of government may be negotiated. It also unilaterally defines those that are not negotiable. In a very real sense this arrangement cannot and does not achieve a workable form of Aboriginal self-government.

The *third* format of Aboriginal self-government has been to recognize legislative authority through parliamentary action for First Nations self-government on reserve lands. Asch (2000: 67) indicates that this was achieved by the Sechelt Band of British Columbia in 1986, and it serves as a model for other bands to consider. Currently the Sechelt Band has power to legislate matters that range from zoning and land use to education on their reserve. This right is respected by the federal and provincial governments even when Sechelt laws are inconsistent with those of both federal and provincial governments. As may be expected, there are certain areas of law in which the Sechelt Band does not have jurisdiction.

According to available literature, the most discussed form of Aboriginal self-government to be implemented is that of a third order government to differentiate it from federal and provincial forms. This form was proposed in the RCAP and has been partially implemented by various bands across the country. Russell (2000: 163) maintains that the third order does nothing more than to recognize the right to negotiate for the right to exercise sovereign authority. Even then, it is hypothesized that negotiations will be undertaken only with regard to peripheral matters. On the practical side this may mean, for example, that if Aboriginal nations have resources and their respective provincial governments have no interest in helping develop them, or negotiate them, nothing will happen. Another closely related inhibiting feature is that neither federal nor provincial governments are required to negotiate with each other before exercising their respective powers.

Russell (2000: 163) emphasizes that generally speaking Indian bands are required to negotiate with governments even over peripheral matters. This is what makes case of the Sechelt Band so significant. In fact, the Royal Commission on Aboriginal Peoples upheld the notion that peripheral authority must be negotiated, thereby reducing hope for anything more powerful. If indeed the First Peoples of Canada have an inherent right to self-government, why was the commission so swift to suggest that they first need to negotiate with government on matters pertaining to their culture practice and future?

# Projections

Ponting and Henderson (2005) suggest that since the process of negotiating Aboriginal self-government is such a tedious and complex process, it might be beneficial to add the element of hard-core academic research to the mix as a trilateral party. Collaborating with academic social scientists might assist both government policy units and Aboriginal organizations in realizing valuable input. After all, academics typically identify many possible explanatory factors pertaining to specific human behavior – often called independent variables. Ponting and Henderson observe that academics appear to have an insatiable appetite for independent variables, and their rigorous methodological training allows them to formulate and test complicated theoretical models with a full explanation as their ultimate goal. Surely this kind of input could speed the process as well as providing valuable insights and possibly clarify future objectives.

The current process has been slow; government policy makers do not usually like to yield power too quickly. With this added source of input, they may be able to proceed more in keeping with their visualized mandate as well as be of immense aid to the Aboriginal community. To do anything else implies either a wish to deliberately slow up the process or an unwillingness to consider utilizing the input of relevant data from a valuable reliable source.

# References

Asch, Michael. (2000). Self-Government in the New Millenium. *Nation to Nation: Aboriginal Sovereignty and the Future of Canada.* John Bird, Lorraine Land, and Murray McAdam, eds. Toronto, ON: Irwin Publishing, 65-73.

Berger, Thomas R. (1982). *Fragile Freedoms: Human Rights and Dissent in Canada.* Toronto, ON: Irwin Publishing.

Buckley, Helen. (1993). *From Wooden Ploughs to Welfare: Why Indian Policy Failed in the Prairie Provinces.* Montreal, PQ: McGill-Queen's University Press.

Conrad, Margaret, Alvin Finkel, and Cornelius Jaenen. (1993). *History of the Canadian Peoples: Beginnings to 1867.* Toronto, ON: Copp Clark Pitman.

Dickason, Olive Patricia. (2006). *A Concise History of Canada's First Nations.* Toronto, ON: Oxford University Press.

Dickason, Olive Patricia. (1984). *The Myth of the Savage and the Beginnings of French Colonialism in the Americas.* Edmonton, AB: University of Alberta Press.

Driver, Harold E. (1968). *Indians of North America.* Chicago, IL: University of Chicago Press.

Goldenweiser, Alexander A. (1968). Iroquois Social Organization. *The North American Indians: A Sourcebook.* Roger C. Owen, James J. F. Deetz, and Anthony Fisher, eds. New York: Macmillan, 565-575.

Hylton, John H. (2001). *Aboriginal Self-Government in Canada: Current Trends and Issues.* Saskatoon, SK: Purich Publishing.

Kulchyski, Peter. (2005). *Like the Sound of a Drum: Aboriginal Cultural Politics in Denendeh and Nunavut.* Winnipeg, MB: University of Manitoba Press.

Miller, Virginia P. (1995). The Micmac: A Maritime Woodland Group. *Native Peoples: The Canadian Experience.* R. Bruce Morrison and C. Roderick Wilson, eds. Toronto, ON: McClelland and Stewart, 444-470.

Penner, Keith. (1983). *Report of the Special Committee on Indian Self-Government in Canada.* Ottawa, ON: Ministry of Supply and Services.

Ponting, J. Rick, and Linda J. Henderson. (2005). Contested Visions of First Nations Governance: Secondary Analysis of Federal Government Research on the Opinions of On-Reserve Residents. *Canadian Ethnic Studies,* XXXVII:1, 63-86.

Russell, Dan. (2000). *A People's Dream: Aboriginal Self-Government in Canada.* Vancouver, BC: UBC Press.

Schouls, Tim. (2003). *Shifting Boundaries: Aboriginal Identity, Pluralist Theory, and the Politics of Self-Government.* Vancouver, BC: UBC Press.

Snow, Chief John. (2005). *These Mountains Are Our Sacred Places: The Story of the Stoney People.* Calgary, AB: Fitzhenry and Whiteside.

Warry, Wayne. (2007). *Unfinished Dreams: Community Healing and the Reality of Aboriginal Self-Government.* Toronto, ON: University of Toronto Press.

# Fifteen
## The Quest for Justice

Native people are greatly over-represented in all phases of the criminal justice system, from arrest through to incarceration. Aboriginal people are twice as likely as non-Natives to become involved with the criminal justice system, and constitute one-quarter of the combined federal and provincial inmate population. Although they constitute roughly 3% of the Canadian population, they comprise 10% of the federal inmate population. (Warry, 2007: 166-167)

Canada has no reason to be proud of its treatment of Aboriginal people, and their over-representation in the criminal justice system is a reflection of that poor record. My experience suggests that the federal justice system is responding to the pressure for change, that it continues to put effort into addressing the situation, and that is doing a credible job, considering the circumstances of most convicted Aboriginal offenders. (Irene Fraser, 2002: 109).

Any discussion of justice has to begin with the subject of rights – in this case, Aboriginal rights. Thomas Berger (1982: 219) has defined Aboriginal rights as rights to which Native people are entitled because they are the original peoples of Canada. This may not mean much to the average Canadian, but it has recently come to light that this truth is the axis on which the dealings of the Canadian government with First Nations rest. Justice, on the other hand, is the realization of those rights in the context of fair treatment. As Zion (2006: 51) notes;

Justice is . . . a feeling or affect. It is confidence in the integrity of processes, institutions, and actors who control and facilitate the resolution of conflict, and it is able to live with the result because of that confidence. It is a feeling of satisfaction – or at least acceptance – of the process.

Although the first few generations of contact between Canada's First Nations and their new European neighbors were fairly uneventful in so far as the honoring of rights was concerned, the end of the fur trade caused a major shift in relations between the two parties. While the fur trade was in process, everyone seemed to benefit from the industry. Fur traders brought loads of produce back to Europe and reaped great profits. Native Americans now had access to goods not locally obtainable, and many of them entered rewarding occupations as providers of furs and food supplies, guides, and interpreters. The question of fair treatment was hardly a concern because both parties were too heavily involved in economic matters. As time went on and the socioeconomic picture changed, a variety of other factors came into play, not the least of which was a major revamping of Native economies and the devastating effects of alcohol and imported diseases. Since then it seems that the deterioration of Indigenous rights continued until the emergence of a vital Native renaissance during the 1960s.

## Traditional Aboriginal Justice

The issue of Aboriginal rights poses a difficult challenge for nonNative politicians because they cannot begin to understand its bases. In the first instance, Native people believe that Aboriginal rights were given to them by the Creator. They were given the right to respect Mother Earth and receive her gifts with thanksgiving. Natural law, not man-made legislation, unless it concludes with natural law, must be respected and obeyed. Without the cooperation of Mother Earth there would be no sustenance, no form of life of any kind. All life is subject to the authority of nature. People are nourished by Mother Earth from whom springs all life. As Elder Oren Lyons (1988: 21) states; "The faces of our future generations are looking up from the earth and we step with great care not to disturb our grandchildren."

Cajete (1994: 75) posits that in contrast to the relatively one-dimensional reductionist Newtonian-Cartesian perception of nature, First Nations perceive multiple realities in nature. Those perceived by the five senses are only one of the possibilities of obtaining knowledge. A serious seeker, for example, can receive knowledge directly from animals, plants, and other living entities. The entities have ritual ways of behavior when they interact with one another. All life has a "personhood," and must be respected for it. Personhood provides each live entity with a sense of purpose and inherent meaning that can be expressed in a variety of ways and at all times. Chief John Snow (2005: 2) states it this way:

We talked to the rocks, the streams, the trees, the plants, the herbs, and all nature's creations. We called the animals our brothers. They understood our language; we too, understood theirs. Sometimes they talked to us in dreams and visions. At times they revealed important events or visited us on our vision quests to the mountain top. Truly we were part of and related to nature, and these animals were a very special part of the Great Spirit's creation.

Obviously it would take only a mild familiarity with the Canadian legal system to see how unreal the above description would seem in comparison. On the other hand, as Henderson (1988: 221) has observed, "The foundation of Aboriginal rights, in legal history, is not so much common-law as it is common sense." If that is true, a look back should inform us as to how far we have come since the days when only First Nations occupied this country. When the first Europeans arrived their initial perception of North America was as a wilderness occupied by uncivilized folk. The latter saw the earth as the most pristine and rich environment – a gift from the Creator to His children. Incoming Europeans looked upon the land primarily as a material object, a commodity from which they could gain economically. They viewed the occupants of the territory as another resource which they would either use or abuse according to their agenda for material gain (Cajete, 1994: 75).

Henderson (1988) appears somewhat undaunted by discrepancy, and outlines three basic schools of jurisprudence, the *first* of which is the natural-law or Aboriginal school. Adherents to this line of thinking posit that there are immutable principles inherent in human societies that cannot be ignored by law. Any law that runs counter to those immutable principles is therefore automatically invalid. The *second* school of law is the positivist school, which views the law as a closed system. Thus, in judging a case, a jurist simply looks at the formality of its enactment to ascertain whether or not it is a law. Henderson (1988: 223) observes:

The difference between the positive school and the natural-law school is illustrated by the traditional Iroquois belief that the world is an island resting on the back of a turtle. The positivist will never look beneath the turtle to see what the turtle is standing on; the natural law lawyer is interested in little else.

The *third* school of law is the realist school. A realist takes the approach that justice may be blind, but judges are not. A realist acknowledges the idealistic aspirations and goals of the legal system as desirable, but recognizes that judges are fallible and often function according to their own training, experience, and personal perceptions. As a result, from time to time they will make less than desirable decisions in judging cases. Henderson cautions that when judges are required to render a decision on a matter, they tend to select theories that more nearly match their own inclinations.

All of this necessitates a deeper look into the metaphysical background of traditional First Nations thinking. Clearly a look at general traditional societal regulations may prove helpful. One of the most widely read interpretations of traditional Aboriginal societal regulations in recent times was Rupert Ross' book, *Dancing With a Ghost: Exploring Indian Reality* (1992). Trained in law and later functioning as an Assistant Crown Attorney, Ross spent eleven years working among the Ojibway people of Ontario and then writing about his experiences. In his work among the Ojibway, Ross identified five "rules of traditional times," the *first* of which is called the ethic of non-interference. Sometimes considered one of the oldest and most pervasive of all the ethics by which First Nations used to live, Ross contends that this ethic has been practiced for more than twenty-five thousand years. Basically it means that a Native individual will never interfere in any way with the rights, privileges, and activities of another person.

The *second* ethic may be called the ethic that anger never be shown. Ross goes on to explain that this ethic actually applies to all human emotions including grief and sorrow. There are a number of reasons for this behavior, primary among them being that an individual is never alone; community life is everything. Therefore, anything that an individual does, particularly in emotional terms, affects the entire community. Some emotions, if indulged, can threaten a group and incapacitate them when a normal state of mind is required. When an individual dies, for example, his or her name is never mentioned because that might serve as a way to too directly remind people of their loss. One young man guilty of violent behavior, who was sentenced by the court to participate in therapy, refused to do so because it was considered wrong to discuss such a negative happening. To do so could stir strong emotions that might have negative or unfortunate repercussions in the community

The *third ethic,* really a form of taboo, is closely related to the second, and has to do with praise and gratitude. The roots of this taboo go back to survival times when the belief was that when each individual in the community did his or her best, there was no need to affirm their particular gift, aptitude, or calling. Fulfilling one's calling was viewed as a required responsibility; it was (and is) a gift given by the Creator to each individual. If someone neglects their duty or responsibility, there could be disastrous consequences for the community.

The *fourth* ethic is the conservation-withdrawal tactic which requires that individuals carefully think things through before they act. Sometimes known as "taking an Aboriginal moment," it implies that hasty responses to potentially-related situations could result in severe harm or even death. This perspective carries over to everyday matters, particularly with regard to behaviors that might affect others. In a deeper sense, this ethic seems to derive from an intentional slowing down to conserve both physical and psychic energy – being careful to consider all aspects of a new situation before responding to it. It is no doubt an ethic that could well serve citizens of the twenty-first century, regardless of cultural orientation. Exactness in timekeeping is a very valued commodity in contemporary society.

The *fifth ethic,* often equated with the popular notion of "Indian time," is better labelled the notion that "the time must be right." Individuals whose livelihood is geared to the cycles of nature, like the farmers of every century including this one, learn to respect the rhythms of nature. These individuals plant, water, and harvest in accordance with times dictated by the seasons. In other words, people learn how to wait patiently until the time is right, until all variables came together to provide the best results (Ross, 1992: 38). These five ethics formed the framework within which such concepts as equality, justice, respect for the individual, and the good of the community were worked out.

Traditionally, the methods of keeping individuals in line utilized by Canada's First Nations included storytelling, ridicule, shaming, and in a more serious cases, putting individuals into a circle of elders who would offer their advice to the offender. Members of the circle would demand change in the accused's behavior, and determine an appropriate punishment for the misdeed (Warry, 2007: 173-174). One particular practice that has recently been revived in some Aboriginal communities is the Native sentencing circle (Russell, 2000: 105). The participation in sentencing circles has varied in communities across Canada. After they became popular, some Native communities of the country adopted them in very significant numbers. For example, by the end of 1994, the Yukon had under-

taken about 300 sentencing circles, more than any other community in Canada. In Saskatchewan, about 100 sentencing circles had
been initiated, plus a few in British Columbia, Manitoba, and
Quebec (Steckley and Cummins, 2008: 241).

The procedure in a sentencing circle is as follows: the offender
is required to sit in the centre of a circle made up of members of
his or her family, community representatives, and members of the
judiciary (often elders). The offender is also considered to be part
of the decision-making process, and he or she may be surrounded
by as many as seventy-five people (Warry: 2007: 185). Essentially
the procedure of the sentencing circle was to remove the individual
from the community, often to an isolated location like an island, and
allowing him or her to be responsible for his or her own survival.
Prayer was a vital ingredient of the process, and everyone participating in some aspect of circle sentencing was viewed as an equal
partner. As Fraser (2002: 114). points out; "The process is less
intimidating, garners more information, and empowers the community. It makes it less easy for ego to prevail."

Initial reports on the effectiveness of sentencing circles, or circle courts, has been overwhelmingly positive. Today many Canadian
courts have welcomed the introduction of sentencing circles,
although research regarding their effectiveness is scant. There
appear to be no clear guidelines as to how to construct workable
sentencing circles or how the should operate. There seems to be a
need to develop such guidelines if the approach is to be adopted by
other communities. A standard form of evaluation is also a real need
so the end result can withstand any scrutiny by jurists, legalists and
other members of the court system.

Warry (2007: 185) observes that the "circle court," as it is sometimes known today, functions quite informally in that when it is
enacted, chairs and tables are located so as to create  as hospitable
an environment as possible. The goal is to increase participation by
community members, particularly in the final sentencing phase of
the process. When sentence is passed it is possible that those
offended by any of the offender's actions, may be awarded compensation in some form. As Warry (2007: 186) notes:

> The potential of sentencing circles lies in its use as a forum for
> community development. . . . Perhaps the greatest potential of
> such procedures lies in the creation of support groups and refer-
> ral networks among justice and social-service personnel, which

offer the promise of local rehabilitation rather than externally imposed punishment or incarceration for offenders.

# The Current Situation

*The Canadian Charter of Rights and Freedoms* is the document that allegedly guarantees certain rights to all Canadians. Russell (2000), a practicing Aboriginal lawyer in Toronto, identifies a series of legal areas in which Charter rights seem to apply differently to Indian and nonIndians. These include "due process of law," which seems to have a different meaning when applied to cases involving individuals of Aboriginal background. An important concept in this context is the motivational ethic which comes to the fore in cases of offenses committed by Aboriginals on behalf of someone else. The value of care and sense of responsibility in First Nations communities have created ties bound together by a complex web of relationships. This responsibility has also shaped the traditional sense of justice that continues to be operant in Indian communities to this day. Many behaviors, judged to be offenses by nonNative standards, may not be such because of the underlying motivational ethic. Was the "crime" committed to fulfill someone else's need and the "offender" undertook the action simply because he or she felt an obligation to meet someone else's need? The Canadian justice system does not readily acknowledge the validity of such an argument.

A closely related concept is what has been called "Aboriginal silence" in so far as proceedings of justice are concerned. Traditionally, Aboriginal cultures valued highly the decision of an individual not to share any more information regarding a specific incident than he or she felt obligated to do. This orientation has made it exceedingly difficult for nonNative justice systems to operate, especially since ours is essentially a verbal society. Unless a way is devised by which to take these values into account, the Canadian justice system will continue to be misapplied to Aboriginal individuals.

Generally speaking, all Canadians have a fairly positive view of the criminal justice system. They believe that the system should prevent crime, resolve disputes between members of a community, and rehabilitate those who offend. Aboriginal people, on the other hand, have a great fear of the courts and for good reason. The numbers indicate that their fears are well justified (Ponting and

Kiely, 1997: 152f). In 2000, for example, statistics furnished by the National Parole Board Monitoring Report show that the total number of Aboriginals sentenced to two years or more was 21 935. Of those, 12 800 were incarcerated, and the rest were conditionally released. Thus a population comprising only three percent of the nation's total, constituted ten percent of the federal inmate population.

There can be no debate that the Canadian criminal justice system has failed the nation's Indigenous peoples. Some Aboriginal leaders are calling for restorative justice because their people are still suffering from centuries of mass post-traumatic stress disorder (Zion, 2006: 60). They are now aware of the extent of injuries caused by law as conquest. They know that they cannot rely on dominant society to clean up the messes created, including high rates of crime and violence, substance abuse, suicide and the resulting anomie caused by failed attempts at assimilation. Preferably, they want to restore and apply their own principles of equality and justice.

A good example of neglect regarding First Nations justice in Canada is section 67 of the *Canadian Human Rights Act.* Today, for example, there is legislation before parliament to repeal section 67 because it denies First Nations people living on or off a reserve from filing a complaint with the Canadian Human Rights Commission relating to any action arising from or pursuant to the *Indian Act.* Section 67 was included in the *Canadian Human Rights Act* when it was first drafted in 1977, the argument being that it would allow the federal government time to address issues regarding sexual discrimination against Aboriginal women who had married nonStatus men. It was intended to be a temporary measure, but now, thirty years after, First Nations are still awaiting access to full human rights protection (*Alberta Native News,* February, 2008: 3). Many Aboriginal leaders believe that an immediate appeal of section 67 is mandatory.

As a result of this kind of treatment, there are strained relations between the federal government and First Nations. The practicality of such treatment is also reflected in police disregard of First Nations concerns. There is often a lack of clearly defined and accepted rules and understandings between the two parties which leads to frustration on both sides. Sometimes police officers have difficulty responding to requests made by members of an Indian community because their mandate is limited or because police officers lack appropriate intercultural training and understanding. Aboriginal communities still need those services, however, and they believe that the police are failing them when services are not provided. There is also the matter of written law which cannot necessarily be applied in all situations, particularly when specific ethnicities are involved (La Prairie, 1997: 109).

Perhaps the most common criticisms of the Canadian criminal justice system are that it is racist. In the first place, there are very few people of Aboriginal ancestry employed in the justice system. Too often nonAboriginal individuals who work in the system lack sufficient knowledge of Indigenous ways for them to be sensitive to Aboriginal needs. Therefore they are not as effective as they might be. There are indications that the situation is slowly changing. Educational requirements for federal workers in criminal justice are changing, and relevant workshops are being held, but progress has been slow.

Ideally, the First Nations of Canada would prefer to be able to exercise greater control over family, civil, and criminal justice matters in their communities. They do not necessarily want extensive jurisdiction, but they would prefer to see significant changes in the way laws are made and enforced, as well as in the way alleged transgressions are adjudicated and the way offenders are treated (La Prairie, 1997: 109). Challenging jurisdictional issues that must be addressed include, *first* of all, whether or not Aboriginal people living off reserve will be dealt with by Aboriginal justice systems, even if they commit offenses in other communities. *Second,* will there be some mechanism by which to return Aboriginal offenders to their own communities? *Third,* will the authority of local Aboriginal justice systems extend to transients, or others, who commit offenses on, but are not resident on Indian reserves? Fourth, if sentence options are honored on Indian reserves, will they be restricted to offenses committed on reserve or will they also be permitted to apply to offenses committed in non-reserve communities?

# Projections

The Canadian justice system is not presently geared to meting out fair treatment to Canada's Aboriginal peoples, but there are signs of positive change. One of them will be to increase opportunities for Aboriginal communities to regain their self-governing authority. If granted, their proceedings could for a time be subject to close scrutiny by enlightened mainline barristers, solicitors, and judges, to be sure. However, the emphasis is on the word "enlightened," implying that individuals who work in those capacities will need to undertake special training, preferably on the job with Aboriginal leaders and elders. Relevant courses in university law schools can certainly be of assistance, but they will not substitute for meaningful apprenticeship in a First Nations community. Faculties of education and social work have responded to this reality for some time, and it is encouraging to witness a similar development in the area of law and justice.

When it's time, it will happen. It is time.

## References

Berger, Thomas R. (1982). *Fragile Freedoms: Human Rights and Dissent in Canada.* Toronto, ON: Irwin Publishing.

Cajete, Gregory. (1994). *Look to the Mountain: An Ecology of Indigenous Education.* Durango, CO: Kiva Press.

Fraser, Irene. (2002). Honouring Alternatives in the Criminal Justice System. *Nation to Nation: Aboriginal Sovereignty and the Future of Canada.* John Bird, Lorraine Land, and Murray McAdam, eds. Toronto, ON: Irwin Publishing, 109-119.

Henderson, William B. (1988). Canadian Legal and Judicial Philosophies on the Doctrine of Aboriginal Rights. *The Quest for Justice: Aboriginal Peoples and Aboriginal Rights.* Menno Boldt and J. Anthony Long, eds. Toronto, ON: University of Toronto Press, 221-229.

La Prairie. (1997). Self-Government and Criminal Justice: Issues and Realities. *Aboriginal Self-Government in Canada: Current Trends and Issues.* John H. Hylton, ed. Saskatoon, SK: Purich Publishing, 108-129.

Lyons, Oren. (1988). Traditional Native Philosophies Relating to Aboriginal Rights. *The Quest for Justice: Aboriginal Peoples and Aboriginal Rights.* Menno Boldt and J. Anthony Long, eds. Toronto, ON: University of Toronto Press, 19-23.

Ponting, J. Rick., and Jerilynn Kiely. (1997). Disempowerment: "Justice," Racism, and Public Opinion. *First Nations in Canada: Perspectives on Opportunity, Empowerment, and Self-Determination.* J. Rick Ponting, ed. Toronto, ON: McGraw-Hill Ryerson Limited, 152-192.

Ross, Jeffrey Ian, and Larry Gould, eds. (2006). *Native Americans and the Criminal Justice System.* Boulder, CO: Paradigm Publishers.

Ross, Rupert. (1992). *Dancing With a Ghost: Exploring Indian Reality.* Markham, ON: Reed Books.

Russell, Dan. (2000). *A People's Dream: Aboriginal Self-Government Canada.* Vancouver, BC: UBC Press.

Snow, Chief John. (2005). *These Mountains Are Our Sacred Places: The Story of the Stoney People.* Calgary, AB: Fitzhenry and Whiteside.

Steckley, John I., and Bryan D. Cummins. (2008). *Full Circle: Canada's First Nations.* Toronto, ON: Pearson Education Canada.

Warry, Wayne. (2007). *Unfinished Dreams: Community Healing and the Reality of Aboriginal Self-Government.* Toronto, ON: University of Toronto Press.

Zion, James W. (2006). Justice as Phoenix: Traditional Indigenous Law, Restorative Justice, and the Collapse of the State. *Native Americans and the Criminal Justice System.* Jeffrey Ian Ross and Larry Gould, eds. Boulder, CO: Paradigm Publishers, 51-66.

# Bibliography

Adams, Howard. (1999). *Tortured People: The Politics of Colonization.* Revised edition. Penticton, BC: Theytus Books.

Adams, Howard. (1975). *Prison of Grass: Canada From the Native Point of View.* Toronto, ON: New Press.

Akan, Linda. (1992). Pimosatamowin Sikaw Kakeequaywin: Walking and Talking; Asaukteaux Elder's View of Native Education. *Canadian Journal of Native Education,* 19:2, 191-214.

Allport, Gordon W. (1958). *The Nature of Prejudice: A Comprehensive and Penterating Study of the Origin and Nature of Prejudice.* New York: Doubleday.

Anderson, T.G. (1863). *General Tuition Agreement.* Edmonton, AB: Department of Indian Affairs and Northern Development, Alberta Region.

Antone, Eileen. (2003). Culturally Framing Aboriginal Literacy and Learning. *Canadian Journal of Native Education,* 27:1, 7-15.

Archambault, Reginald, ed. (1964). *John Dewey on Education: Selected Writings.* New York: The Modern Library.

Armstrong, Jeanette. (2001). Invocation: The Real Power of Aboriginal Women. *Women of the First Nations: Power, Wisdom, and Strength.* Christine Miller and Patricia Chuchryk, eds. Winnipeg, MB: University of Manitoba Press, x-xii.

Asch, Michael. (2000). Self-Government in the New Millenium. *Nation to Nation: Aboriginal Sovereignty and the Future of Canada.* John Bird, Lorraine Land, and Murray McAdam, eds. Toronto, ON: Irwin Publishing, 65-73.

Banton, Michael, ed. (1966). *Anthropological Approaches to the Study of Religion.* London, UK: Tavistock.

Barman, Jean, Yvonne Hébert, and Don McCaskill, eds. (1986). The Legacy of the Past: An Overview. *Indian Education in Canada, Volume 1: The Legacy.* Vancouver, BC: University of British Columbia Press, 1-22.

Barron, F. Laurie, and Joseph Garcea, eds. (1999). Introduction. *Urban Indian Reserves: Forging New Relationships in Saskatchewan.* Saskatoon, SK: Purich Publishing.

Barron, F. Laurie, and Joseph Garcea. (1999). The Genesis of Urban Reserves. *Urban Indian Reserves: Forging New Relationships in Saskatchewan.* F. Laurie Barron, and Joseph Garcea, eds. Saskatoon, SK: Purich Publishing, 22-52.

Baruth, Leroy, and M. Lee Manning. (1992) *Multicultural Education of Children and Adolescents.* Needham Heights, MA: Allyn and Bacon.

Battiste, Marie, and James [Sa'ke'j) Youngblood Henderson. (2000). *Protecting Indigenous Knowledge and Heritage: A Global Challenge.* Saskatoon, SK: Purich Publishing Company.

Battiste, Marie. (2000). Maintaining Aboriginal Identity, Language and Culture in Modern Society. *Reclaiming Indigenous Voice and Vision.* Marie Battiste, ed. Vancouver, BC: UBC Press, 192-208.

Battiste, Marie, and James (Sa'ke'j) Youngblood Henderson. (2000). *Protecting Indigenous Knowledge and Heritage: A Global Challenge.* Saskatoon, SK: Purich Publishing Ltd.

Bayles, Ernest E., and Bruce L. Hood. (1966). *Growth of American Educational Thought and Practice.* New York: Harper & Row.

Benedict, Ruth. (1934). *Patterns of Culture.* New York: The New American Library.

Bennett, Christine. (1990). *Comprehensive Multicultural Education: Theory and Practice.* Second edition. Boston, MA: Allyn and Bacon.

Berger, Paul, Juanita Ross Epp, and Helle Møller. (2006). The Predictable Influences of Culture Clash, Current Practice, and Colonialism on Punctuality, Attendance, and Achievement in Nunavut Schools. *Canadian Journal of Native Education,* 29:2, 182-205.

Berger, Thomas R. (1982). *Fragile Freedoms: Human Rights and Dissent in Canada.* Toronto, ON: Irwin Publishing.

Berlo, Janet Catherine. (1992). Introduction: The Formative Years of Native American Art History. *The Early Years of Native American Art History: The Politics and Scholarship and Collecting.* Janet Catherine Berlo, ed. Seattle, WA: University of Washington Press, 1-21.

Berlo, Janet Catherine, and Ruth B. Phillips. (1998). *Native North American Art.* New York: Oxford University Press.

Bernstein, Bruce. (1999). Contexts for the Growth and Development of the Indian Art World in the 1960s and 1970s. *Native American Art in the Twentieth Century: Makers, Meanings, Histories.* W. Jackson III, ed. London, UK: Routledge, 57-74.

Berry, John W. (1981). Native People and the Larger Society. *A Canadian Social Psychology of Ethnic Relations.* Robert C. Gardner and Rudolf Kalin, eds. Toronto, ON: Methuen, 214-230.

Bird, John, Lorraine Land, and Murray Macadam. (2002). *Nation to Nation: Aboriginal Sovereignty and the Future of Canada.* Toronto, ON: Public Justice Resource Centre.

Bobiwash, A. Rodney. (1997). Native Urban Self-Government in Toronto and the Politics of Self Determination. *The Meeting Place: Aboriginal Life in Toronto.* Frances Sanderson & Heather Howard-Bobiwash, eds. Toronto, ON: Native Canadian Centre of Toronto, 84-94.

Boldt, Menno (1993). *Surviving as Indians: The Challenge of Self-Government.* Toronto, ON: University of Toronto Press.

Bone, Robert M. (1992). *The Geography of the Canadian North: Issues and Challenges.* Toronto, ON: Oxford University Press.

Bordewich, Fergus. (1996). *Killing the White Man's Burden: Reinventing Native Americans at the End of the Twentieth Century.* New York: Anchor Books.

Brickman, William W., and Stanley Lehrer. (1961). *John Dewey: Master Educator.* New York: Atherton Press.

Brookes, Sonia. (1991). The Persistence of Native Education Policy in Canada. *The Cultural Maze: Complex Questions on Native Destiny in Western Canada.* John W. Friesen, ed. Calgary, AB: Detselig Enterprises, 163-180.

Brown, Dee. (1981). *Bury My Heart at Wounded Knee.* New York: Holt, Rinehart & Winston.

Buckley, Helen. (1993). *From Wooden Ploughs to Welfare: Why Indian Policy Failed in the Prairie Provinces.* Montreal, PQ: McGill-Queen's University Press.

Bull, Linda R. (1991). Indian Residential Schooling: The Native Perspective. *Canadian Journal of Native Education,* 18: Supplement, 1-64.

Burns, George F. (1998). Factors and Themes in Native Education and School Boards/First Nations Tuition Negotiations and Tuition Agreement Schooling. *Canadian Journal of Native Education,* 22:1, 53-66.

Cajete, Gregory. (1994). *Look to the Mountain: An Ecology of Indigenous Education.* Durango, CO: Kiva Press.

Callahan, Marilyn. (2005). Beyond Stereotypes of Old Maids and Grand Dames: Women as Insurgents in Child Welfare in British Columbia. *Child and Family Welfare in British Columbia.* Diane Purvey and Christopher Walmsley, eds. Calgary, AB: Detselig Enterprises, 235-258.

Calliou, George D. (1997) Urban Indians: Reflections on Participation of First Nation Individuals in the Institutions of the Larger Society. *First Nations in Canada: Perspectives on Opportunity, Empowerment, and Self-Determination.* J. Rick Ponting, ed. Toronto, ON: McGraw-Hill Ryerson, 222-244.

Cardinal, Harold. (1977). *The Rebirth of Canada's Indians.* Edmonton, AB: Hurtig Publishers.

Cardinal, Harold. (1969). *The Unjust Society: The Tragedy of Canada's Indians.* Edmonton, AB: M. G. Hurtig.

Cardinal, Harold, and Walter Hildebrandt. (2000). *Treaty Elders of Saskatchewan.* Calgary, AB: University of Calgary Press.

Carter, Sarah. (2001). First Nations Women of Prairie Canada in the Early Reserve Years, the 1870s to the 1920s: A Preliminary Inquiry. *Women of the First Nations: Power, Wisdom, and Strength.* Christine Miller and Patricia Chuchryk, eds. Winnipeg, MB: The University of Manitoba Press, 51-76.

Castellano, Marlene Brant, Lynne Davis, and Louise Lahache.(2000). Innovations in Education Practice. *Aboriginal Education: Fulfilling the Promise.* Marlene Brant Castellano, Lynne Davis, and Louise Lahache, eds. Vancouver, BC: University of British Columbia Press, 97-100.

Chalmers, John W. (1974). Marguerite Bourgeoys, Preceptress of New France. *Profiles of Canadian Educators.* Robert S. Patterson, John W. Chalmers, and John W. Friesen, eds. Toronto, ON: D. C. Heath Canada, Ltd., 4-20.

Chief Dan George. (1974). *My Heart Soars.* Toronto, ON: Hancock House Publishers.

Cockerill, Jodi, and Roger Gibbins. (1997). Reluctant Citizens? First Nations in the Canadian Federal State. *First Nations in Canada: Perspectives on Opportunity, Empowerment, and Self-Determination.* Toronto, ON: McGraw-Hill Ryerson, 383-403.

Conrad, Margaret, Alvin Finkel, and Cornelius Jaenen. (1993). *History of the Canadian Peoples: Beginnings to 1867.* Toronto, ON: Copp Clark Pitman.

Cooke-Dallin, Bruce, Trish Rosborough, and Louise Underwood. (2000). The Role of Elders in Child and Youth Care Education. *Canadian Journal of Native Education,* 24:2, 82-91.

Cooper, Michael L. (1999). *Indian School: Teaching the White Man's Way.* New York: Clarion Books.

Copley, John. (February, 2006). Bigstone Ventures Puts Community Members at Work. *Alberta Native News,* 23:2, 11, 16.

Copley, John. (March, 2006). Companies and Communities Benefit from Access Agreements. *Alberta Native News,* 23:3, 21.

Couture, Joseph E. (1991). Explorations in Native Knowing. *The Cultural Maze: Complex Questions on Native Destiny in Western Canada.* John W. Friesen, ed. Calgary, AB: Detselig Enterprises, 53-73.

Couture, Joseph E. (1991). The Role of Native Elders: Emergent Issues. *The Cultural Maze: Complex Questions on Native Destiny in Western Canada.* John W. Friesen, ed. Calgary, AB: Detselig Enterprises, 201-218.

Craig, Susan E. (September, 1992). The Educational Needs of Children Living with Violence. *Phi Delta Kappan,* 24:1, 67-71.

Crow Chief, Lillian. (2006). Indigenous Ideas on Instruction. Calgary, AB: University of Calgary, Unpublished paper. Faculty of Communication and Culture. 3pp.

Cross, Martin. (December 17, 2001). Aboriginal Leaders Exploiting Their Own Communities. *Mennonite Reporter,* 5:24, 11.

Cummins, J., and M. Swain. (1986). *Bilingualism in Education.* London, UK: Longman.

Daniel, Richard. (1999). The Spirit and Terms of Treaty Eight. *The Spirit of the Alberta Treaties.* Third edition. Richard T. Price, ed. Edmonton, AB: The University of Alberta Press, 47-100.

Deloria, Vine, Jr. (1995). *Red Earth, White Lies: Native Americans and the Myth of Scientific Fact.* New York: Scribner.

Dempsey, Hugh A. (1997). *Indian Tribes of Alberta.* Calgary, AB: Glenbow Museum.

Dempsey, Hugh A. (1997). Tribal Honors: *A History of the Kainai Chieftainship.* Calgary, AB: Kainai Chieftainship.

Denig, Edwin Thompson. (2000). *The Assiniboine.* Edited by J.N.B. Hewitt. Regina, SK: Canadian Plains Research Center.

Dickason, Olive Patricia. (2006). *A Concise History of Canada's First Nations.* Toronto, ON: Oxford University Press.

Dickason, Olive Patricia. (2000). Toward a Larger View of Canada's History: The Native Factor. *Visions of the Heart: Canadian Aboriginal Issues.* David Long and Olive Patricia Dickason, eds. Toronto, ON: Harcourt Canada, 11-30.

Dickason, Olive Patricia. (1993). *Canada's First Nations: A History of Founding Peoples from Earliest Times.* Toronto, ON: McClelland and Stewart.

Dickason, Olive Patricia. (1984). *The Myth of the Savage and the Beginnings of French Colonialism in the Americas.* Edmonton, AB: University of Alberta Press.

Dion, Joseph F. (1979). *My Tribe, The Crees.* Calgary, AB: Glenbow Museum.

Dissanayake, Ellen. (1990). *What is Art For?* Seattle, WA: University of Washington Press.

Dossey, Larry. (1997). *Prayer is Good Medicine.* New York: HarperCollins.

Dossey, Larry. (1997). *Healing Words: The Power of Prayer and the Practice of Medicine.* New York: HarperCollins.

Driver, Harold E. (1968). *Indians of North America.* Chicago, IL: University of Chicago Press.

Dunsmore, Frances. (1979). *Chippewa Customs.* St. Paul, MN: Minnesota Historical Society Press.

Dyck, Noel. (1997). *Differing Visions: Administering Indian Residential Schooling in Prince Albert, 1867-1995.* Halifax, NS: Fernwood Publishing and Prince Albert, SK: The Prince Albert Grand Council.

Eastman, Charles A. (Ohiyesa). (1980). *The Soul of the Indian: An Interpretation.* Lincoln, NE: University of Nebraska Press.

Ewers, John C. (1989). *The Blackfeet: Raiders of the Northwestern Plains.* Norman, OK: University of Oklahoma Press.

Ewing, Douglas C. (1982). *Pleasing the Spirits: A Catalog of a Collection of American Indian Art.* New York: Ghylen Press.

Fain, Stephen M., Robert Shostak, and John F. Dean. (1979). *Teaching in America.* Glenview, IL: Scott, Foresman and Company.

Feder, Norman. (1971). *Two Hundred Years of North American Art.* New York: Praeger.

Fisher, Robin. (1977). *Contact & Conflict: Indian-European Relations in British Columbia, 1774-1890.* Vancouver, BC: University of British Columbia Press.

Fiske, JoAnne. (2001). Gender and the Paradox of Residential Education in Carrier Society. *Women of the First Nations: Power, Wisdom, and Strength.* Christine Miller and Patricia Chuchryk, eds. Winnipeg, MB: The University of Manitoba Press, 167-182.

Flanagan, Thomas. (2000). *First Nations? Second Thoughts?* Montreal, PQ: McGill-Queen's University Press.

Fleras, Augie, and Jean Leonard Elliott. (2007). *Unequal Relations: An Introduction to Race, Ethnic, and Aboriginal Dynamics in Canada.* Fifth edition. Toronto, ON: Pearson Canada.

42eXplore. http://42explore.com/story.htm

Fraser, Irene. (2002). Honouring Alternatives in the Criminal Justice System. *Nation to Nation: Aboriginal Sovereignty and the Future of Canada.* John Bird, Lorraine Land, and Murray McAdam, eds. Toronto, ON: Irwin Publishing, 109-119.

Freeland, Cynthia. (2001). *But Is It Art?* London: Oxford University Press.

Frideres, James S., and René R. Gadacz. (2001). *Aboriginal Peoples in Canada: Contemporary Conflicts.* Sixth edition. Toronto, ON: Pearson Canada.

Friesen, John W. (2000). *Aboriginal Spirituality and Biblical Theology: Closer Than You Think.* Calgary, AB: Detselig Enterprises.

Friesen, John W. (2000). *Legends of the Elders.* Calgary, AB: Detselig Enterprises.

Friesen, John W. (1999). *First Nations of the Plains: Creative, Adaptable and Enduring.* Calgary, AB: Detselig Enterprises.

Friesen, John W. (1998). *Sayings of the Elders: An Anthology of First Nations Wisdom.* Calgary, AB: Detselig Enterprises.

Friesen, John W. (1997). *Rediscovering the First Nations of Canada.* Calgary, AB: Detselig Enterprises.

Friesen, John W. (1995). *You Can't Get There From Here: The Mystique of North American Plains Indians Culture & Philosophy.* Dubuque, IA: Kendall/Hunt.

Friesen, John W. (1995). *Pick One: A User-Friendly Guide to Religion.* Calgary, AB: Detselig Enterprises.

Friesen, John W. (1993). Formal Schooling Among the Ancient Ones: The Mystique of the Kiva. *American Indian Culture and Research Journal,* 17:4, 55-68.

Friesen, John W. (1993). *When Cultures Clash: Case Studies in Multiculturalism.* Second edition. Calgary, AB: Detselig Enterprises.

Friesen, John W. (1991). *The Cultural Maze: Complex Questions on Native Destiny in Western Canada.* Calgary, AB: Detselig Enterprises.

Friesen, John W. (1991). Native Cultures in a Cultural Clash. *The Cultural Maze: Complex Questions on Native Destiny in Western Canada.* John W. Friesen, ed. Calgary, AB: Detselig Enterprises, 23-38.

Friesen, John W. (1991). The Persistence of Cultural Destiny: The Role of Language. *The Cultural Maze: Complex Questions on Native Destiny in Western Canada.* John W. Friesen, ed. Calgary, AB: Detselig Enterprises, 147-162.

Friesen, John W. (1989). Institutional Response to Multicultural Policy: A Pilot Study of the Business Sector. *Multicultural and Intercultural Education: Building Canada.* Proceedings of the November, 1987, Canadian Council for Multicultural and Intercultural Education. Sonia V. Morris, ed. Calgary, AB: Detselig Enterprises, 13-24.

Friesen, John W. (1983). *Schools With a Purpose.* Calgary, AB: Detselig Enterprises.

Friesen, John W. (1977). *People, Culture & Learning.* Calgary, AB: Detselig Enterprises.

Friesen, John W., and Virginia Lyons Friesen. (2006). *Canadian Aboriginal Art and Spirituality: A Vital Link.* Calgary, AB: Detselig Enterprises.

Friesen, John W., and Virginia Lyons Friesen. (2005). *First Nations in the Twenty-First Century: Contemporary Educational Frontiers.* Calgary, AB: Detselig Enterprises.

Friesen, John W., and Virginia Lyons Friesen. (2005). *Even More Legends of the Elders.* Calgary, AB: Detselig Enterprises.

Friesen, John W., and Virginia Lyons Friesen. (2004). *Still More Legends of the Elders.* Calgary, AB: Detselig Enterprises.

Friesen, John W., and Virginia Lyons Friesen. (2004). *We Are Included: The Métis People of Canada Realize Riel's Vision.* Calgary, AB: Detselig Enterprises.

Friesen, John W., and Virginia Lyons Friesen (2002). *Aboriginal Education in Canada: A Plea for Integration.* Calgary, AB: Detselig Enterprises.

Friesen, John W., and Virginia Lyons Friesen. (2001). *In Defense of Public Schools in North America.* Calgary, AB: Detselig Enterprises.

Friesen, Virginia Lyons, and John W. Friesen. (2005). *Legends of the Elders Handbook for Teachers, Homeschoolers, and Parents.* Calgary, AB: Detselig Enterprises.

Fultz, Joanna. (March / April, 2007). Keepers of the Forest. *Canadian Geographic,* 127:2, 52-61.

Furniss, Elizabeth. (1995). *Victims of Benevolence: The Dark Legacy of the Williams Lake Residential School.* Vancouver, BC: Arsenal Pulp Press.

Garcia, Eugene. (1994). *Understanding and Meeting the Challenge of Student Cultural Diversity.* Boston, MA: Houghton-Mifflin.

Garnier, Karie. (1990). *Your Elders Speak: A Tribute to Native Elders.* Volume One. White Rock, BC: Published by Karie Garnier.

Gebhard, David. (1974). *Indian Art of the Northern Plains.* Santa Barbara, CA: University of Santa Barbara.

Ghosh, Ratna. (1996). *Redefining Multicultural Education.* Toronto, ON: Harcourt & Brace.

Gibson, Margaret. (1976). Approaches to Multicultural Education in the U.S.A.: Some Concepts and Assumptions. *Anthropology and Education Quarterly,* 7:4, 7-18.

Goldenweiser, Alexander A. (1968). Iroquois Social Organization. *The North American Indians: A Sourcebook.* Roger C. Owen, James J. F. Deetz, and Anthony Fisher, eds. New York: Macmillan, 565-575.

Goldfrank, Esther S. (1945). Changing Configurations on the Social Organization of a Blackfoot Tribe during the Reserve Period (The Blood Indians of Alberta, Canada). *Monographs of the American Ethnological Society.* No. 8, A. Irving Hollowell, ed. Seattle, WA: University of Washington Press.

Gollnick, Donna M., and Philip C. Chinn. (1986). *Multicultural Education in a Pluralistic Society.* Second edition. Columbia, OH: Charles E. Merrill.

Goodstriker, Wilton. (1996). Introduction. *The True Spirit and Original Intent of Treaty 7.* Treaty 7 Elders and Tribal Council with Walter Hildebrandt, Sarah Carter, and Dorothy First Rider. Montreal, PQ: McGill-Queen's University Press

Goulet, Linda. (2001). Two Teachers of Aboriginal Students: Effective Practice in Sociocultural Realities. *Canadian Journal of Native Education,* 25:1, 68-82.

Grant, Agnes, ed. (2004). Shirley Sterling. *Finding My Talk: How Fourteen Native Women Reclaimed Their Lives after Residential School.* Calgary, AB: Fitzhenry and Whiteside, 87-100.

Grant, Agnes. (1996). *No End of Grief: Indian Residential Schools in Canada.* Winnipeg, MB: Pemmican Publications.

Grant, Agnes. (1993). *Our Bit of Truth: An Anthology of Canadian Native Literature.* Winnipeg, MB: Pemmican Publications.

Grant, Carl A., ed. (1995). *Educating for Diversity: An Anthology of Multicultural Education.* Needham Heights, MA: Allyn and Bacon.

Grinnell, George Bird. (1900). *The North American Indians of Today.* London, UK: C. Arthur Pearson, Ltd.

Haig-Brown, Celia. (1993). *Resistance and Renewal: Surviving the Indian Residential School.* Vancouver, BC: Tillacum Books.

Hale, Horatio (1965). *The Iroquois Books of Rites.* Toronto, ON: University of Toronto Press, originally published in 1883.

Hare, Jan. (2003). Aboriginal Families and Aboriginal Education: Coming Full Circle. Second edition. *Children, Teachers and Schools in the History of British Columbia.* Jean Barman and Mona Gleason, eds. Calgary, AB: Detselig Enterprises, 411-430.

Harrison, Trevor W., and John W. Friesen. (2004). *Canadian Society in the Twenty-First Century.* Toronto, ON: Pearson Canada.

Harrod, Howard L. (1995). *Becoming and Remaining a People: Native American Religions on the Northern Plains.* Tucson, AZ: University of Arizona Press.

Haycock, Ronald G. (1971). *The Image of the Indian.* Waterloo, ON: Waterloo Lutheran University.

Henderson, William B. (198). Canadian Legal and Judicial Philosophies on the Doctrine of Aboriginal Rights. *The Quest for Justice: Aboriginal Peoples and Aboriginal Rights.* Menno Boldt and J. Anthony Long, eds. Toronto, ON: University of Toronto Press, 221-229.

Hendry, Graham D. (April, 1996). Constructivism and Educational Practice. *Australian Journal of Education,* 40:1, 19-45.

Henlin, Calvin. (2006). *Dances with Dependency: Indigenous Success Through Self-Reliance.* Vancouver, BC: Orca Spirit Publishing and Communications.

Herrick, C.J. (1924). *Neurological Foundations of Animal Behavior.* New York: Holt, Rinehart and Winston.

Hewitt, W. E., ed. (1993). *The Sociology of Religion: A Canadian Focus.* Toronto, ON: Butterworths.

Hirst, L., and C. Slavik. (1990). Cooperative Approaches to Language Learning. In J. Reyhner (Ed.), Effective Language Education Practices and Native Language Survival. Choctaw, OK: *Native American Language Issues.* Proceedings of the Ninth Annual International Native American Language Issues Institute, 133-142. (ERIC Document Reproduction Service No. ED 342, 512).

Hodgson-Smith. (2000). Issues of Pedagogy in Aboriginal Education. *Aboriginal Education: Fulfilling the Promise.* Marlene Brant Castellano, Lynne Davis, and Louise Lahache, eds. Vancouver, BC: UBC Press, 156-170.

Hookimaw-Witt, J. (1998). Keenabonoh Keemoshominook Kaeshge Peemishishik Odaskiwakh [we stand on the graves of our ancestors]: Native interpretations of Treaty #9 with Attawapiskat Elders. Unpublished Master's Thesis. Peterborough, ON: Trent University

Houle, Robert. (1991). The Spiritual Legacy of the Ancient Ones. *Land Spirit Power: First Nations at the National Gallery of Canada.* Diana Nemiroff, Robert Houle, and Charlotte Townsend-Gault, eds. Ottawa, ON: National Gallery of Canada, 43-73.

Hungry Wolf, Beverly. (2001). Life in Harmony with Nature. *Women of the First Nations: Power, Wisdom, and Strength.* Christine Miller and Patricia Chuchryk, editors. Winnipeg, MB: The University of Manitoba Press, 77-82.

Hungry Wolf, Beverly. (1996). Living in Harmony with Nature. *Women of the First Nations: Power, Wisdom, and Strength.* Christine Miller and Patricia Chuchryk, eds. Winnipeg, MB: The University of Manitoba Press, 77-82.

Hungry Wolf, Beverly. (1982). *The Ways of My Grandmothers.* New York: Quill.

Hylton, John H. (2001). *Aboriginal Self-Government in Canada: Current Trends and Issues.* Saskatoon, SK: Purich Publishing.

Indian Affairs and Northern Development website. http://www.ainc-inac.gc.ca

Jaenen, Cornelius J. (1986). Education for Francisation: The Case of New France in the Seventeenth Century. *Indian Education in Canada,*

*Volume 1: The Legacy.* Jean Barman, Yvonne Hébert, and Don McCaskill, eds. Vancouver, BC: University of British Columbia Press, 45-63.

Jenness, Diamond. (1977). *The Indians of Canada.* Seventh edition. Toronto, ON: University of Toronto Press.

Jordan, C. (1984). Cultural Compatibility and the Education of Hawaiian Children: Implications for Mainland Educators. *Educational Research Quarterly,* 8:4, 59-71.

Josephy, Alvin M., Jr. (1968). *The Indian Heritage of America.* New York: Alfred A. Knopf.

Kaltreider, Kurt. (1998). *American Indian Prophecies: Conversations with Chasing Deer.* Carlsbad, CA: Hay House.

Kennedy, Dan (Ochankugahe). (1972). *Recollections of an Assiniboine Chief.* Toronto, ON: McClelland and Stewart.

Kirkness, Verna J. (1998). The Critical State of Aboriginal Languages in Canada. *Canadian Journal of Native Education.* 22:1, 93-107.

Knockwood, Isabelle. (1994). *Out of the Depths: The Experiences of Mi'kmaw Childeren at the Indian Residential School at Shubenacadie, Nova Scotia.* Lockeport, NS: Roseway Publishing.

Knowles, T., J. Gill, A. Beauvais, and C. Medearis. (1992). *Teacher Education and the Rosebud Tribal Education Code.* Tribal College, 4:2, 21-23.

Knudtson, Peter, and David Suzuki. (1992). *Wisdom of the Elders.* Toronto, ON: Stoddart.

Kulchyski, Peter. (2005). *Like the Sound of a Drum: Aboriginal Cultural Politics in Denendeh and Nunavut.* Winnipeg, MB: University of Manitoba Press.

La Prairie. (1997). Self-Government and Criminal Justice: Issues and Realities. *Aboriginal Self-Government in Canada: Current Trends and Issues.* John H. Hylton, ed. Saskatoon, SK: Purich Publishing, 108-129.

Leavitt, Robert. (1995). Language and Cultural Change Content in Native Education. *First Nations Education in Canada: The Circle Unfolds.* Marie Battiste and Jean Barman, eds. Vancouver, BC: University of British Columbia Press, 124-138.

Lincoln, Kenneth. (1985). *Native American Renaissance.* Berkeley, CA: University of California Press.

Lischke, Ute, and David T. McNab. (2007). Introduction. *Walking a Tightrope: Aboriginal People and Their Representations.* Ute Lischke and David T. McNab, eds. Waterloo, ON: Wilfred Laurier University Press, 1-18.

Little Soldier, L. (1989). Cooperative Learning and the Native American Student. *Phi Delta Kappan,* 7:2, 161-163.

Lowie, Robert. (1963). *Indians of the Plains.* New York: The American Museum of Natural History.

Lowie, Robert. (1924). *Primitive Religion.* New York: Grosset and Dunlop.

Lyons, Oren. (1988). Traditional Native Philosophies Relating to Aboriginal Rights. *The Quest for Justice: Aboriginal Peoples and Aboriginal Rights.* Menno Boldt and J. Anthony Long, eds. Toronto, ON: University of Toronto Press, 19-23.

Maclean, John. (1980). *Native Tribes of Canada.* Toronto, ON: William Briggs. Reprinted by Coles Publishing Company, Toronto, ON.

Maclean, John. (1896). *Canada's Savage Folk.* London, UK: William Briggs. Reprinted in 1980 by Coles Publishing Company of Toronto, ON.

Mails, Thomas E. (1997). *Creators of the Plains.* Tulsa, OK: Council Oak Books.

Makela, Kathleen. (1999). Legal and Jurisdictional Issues of Urban Reserves. *Urban Indian Reserves: Forging New Relationships in Saskatchewan.* Barron F. Laurie, and Joseph Garcea, eds. Saskatoon, SK: Purich Publishing, 78-95.

Mandelbaum, David G. (1979). *The Plains Cree: An Ethnographic, Historical and Comparative Study.* Regina, SK: Canadian Plains Research Center.

Mason, Jim (1997). The kind of reward you put into your heart. *The Meeting Place: Aboriginal Life in Toronto.* Frances Sanderson & Heather Howard-Bobiwash, eds. Toronto, ON: Native Canadian Centre of Toronto, 97-105.

McConnell, Andrew. (1997). To know where you are going, you have to know where you've been. *The Meeting Place: Aboriginal Life in Toronto.* Frances Sanderson & Heather Howard-Bobiwash, eds. Toronto, ON: Native Canadian Centre of Toronto, 149-155.

McFarlane, Peter. (2000). Aboriginal Leadership. *Visions of the Heart: Canadian Aboriginal Issues, Second Edition. David A. Long and Olive P. Dickason, eds..* Toronto, ON: Harcourt Canada, 49-80.

McKay, Eva. (1999). If they read what you are writing, this is the teachings, this is some of the teachings that we want them to read about. *In the Words of Elders.* Peter Kulchyski, Don McCaskill, and David Newhouse, eds. Toronto, ON: University of Toronto Press, 289-310.

McMillan, Alan D. (1995). *Native Peoples and Cultures of Canada.* Second edition. Vancouver, BC: Douglas and McIntyre.

McNeill, John L. (1974). Egerton Ryerson, Founder of (English-Speaking) Education. *Profiles of Canadian Educators.* Robert S. Patterson, John W. Chalmers, and John W. Friesen, eds. Toronto, ON: D. C. Heath Canada, Ltd., 118-140.

Medicine, Beatrice. (1987). My Elders Tell Me. *Indian Education in Canada: Volume Two, The Challenge.* Jane Barman, Yvonne Hébert, and Don McCaskill, eds. Vancouver, BC: University of British Columbia Press, 142- 152.

Meili, Dianne. (1991). *Those Who Know: Profiles of Alberta Elders.* Edmonton, AB: NeWest.

Melling, John. (1967). *Right to a Future: The Native Peoples of Canada.* Don Mills, ON: T. H. Best Printing Company.

Mercer, Geoffrey. (2001). Aboriginal Peoples: Health and Healing. *Aboriginal People and Other Canadians.* Martin Thornton and Roy Todd, eds. Ottawa, ON: University of Ottawa Press, 131-160.

Miller, Christine, and Patricia Chuchryk, eds. (2001). *Women of the First Nations: Power, Wisdom, and Strength.* Winnipeg, MB: University of Manitoba Press.

Miller, J.R. (2004). *Reflections on Native-Newcomer Relations: Selected Essays.* Toronto, ON: University of Toronto Press.

Miller, J.R. (2000). *Skyscrapers Hide the Heavens: A History of Indian-White Relations in Canada.* Third edition. Toronto, ON: University of Toronto Press.

Miller, J.R. (1997). *Shingwauk's Vision: A History of Native Residential Schools.* Toronto, ON: University of Toronto Press.

Miller, Virginia P. (1995). The Micmac: A Maritime Woodland Group. *Native Peoples: The Canadian Experience.* R. Bruce Morrison and C. Roderick Wilson, eds. Toronto, ON: McClelland and Stewart, 444-470.

Miller-Lauchmann, Lynn, and Lorraine S. Taylor. (1995). *Schools for All: Educating Children in a Diverse Society.* Albany, NY: Delmar Publishers.

Milloy, John S. (1999). *A National Crime: The Canadian Government and the Residential School System, 1879 to 1986.* Winnipeg, MB: University of Manitoba Press.

Milloy, John S. (1990). *The Plains Cree: Trade, Diplomacy and War, 1790 to 1870.* Winnipeg, MB: The University of Manitoba Press.

Morgan, Lewis H. (1963). *Ancient Society.* Cleveland, OH: World Publishing.

Mountain Horse, Mike. (1989). *My People, The Bloods.* Calgary, AB: Glenbow Museum.

NA. (2004). *Our Story: Aboriginal Voices on Canada's Past.* Toronto, ON: Doubleday Canada.

Nagler, Mark. (1973). *Indians in the City: A Study of the Urbanization of Indians in Toronto.* Ottawa, ON: Canadian Research Centre for Anthropology, Saint Paul University.

Newhouse, David R., Cora J. Voyageur, and Dan Beavon. eds. (2004). *Hidden in Plain Sight: Contributions of Aboriginal Peoples to Canadian Identity and Culture.* Toronto, ON: University of Toronto Press.

Newhouse, David R., Cora J. Voyageur, and Dan Beavon. (2005). Introduction. *Contributions of Aboriginal Peoples to Canadian Identity and Culture.* David R. Newhouse, Cora J. Voyageur, and Dan Beavon, eds. Toronto, ON: University of Toronto Press, 3-13.

Norton, Ruth W. (1989) Analysis of Policy on Native Languages: A Comparison of Government Policy and Native Preferences for a Native Language Policy. Unpublished paper, University of Calgary, 35pp.

Obonsawin, Roger, and Heather Howard-Bobiwash. (1997). The Native Canadian Centre of Toronto: The Meeting Place for the Aboriginal Community for 35 Years. *The Meeting Place: Aboriginal Life in Toronto.* Frances Sanderson & Heather Howard-Bobiwash, eds. Toronto. ON: The Native Canadian Centre of Toronto, 25-59.

Ornstein, Allan. C. (1990). *Strategies for Effective Teaching.* New York: Harper and Row.

O'Toole, Roger. (1984). *Religion: Classic Sociological Approaches.* Toronto, ON: McGraw-Hill Ryerson.

Ozmon, Howard A., and Samuel M. Craver. (2003). *Philosophical Foundations of Education.* Upper Saddle River, NJ: Merrill Prentice-Hall.

Palliser, Brian. (September 8, 2003). Canadian Aboriginal Policy: Where to From Here? *The Carberry News.*

Palmer, Howard H. (1981). *Patterns of Prejudice: A History of Nativism in Alberta.* Toronto, ON: McClelland and Stewart.

Parkerson, Donald H., and Jo Ann Parkerson. (2001). *Transitions in American Education: A Social History of Teaching.* New York: Routledge-Falmer.

Patterson, E. Palmer. (1972). *The Canadian Indian.* Toronto, ON: Macmillan.

Paupanekis, Kenneth, and David Westfall. (2001). Teaching Native Language Programs: Survival Strategies. *Aboriginal Education in Canada: A Study in Decolonization.* K. P. Binda and Sharilyn Calliou, eds. Mississauga, ON: Canadian Educators' Press, 89-104.

Peers, Laura. (1994). *The Objiway of Western Canada, 1780 to 1870.* St. Paul, MN: Minnesota Historical Society Press.

Penner, Keith. (1983). *Report of the Special Committee on Indian Self-Government in Canada.* Ottawa, ON: Ministry of Supply and Services.

Penney, David W. (2004). *North American Indian Art.* London, UK: Thames & Hudson.

Peters, Evelyn. (2000). Aboriginal People in Urban Areas. *Visions of the Heart: Canadian Aboriginal Issues.* Second edition. David Long and Olive Patricia Dickason, eds. Toronto, ON: Harcourt Brace, 237-270.

Phillips, Ruth B. (1989). What is 'Huron Art'?: Native American Art and the New Art History. *The Canadian Journal of Native Studies,* IX:2, 161-186.

Ponting, J. Rick, and Linda J. Henderson. (2005). Contested Visions of First Nations Governance: Secondary Analysis of Federal Government Research on the Opinions of On-Reserve Residents. *Canadian Ethnic Studies,* XXXVII:1, 63-86.

Ponting, J. Rick, and Cora J. Voyageur. (2004). Multiple Points of Light: Grounds for Optimism among First Nations in Canada. *Hidden in Plain Sight: Contributions of Aboriginal Peoples to Canadian Identity and Culture.* David R. Newhouse, Cora J. Voyageur, and Dan Beavon, eds. Toronto, ON: University of Toronto Press, 425-454.

Ponting, J. Rick, and Jerilynn Kiely. (1997). Disempowerment: "Justice", Racism, and Public Opinion. *First Nations in Canada: Perspectives on Opportunity, Empowerment, and Self-Determination.* J. Rick Ponting, ed. Toronto, ON: McGraw-Hill Ryerson Limited, 152-192.

Prest, J. (January, 1922). Alberta Indians. *The Beaver,* 2:4, 5-6.

Purich, Donald. (1988). *The Métis.* Toronto, ON: James Lorimer.

Purvey, Diane. (2005). "Must a Wife do all the Adjusting?" Attitudes and Practices of Social Workers Toward Wife Abuse in Vancouver, 1945-1960. *Child and Family Welfare in British Columbia: A History.* Diane Purvey and Christopher Walmsley, eds. Calgary, AB: Detselig Enterprises, 259-282.

Radin, Paul. (1937). *The Story of the American Indian.* Garden City, NY: Garden City Publishing Company.

Ray, Arthur J. (1974). *Indians in the Fur Trade: Their Role as Hunters, Trappers and Middlemen in the Lands Southwest of the Hudson Bay.* Toronto, ON: University of Toronto Press.

Red Gun, Pam. (2006). The Teachings in Blackfoot Stories Through Our Elders. Calgary, AB: University of Calgary, Unpublished paper. Faculty of Communication and Culture. 3pp.

Robertson, Heather. (1970). *Reservations Are For Indians.* Toronto, ON: James, Lewis & Samuel.

Ross, Jeffrey Ian, and Larry Gould, eds. (2006). *Native Americans and the Criminal Justice System.* Boulder, CO:Paradigm Publishers.

Ross, Rupert. (1992). *Dancing With a Ghost: Exploring Indian Reality.* Markham, ON: Reed Books.

Rousseau, Jean Jacques. (1911). *Emile.* Translated by Barbara Foxley. New York: Dutton.

Runes, Dagobert D. (1967). *Dictionary of Philosophy.* Totowa, NJ: Littlefield, Adams & Co.

Rushing III, W. Jackson. (1999). Editor's Introduction to Part III. *Native American Art in the Twentieth Century: Makers, Meanings, Histories.* W. Jackson Rushing III, ed. London, UK: Routledge, 169-173.

Russell, Dan. (2000). *A People's Dream: Aboriginal Self-Government in Canada.* Vancouver, BC: UBC Press.

Schissel, Bernard, and Terry Wotherspoon. (2003). *The Legacy of School for Aboriginal People.* Don Mills, ON: Oxford University Press.

Schouls, Tim. (2003). *Shifting Boundaries: Aboriginal Identity, Pluralist Theory, and the Politics of Self-Government.* Vancouver, BC: UBC Press.

Scott, Duncan C. (1914). *Indian Affairs. Canada and Its Provinces. Volume Four in Adam Short and Arthur Doughy.* Toronto, ON: Brook and Company, 714-715.

Sealey, D. Bruce, and Antoine S. Lussier. (1975). *The Métis: Canada's Forgotten People.* Winnipeg, MB: Manitoba Métis Federation Press.

Siccone, Frank. (1995). *Celebrating Diversity: Building Self-Esteem in Today's Multicultural Classrooms.* Boston, MA: Allyn and Bacon.

Scott, Duncan C. (1914). *Indian Affairs. Canada and Its Provinces. Volume Four in Short and Doughy.* Toronto, ON: Brook and Company, 714-715.

Slobodin, Richard. (1966). *Métis of the MacKenzie District.* Ottawa, ON: Centre Canadien de Reserches en Anthropologie, Universite Saint-Paul.

Snow, Chief John. (2005). *These Mountains Are Our Sacred Places: The Story of the Stoney People.* Calgary: AB: Fitzhenry and Whiteside.

Solway, Louann. (2006). Indigenous Ideas on Instruction. Calgary, AB: Unpublished Paper. University of Calgary, Faculty of Communication and Culture. 3pp.

Steckley, John I., and Bryan D. Cummins. (2008). *Full Circle: Canada's First Nations.* Second edition. Toronto, ON: Pearson Education Canada.

Steigelbauer, S. M. (1996) What is an Elder? What do Elders Do? First Nations Elders as Teachers in Culture-based Urban Organizations. *The Canadian Journal of Native Studies,* XVI: 37-66.

Sterling, Shirley. (2002). Yetko and Sophie: Nlakapamux Cultural Professors. *Canadian Journal of Native Education,* 26:1, 4-10.

Sterling, Shirley. (1992). Quaslametko and Yetko: Two Grandmother Models for Contemporary Native Pedagogy. *Canadian Journal of Native Education,* 19:2, 165-174.

Stockden, Eric W. (2005) Pluralism, Corporatism, and Educating Citizens. *Educating Citizens for a Pluralistic Society.* Rosa Bruno-Jofré and Natalia Aponiuk, eds. Calgary, AB: Canadian Ethnic Studies, 71-93.

Strong-Boag, Veronica. (2005). Interrupted Relations: The Adoption of Children in Twentieth Century British Columbia. *Child and Family Welfare in British Columbia: A History.* Diane Purvey and Christopher Walmsley, eds. Calgary, AB: Detselig Enterprises, 139-164.

Suzuki, David, with Amanda McConnell. (1997). *The Sacred Balance: Rediscovering our Place in Nature.* Vancouver, BC: Douglas & McIntyre.

Suzuki, David. (1992). A Personal Foreword: The Value of Native Ecologies. *Wisdom of the Elders.* Peter Knudtson and David Suzuki. Toronto, ON: Stoddart.

Taylor, Fraser. (1989). *Standing Alone: A Contemporary Blackfoot Indian.* Halfmoon Bay, BC: Arbutus Bay Publications.

Taylor, John Leonard. (1999). Canada's Northwest Indian Policy in the 1870s: Traditional Premises and Necessary Innovations. *The Spirit of the Alberta Treaties.* Third edition. Richard T. Price, ed. Edmonton, AB: The University of Alberta Press, 3-8.

Taylor, John Leonard. (1999). Two Views on the Meanings of Treaties Six and Seven. *The Spirit of the Alberta Treaties.* Third edition. Richard T. Price, ed. Edmonton, AB: The University of Alberta Press, 9-46.

Tiedt, Pamela L., and Iris M. Tiedt. (1990). *Multicultural Teaching: A Handbook of Activities, Information and Resources.* Third edition. Boston, MA: Allyn and Bacon.

Tiedt, Pamela L., and Iris M. Tiedt. (1986). *Multicultural Teaching: A Handbook of Activities, Information and Resources.* Second edition. Boston, MA: Allyn and Bacon.

Todd, Roy. (2001). Aboriginal People in the City. *Aboriginal People and Other Canadians: Shaping New Relationships.* Martin Thornton and Roy Todd, eds. Ottawa, ON: University of Ottawa, 93-130.

Treaty Days. (1971). Manitoba Indian Brotherhood. Winnipeg, MB: Centennial Commemoration Historial Pageant.

Treaty 7 Elders and Tribal Council, with Walter Hildebrandt, Dorothy First Rider, and Sarah Carter. (1996). *The True Spirit and Original Intent of Treaty 7.* Montreal, PQ: McGill-Queen's University Press.

Underhill, Ruth M. (1953). *Red Man's America: A History of Indians in the United States.* Chicago, IL: University of Chicago Press.

Voyageur, Cora. (1996). Contemporary Indian Women. *Visions of the Heart: Canadian Aboriginal Issues.* David Alan Long and Olive Patricia Dickason, eds. Toronto, ON: Harcourt Brace & Company, 93-116.

Wishart, David J. (2004). *Native American Gender Roles. Encyclopedia of The Great Plains.* David J. Wishart, ed. Lincoln, NB: Centre for Great Plains Studies, University of Nebraska – Lincoln, 333-334.

Wagner, Tony. (March, 1998). Change as Collaborative Inquiry: A Constructivist Methodology for Reinventing Schools. *Phi Delta Kappan,* 79:7, 512-517.

Wallace, Ernest, and E. Adamson Hoebel. (1986). *The Comanches: Lords of the Southern Plains.* Norman, OK: University of Oklahoma Press.

Walmsley, Christopher. (2005). *Protecting Aboriginal Children.* Vancouver, BC: UBC Press.

Walters, Anna Lee. (1989). *The Spirit of Native American Beauty and Mysticism in American Indian Art.* San Francisco, CA: Chronicle Books.

Ward, Angela, and Rita Bouvier. (2001). Introduction. *Resting Lightly on Mother Earth: The Aboriginal Experience in Urban Educational Settings.* Calgary, AB: Detselig Enterprises, 5-16.

Warry, Wayne. (2007). *Ending Denial: Understanding Aboriginal Issues.* Peterborough, ON: Broadview Press.

Warry, Wayne. (2007). *Unfinished Dreams: Community Healing and the Reality of Aboriginal Self-Government.* Toronto, ON: University of Toronto Press.

Webb, Walter Prescott. (1931). *The Great Plains.* New York: Gosset and Dunlop.

Webb, L. Dean, Arlene Metha, and K. Forbis Jordan. (2000). *Foundations of American Education.* Third edition. Upper Saddle River, NJ: Merrill Prentice Hall.

Williams, Lorna. (2000). Urban Aboriginal Education: The Vancouver Experience. *Aboriginal Education: Fulfilling the Promise.* Marlene Brant Castellano, Lynne Davis, and Louise Lahache, eds. Vancouver, BC: UBC Press. 129-146.

Wilson, C. Roderick, and Carl Urion. (1995). First Nations Prehistory and Canadian History. *Native Peoples: The Canadian Experience.* R. Bruce Morrison and C. Roderick Wilson, eds. Toronto, ON: McClelland and Stewart, 22-66.

Wishart, David T. (2004). Native American Gender Roles. *Encylopedia of the Great Plains.* David T. Wishart, ed. University of Nebraska-Lincoln, 333-334.

Wissler, Clark. (1966). *Indians of the United States.* Revised edition. Garden City, NY: Doubleday & Company.

Woolfolk, Anita E., Philip H. Winne, Nancy E. Perry, and Jennifer Shapka. (2009). *Educational Psychology.* Fourth Canadian Edition. Toronto, ON: Pearson Canada.

Wuttunee, William, I.C. (1971). *Ruffled Feathers: Indians in Canadian Society.* Calgary, AB: Bell Books.

Young Man, Alfred. (1992). *îndîgena: Contemporary Native Perspectives.* Gerald McMaster and Lee-Ann Martin, eds. Vancouver, BC: Douglas & McIntyre and Hull, PQ: Canadian Museum of Civilization, 81-99.

Zaharia, Sikotan Flora, and Makai'sto Leo Fox. (1995). *Kitomahkitapiiminnooniks: Stories from our Elders.* Three volumes. Standoff, AB: Kainaiwa Board of Education.

Zaharia, Sikotan Flora, Makai'sto Leo Fox, and Omahksipiitaa Marvin Fox. (2003). *Kitomahkitapiiminnooniks: Stories from our Elders.* Volume Four. Standoff, AB: Kainaiwa Board of Education.

Zimmerman, Larry J., and Brian Leigh Molyneaux. (1996). *Native North America.* Norman, OK: University of Oklahoma Press.

Zion, James W. (2006). Justice as Phoenix: Traditional Indigenous Law, Restorative Justice, and the Collapse of the State. *Native Americans and the Criminal Justice System.* Jeffrey Ian Ross and Larry Gould, eds. Boulder, CO: Paradigm Publishers, 51-66.

# Index